Designing
Intelligent
Front Ends
for Business Software

Dan Shafer

WILEY

JOHN WILEY & SONS
New York Chichester Brisbane Toronto Singapore

Publisher: Stephen Kippur
Editor: Therese A. Zak
Managing Editor: Ruth Greif
Compositor: Production Services

Library of Congress Cataloging-in-Publication Data

Shafer, Dan.
    Designing intelligent front ends for business software/Dan Shafer
      p. cm.
    Bibliography: p.
    ISBN 0-471-60114-4
    1. Business—Data processing. 2. Artificial intelligence. 3. Expert sys-
tems (Computer Science)—Computer programs. 4. Computer software—
Development. I. Title.
HF5548.2.S438 1989
650'.028'5512—dc20

Printed in the United States of America
89 90 10 9 8 7 6 5 4 3 2 1

89-32526
CIP

PREFACE

One of the most important ideas in microcomputing — the interweaving of Artificial Intelligence (AI) technology into everyday business programs to create intelligent solutions to business problems — is discussed in this book. The idea is important from the perspective of both expert systems designers looking for ready markets for the technology and from business users who are not interested in technology but who would like their spreadsheets and databases to be somehow "smarter" than they are.

If you are either a current or hopeful expert systems designer or if you are a power user of a spreadsheet or database program, this book will help you figure out how to make these two aspects of business software work together profitably.

Expert Systems Workers

Practitioners in expert systems have recognized for some time the need to integrate the power embodied in their technology into mainstream business applications if they will ever have a chance of commercial success. But they have not always seen the forest for the trees. However helpful spreadsheets and databases are and however complex the information with which they deal, they are not sufficiently intricate to attract the attention of AI researchers. There is a great deal of lip service to the adage that "People don't buy technology, they buy solutions." But action does not follow statement.

There are literally millions of spreadsheet and database applications being used with microcomputers in this country every day. Many (though certainly not all) could benefit from the application of some simple expert systems technology. They can be made:

- Easier to use

- Less prone to erroneous data

- More helpful in terms of the information they provide

Each of these applications represents a potential use of expert systems: a chance to make software work better for people and a real, commercially viable opportunity.

Power Users

Those people who consider themselves "power users" of one or more spreadsheet or database applications will find three primary benefits in this book.

1. You will see that expert systems technology has the potential to add value to the work you do every day with business applications. You'll believe that AI is not entirely pie in the sky.

2. Your thinking will be spurred and catalyzed as you think of those spreadsheet and database applications with which you are familiar that could benefit from the application of expert systems technology.

3. I hope to demystify expert systems enough so that when you are done reading this book you will say, "I can do that." Because you probably can. Expert systems aren't nearly as complex as they are often made to appear.

Limiting the Scope

In this book, I hope to provide you with the practical tools needed to develop rule-based expert systems that work well with new and existing spreadsheet and database applications. Along the way, we must explore some ideas and concepts in AI, expert systems, database management systems, and spreadsheet tools. But none of these is the primary focus of the book.

Thus, you should not expect to find an in-depth tutorial on expert systems in this book. I have purposely limited the discussion of AI and expert systems concepts to those ideas that will be useful if you decide to build one or more intelligent front ends for a business application.

Similarly, an in-depth tutorial on the use of Lotus 1-2-3 and its workalike spreadsheet applications are not provided here. The same can be said for its treatment of dBASE III Plus and workalike database management systems.

I have chosen to take a step-by-step approach to the actual construction of worksheets (which is what we call spreadsheet documents where data is actually stored), database files, and expert systems. I start with the basics, since this makes it possible for the book to serve the interests and needs of people who have strengths in one or more of these areas but little or no experience in another. However, this step-by-step approach is not tutorial in nature; it is more like a cookbook or a set of construction instructions for a kit.

What's in the Book?

This book progresses from providing you with a foundation in the terms and concepts of AI and expert systems through concrete examples of day-to-day spreadsheet and database applications to which expert systems technology has been applied.

Chapter 1 provides a set of definitions of AI and expert systems. It also defines the components of an expert system and how they relate to one another as well as discussing briefly the question of how knowledge is stored and represented.

Chapter 2 refines our focus as it concentrates on expert system design issues. It discusses the five basic steps in expert system construction and provides some suggestions for classifying and choosing appropriate expert system tools for business problem solving. It concludes with a discussion of two design issues:

1. Understanding your user's needs and expectations

2. Rapid prototyping

Chapter 3 is a brief discussion of problem selection in expert system design. It explains the basic criteria to follow in determining whether a particular problem you are facing is susceptible of expert system solution.

Chapter 4 begins our exploration of intelligent interface design by considering how such design is handled using traditional approaches. It describes the mechanisms for user interface available in spreadsheet and database management systems, pointing out their weaknesses and suggesting potential problem areas.

Chapter 5 describes how to implement the most basic of expert system interface designs for a business application: guided data entry. In such a system, the user is simply hand-held through the process of entering data so that there is no need to be aware of or involved with the underlying business application.

Chapter 6 carries the discussion of intelligent interface design to the next level: intelligent data validation strategies. It is in this area that we will find expert systems most helpful, as they ensure that data being entered into a spreadsheet or database is accurate and consistent with reality.

Chapter 7 presents a small example of a spreadsheet application and describes how an intelligent front end could be written for it using a rule-based approach. We actually build our first full intelligent interface using VP-Expert in this chapter.

Chapter 8 builds on Chapter 7. Using the same example, it examines how another expert system shell, KnowledgePro, might be used to approach the interface design. KnowledgePro takes a different approach to expert system design than VP-Expert, yet it allows for the design of production rules. You can easily compare and contrast the two approaches.

Chapter 9 presents a small example of a database application and describes how an intelligent front end could be written for it using VP-Expert.

Chapter 10 describes a combined spreadsheet-database example with a VP-Expert intelligent interface. The approach solves not only data entry and validation problems but also addresses the question of how to make these two seemingly incompatible applications work together.

Chapter 11 explains how the ideas of an intelligent interface can be extended by using a state-of-the-art approach called hypertext. We use both VP-Expert and KnowledgePro to show how an interface can be made to act and seem more intelligent than it really is by providing well-designed connecting links between related pieces of data in the interface.

Chapter 12 describes how to extend intelligent interfaces using "hot" graphics (i.e., graphics that respond to the users pressing on them with a mouse or other input device). Again, we will use VP-Expert and KnowledgePro to demonstrate this capability, as well as discussing a Personal Consultant series add-in product called PC Images to achieve a similar result.

Chapter 13 concludes our examination of the subject by briefly describing other ways that spreadsheets, databases, and expert systems might work together. A major focus is on the issue of designing intelligent "back" ends: expert systems that analyze information stored in databases and spreadsheets and provide the user with advice and counsel about policy and other decisions to make.

There are three appendices in this book.

- Appendix A describes how you can create an expert system rule set from an existing database or spreadsheet using a process known as induction.

- Appendix B discusses expert system shells and compares their capabilities in view of the class of application we are interested in here.

- Appendix C is a sample spreadsheet.

The book concludes with a glossary and index. Terms that appear in italics in the text can be found in the glossary.

Tools We've Chosen

Throughout this book, whenever an example is presented, I use a more or less "typical" production rule system (see Chapter 2 for a full explanation of this term). This makes it possible to build these rules in any expert system shell you choose to use. However, there are obviously differences among these shells and how they interact with spreadsheets and databases. An entirely generic book would have been less than useful. I have therefore chosen to use Paperback Software's VP-Expert as the primary shell of choice throughout this book. The *rules* that are presented here can be built in any of several systems, but the interaction with the spreadsheet and database will be quite system-specific.

Of the widely available expert system shells for desktop computers, no other offers the flexibility and total, seamless integration of interface with database and spreadsheet files of VP-Expert. Texas Instruments' Personal Consultant Plus, easily one of the best and most widely used expert system shells on the market, for example, has very powerful database access but very limited direct spreadsheet use. The same is true of Level 5, a Pascal-flavored shell from Information Builders. Other expert system shells have been slow to realize what VP-Expert designer Brian Sawyer and Paperback Software chief executive officer Adam Osborne noted from the beginning of their design: Full-scale use of database and spreadsheet files is as powerful an idea as the concept of an expert system itself.

Still, I did not want to narrow the focus of the book too much. There are approaches to spreadsheet and database interaction other than those embodied in VP-Expert. That is why in Chapter 8 I have presented alternate solutions to some of the problems in this book that might be created by the use of other tools, specifically Knowledge-Pro.

In Appendix B, I examine briefly other expert system shells with some "hooks" into spreadsheets and databases. To the extent that they are rule-based and have the ability to interact with spreadsheets/databases, the examples in the book will work with them, albeit with some modifications.

One Other Product

There is another program you should know about if you are interested in expert systems and their involvement with day-to-day business software.

The other program is called "if/then." It is not a development tool but rather an educational one. It permits a person familiar with Lotus 1-2-3 to learn a great deal about expert systems by observing how they work in a spreadsheet environment. The program is not designed to be used to "build" anything, but using it can provide a good adjunct to the material in this book, particularly if you are an accomplished spreadsheet aficionado with little or no AI background.

Contacting the Author

After you read this book, if you want to correspond with me, please do so. I can be reached on CompuServe Information Service (my ID is 71246,402), on MCI Mail or Genie (my name for both places is DSHAFER) or by U.S. Mail (277 Hillview Ave., Redwood City, CA 94062). I am always interested in hearing from readers who have found errors in the book, or who have suggestions for making the book more useful. I also enjoy hearing from readers who have been inspired by the book to build something useful and interesting.

ACKNOWLEDGMENTS

I am indebted to a number of people who have joined me in the past few years in my quest for a deeper understanding of expert systems technology and how it applies to the real world of business.

Brian Sawyer, who wrote VP-Expert for Paperback Software International, has been a source of help and explanation, particularly as I tried to muddle my way through the early days of experimenting with building systems. Other Paperback Software people have also been helpful, notably founder and former President Adam Osborne, Jennifer Mok, Terry Schussler, and Annie Moose.

A major contribution to this book came from Ron Ogg. Ron was a vice president at Paperback Software when I started this project and an independent consultant by the time I finished it. He not only reviewed the manuscript, pointing out many errors and helping to polish the thoughts, but he also provided the spreadsheet macro and VP-Planner Plus Version 2 material in Chapter 5.

Avron Barr, one of the true luminaries of this industry, has proven to be not only a friend and a helpful colleague but also a source of inspiration as I have put this book together. He believed from the beginning that there are nuggets of opportunity for the kinds of projects described in this book. I might have quit this project any number of times if not for his support.

Laurence Rozier, who developed some of the most impressive expert system technology that was never published, has provided constant inspiration and support for this and other projects on which we have worked together in the past few months. His understanding of some aspects of expert systems technology is clearly superior to that of many other people I know who make their living in this field.

Paul C. Anacker, a former lawyer who's much happier and better off studying AI techniques and expert systems, and who co-authored the revised edition of the book *Understanding Artificial Intelligence* with me, offered many interesting insights in numerous discussions.

Tom J. Schwartz, founder and president of TSA, and I have spent many hours debating the relative merits of various approaches to expert systems design. Those discussions have honed and focused my understanding and appreciation for this technology.

Bev Thompson and Bill Thompson, the geniuses behind Knowledge Garden, Inc., and the developers of KnowledgePro, have been immensely helpful over the years in looking at things I've written and patiently pointing out places where my understanding was lacking. Their colleague John Slade has also contributed to that process more recently.

Jim Chapman of Human Intellect Systems and his programmer *extraordinaire* Esoukan Mouange of Paris have worked through a great many problems and solutions with me over many a lunch-hour napkin on the way to designing and building their Instant-Expert product line.

Keith Weiskamp, founder and former editor of *PC AI* magazine, has passed along some of his not inconsiderable knowledge of the general subject matter and has examined things I've done from time to time as well.

Others who have contributed to my education in this field include: Denny Bollay, President, ExperTelligence; John Forge, Executive Vice-President, ExperTelligence; Lou Giacalone, founder and former publisher of *Intelligent Systems Analyst*; Dennis Chan, co-designer of Intelligent Developer and IntelliCard; Neil McGlone and Mark Linesch of Texas Instruments; Will Hapgood of 1st-CLASS Software; Dan Rasmus, Manager of Advanced Manufacturing Systems at Western Digital Corporation; Steve Weyer and Harald Striepe of Apple Computer; all of the people on CompuServe's AI forum, sponsored by *AI Expert* magazine; and others I'm sure I'm omitting simply because the pressure of time removes them from my mind temporarily.

As usual, none of these people is responsible for any of the errors that may have found their way into this book. I am solely responsible for its content.

My agent Bill Gladstone, John Wiley editor Teri Zak, and assistant editor Ellen Greenberg gave me lots of support and patience when I floundered, delayed, and confused the issue along the way. Karen Watterson wrote a sharply focused review of the first draft of this manuscript and her suggestions made this a far better book. Too often, technical reviewers don't go to the lengths she did for this book and their role is not often appreciated. Ruth Greif shepherded the manuscript through production with sensitivity and aplomb. Don and Rae Huntington read my scribbles and put the book into its final format.

Finally, my wife and family displayed their usual patience with me as I wrote this manuscript. They are by now becoming accustomed, perhaps even inured, to the idea that I'm going to spend hundreds of hours in my little office, clattering away on the keyboard and watching letters appear magically on the TV-like screen in front of me, writing about who knows what. Still, they could make life much more difficult. The fact that they don't should not go unrecognized.

CONTENTS

CHAPTER 3   Problem Selection and Definition   51

CHAPTER 1
Basics of Artificial Intelligence and Expert Systems

This chapter will discuss the meaning of the term *Artificial Intelligence* (AI) and attempt to define it for our purposes. We will talk about the recent history of AI, focusing on how and why it has failed to produce what its practitioners had promised and we had all hoped. The chapter will go on to provide a working definition for the term *expert system*, looking at what an expert system is not, and examining the kinds of problems to which expert systems have been applied. We will discuss the components of an expert system and delve into how its brain, the inference engine, works. We will conclude the chapter by taking a brief look at the issue of *knowledge representation* — how the knowledge that comprises such an important part of an expert system is represented and stored.

Defining Artificial Intelligence

AI is difficult to define because natural intelligence eludes definition. How can we define an artificial anything if we can't describe or define the real version? We know what artificial sweetener is because we can define what a real sweetener is; but what is intelligence? And how will we know when we have achieved its artificial implementation?

There are some deep-seated philosophical undercurrents in the AI arena. What does it mean for a human being to think? How do we store and retrieve information so efficiently and effectively? Why can experts perform a subtly complex task but cannot describe the steps it involves so that their knowledge can be translated into a form other people can use?

It is this realm in which AI lives and attempts to find answers. Broadly stated, AI is a branch of computer science which attempts to emulate or replicate the functioning of the human brain.

However, given that we know little about the human mind and how it works, we should not be surprised that we know very little about what an emulation of a human mind will do or how it will look.

In this book our interest in AI is narrow and practical. We want to focus on a branch of AI known as *expert systems* or *knowledge-based* systems. Specifically, we want to understand how expert systems "behave" in intelligent ways to help us in business. Given this behavioral need, we can propose a working definition of AI which, though wholly unacceptable to most academics, will suit us quite well.

A program will be considered artificially intelligent if it exhibits behavior which, if we saw a human being behaving identically, we would consider required more than ordinary intelligence.

A revamped definition for AI has been circulating for some time. The phrase "more than ordinary," which I suggest adding to the usual description, eliminates such tasks as routine mathematical calculations. Such calculations require intelligence but a program that carries out such calculations (e.g., a spreadsheet) is not an AI program.

I recognize some of the ambiguities of the definition. However, in view of our limited purpose, it will be adequate.

The Promise and Failure of AI

Attempts to create artificially intelligent programs date back more than 30 years. Yet despite the years of research and study, only one major class of usable commercial technology has emerged from the AI laboratories — expert systems. Today expert systems represent the primary visible, tangible evidence that AI is something other than a pipe dream.

One could argue that if nothing else came of AI research but expert systems, the field would have borne abundant fruit. After all, designing and building systems that help us solve complex real-world problems is no mean feat.

The problem is, AI researchers have traditionally set goals and claims that make anything short of miraculous software look like a failure. In the 1960s and 1970s, it was not uncommon for AI researchers to predict outlandish achievements for the field. Visions abounded of world chess champion computer software, all-purpose problem solvers that could deal with any problem we wished to pose, and computers that could deal with us in our own human tongue. Today, we are well short of attaining any of those goals. Indeed, at least the second — that of an all-purpose problem-solving system — has been all but abandoned.

However, if AI's overpromotion has led to unrealistic expectations, its tendency to remain research directed and focused on very difficult problems has kept it from becoming broadly useful.

We will see in this book that a great many business systems can benefit from expert system technology. However, on the whole, they have relatively dull and mundane problems. Most AI work is done in laboratories where the emphasis is either on doing the nearly impossible and thus making a contribution to the body of knowledge or on large-scale projects with six- and seven-figure price tags. The educational world's need to focus on pure research is not only understandable, but valuable. It is more difficult to understand the focus of commercial AI companies on a narrow range of problems.

In part, this high-end focus derives from the fact that until the past year or two, it was all but unthinkable to develop an expert system on a microcomputer. The hardware lacked the power and capacity to deal with expert systems technology in the first place, and most expert systems were being built in LISP, a powerful but cumbersome language that was ill-suited to microcomputer implementation. Both of those conditions have changed. Hardware has leaped forward in both speed and power. At the same time, LISP has been efficiently implemented on microcomputers while shells written in conventional languages such as C and Pascal have also appeared. Today, it is clear that the vast majority of expert systems are being developed on desktop computers.

Solutions, Not Technology

As the microcomputer has come more into its own as a vehicle for expert system technology, knowledge engineers have begun to sense the power of the software and the potential of the market. This has led to some marketing hype that has touted everything from games to music generators, from educational software to programming environments, as embodying AI technology. All of this, however, misses the point.

Business owners and managers who buy microcomputers and software are not particularly interested in technology. They don't care if you call it artificial intelligence or user-friendly interface or intelligent front end. What they "do" care about is a solution to their problem. If they can find a solution that uses AI techniques, that's fine. If they can find an equally viable solution that doesn't use AI techniques but is easier to use or more efficient, they'll buy it.

One strong implication of all of this is that AI, to be successful, is going to have to disappear. Only when it is invisibly embedded into everyday software will AI achieve anything resembling commercial acceptance. This "disappearing act" can take any of several forms.

In its simplest form, it is a recognition by expert systems marketers that they not only do not have to tout their product's intelligence, but they might be better off downplaying it. Some observers of the AI and expert systems communities have suggested, for example, that the term expert systems be replaced by a more approachable term that generates fewer expectations. Such as *advisory systems*. Put simply, selling AI as AI is not a good marketing strategy when you are trying to sell it to a typical business owner or manager.

A second way AI can become embedded is for it to be woven tightly into the code of existing applications. A perceived necessity for such tight integration is behind a recent movement of expert systems shells written in C and Pascal. The real embedded expert system doesn't simply "use" an external program written in another language, it becomes part of it. The *inference engine* (we'll talk more about this part of an expert system in "The Inference Engine" section) is simply integrated right into the database, telecommunications program, or accounting package.

Finally, AI can be made to disappear by attaching it to the front end of existing computer programs making those programs easier to use and better at what they do (the method we will use in this book). The integration here is not tight or necessarily transparent — though it can be nearly so — but the borderline between the "ordinary" business program and the "intelligent" expert system is not well-defined and in any case not visible to the user.

AI in Business Today

It would be wrong to assume that simply because we don't hear very much in the press about expert systems that the technology is not having an impact in the business world. It is. However, today most expert systems work performed commercially is being carried out by in-house development groups. The resulting products are deployed internally. Public discussion of these programs and their capabilities is not encouraged; since the company almost certainly perceives its knowledge base — embodied in an expert system or otherwise — as its competitive advantage. If companies jealously protect their lists of customers and distributors — and they rightfully do — how much more closely can they be expected to safeguard their knowledge of how to make good business and marketing decisions?

Compared to expert systems, the rest of the AI technology family has had a far less noticeable impact on business. There have been some speech recognition systems that have caused interest. Robotic vision systems have seen some limited amounts of application. But, on the whole, the impact has been scattered and diffused.

A Working Definition

Defining the term "expert system" is in some ways easier than the task of defining the broader term, artificial intelligence. An expert system can be thought of as a computer program that furnishes advice about or otherwise assists a user in solving a particular problem or class of problem, usually through a highly interactive process that resembles an interview. This definition has different implications for the three types of people involved in expert systems: users, designers, and knowledge engineers.

This definition implies that users can interact with this computer program, apparently answer some questions and supply information peculiar to a particular case or situation, and expect the system to produce one or more recommendations. From the users' perspective, then, the expert system replaces the human expert to whom they might otherwise turn. Like the human expert, the expert system knows (or seems to know) a great deal about the subject matter at hand. At least, it appears to know more than the users who are seeking its advice. Like the human expert, the expert system asks a series of questions designed to enable it to focus on the precise nature of the problem or question the users bring to the process. And like the human expert, the expert system recommends a course of action as a consequence of its analysis of the knowledge it has about the subject in general and of the users' particular description of a problem.

When designers look at an expert system they see it from an inside-out perspective. From what designers can tell, an expert system has to have three basic components: a collection of facts and knowledge about the subject matter from which it begins its consultation, a user interface, and some program in the middle that combines the general knowledge and the user-supplied knowledge in such a way that a reasonable conclusion results. This three-part organization of an expert system is depicted in Figure 1-1.

Knowledge Base	**Inference Engine**	**User Infterface**
(Facts, rules, and information about subject)	(General knowledge about how to draw conclusions)	(Mechanism for interacting with user)

Figure 1-1. Expert System from Designers' Perspective

Designers come to refer to the program that handles the analysis of the knowledge and the generation of recommendations and conclusions as the *inference engine*. (We'll discuss the inference engine in detail in the next section.)

To the experts whose knowledge is being embodied in and emulated by an expert system, the software is somewhat one dimensional. Unless the expert is also, as frequently happens, the designer, the expert's view of the expert system is that of a software product into which he directly or indirectly places his knowledge. Experts might accomplish this by directly interacting with a *knowledge acquisition* module. In many expert system projects, the domain expert interacts with a person called the knowledge engineer, who is generally a trained programmer. The knowledge engineer's job is to extract the expert's knowledge and put it into a form the expert system program can use with its inference engine. So it is conceivable that the domain expert might never actually see the expert system software itself while the expert system is being constructed.

The Inference Engine

The *inference engine* is the software program "brain" of an expert system. It is designed so that it draws conclusions (inferences) from information passed to it, allowing it to appear to act intelligently by "understanding" things that it has not been explicitly told.

For example, provide an inference engine with these two facts:

> All worksheets have cells
> File THING1.WKS is a worksheet

The inference engine will conclude that the file THING1.WKS has cells. Notice that you haven't explicitly stated that fact. The inference engine had to draw its own conclusion from information you provided. This is a very powerful idea.

Working with a combination of facts and rules about how to extrapolate facts, an inference engine can help us to deal more intelligently with the information stored in our computer systems.

An expert system's inference engine reasons along one of two basic lines: backward chaining or forward chaining.

In backward chaining, the expert system uses facts to prove (or disprove) hypotheses, which are usually stated in the form of goals. Here's a brief example:

> Rule 1: IF it is raining AND you forgot your umbrella
>
> THEN you will get wet.
>
> Rule 2: IF it is Wednesday
>
> THEN you forgot your umbrella.
>
> Fact 1: It is raining.
>
> Fact 2: It is Wednesday.

An expert system that was set up to backward chain through such a limited knowledge base would be started out with a goal statement to prove. In this case, let's assume we've told the system we want it to find out if you will get wet. In other words, we've given it the hypothesis that you will get wet. It looks through its knowledge base to see if it has any way of drawing that conclusion. Sure enough, there in Rule 1, it has a conclusion it can reach that exactly matches your hypothesis. Now all it has to do is figure out if the conclusion is true.

It looks at the conditions that have to be met for the goal hypothesis to be proven and sees that there are two, both of which must be true for the goal to be proven. It must be raining and you must have forgotten your umbrella. Now it looks into the fact portion of its knowledge base to see if it can prove or disprove either of these facts. Fact 1 matches the first fact in the rule the expert system is examining (Rule 1). So we're halfway home.

Now the system looks at the second condition that must be true (i.e., you forgot your umbrella). It has no facts that tell it whether you have forgotten your umbrella or not, so it looks through its rules to see if it can draw a conclusion that matches this new condition. It does indeed have a rule (Rule 2) that will allow it to reach the conclusion. To do so, it must prove that it is Wednesday. It temporarily sets aside its original goal of finding out if you will get wet to find out if it is Wednesday. So it looks through its knowledge base and finds a fact (Fact 2) that supplies this missing link. Now the system knows you forgot your umbrella. (Don't ask me why you'd forget your umbrella every Wednesday; it's "your" umbrella!) It can now chain back to the previous goal of proving that you will get wet. (This chaining back to previously examined goals that have been set aside to solve subsequent ones is where the concept of backward chaining gets its name.)

Now it can see that both of the conditions in Rule 1 have been satisfied. So it can now tell you that the conclusion of Rule 1, namely that you will get wet, is indeed true.

A forward-chaining expert system design generally begins not with a goal or goals as does a backward-chaining system, but rather with a situation described by one or more facts. The system then reasons from these facts to achieve a goal whose identity the system does not know at the outset of a session. In our example, we could set up the knowledge base of rules about rain and getting wet so that we tell the expert system at the outset that it is raining outside and that today is Wednesday. Then we turn it loose, in essence asking it, "What can you conclude from these facts?"

The forward-chaining inference engine looks through the knowledge base, typically from start to finish, and finds in our example that it can make one new assertion of facts as a result of what we've told it: that you forgot your umbrella (thanks to Rule 2). Having traversed the knowledge base, the system looks at its new base of facts. Determining that it has changed since the last pass through the rules, the inference engine makes another pass. This time, Rule 1's conditions are both met, so it asserts that it is true that you will get wet.

It has now exhausted all the rules and possibilities, so the inference engine quits (perhaps after a final pass through the rules, depending on the design used). In most systems, it will simply announce, "No new inferences can be drawn," or words to that effect.

All inference engines use forward or backward chaining, or some combination. If they combine both methods, they may either allow the designer or user to select the method to be used during a consultation session or the inference engines may be able to switch back and forth during a consultation depending on what logic needs exist.

What an Expert System Is Not

Given these perspectives of an expert system, one way to help us to focus on an appropriate definition for an expert system is to concentrate on differentiating it from other programs that might be similar.

An area of software development that usurped some of the AI mantle is a class of programs called *decision-support systems* (DSS). These take the form of interactive systems that help a manager or executive make a decision about some subject. They may be generic; one manager may use a DSS to help with budgeting decisions and another manager to assist in deciding where to put a new manufacturing facility. DSSs are not really intelligent. They are sophisticated analytical tools that use weighting and other methods of decision making. They present those tools in a way that managers feel comfortable with and and can interact without understanding the underlying structures. DSSs' generality differentiates them from expert systems: an expert system possesses knowledge about a particular domain; a DSS is a tool, like a spreadsheet, that is a tabla rosa — a blank sheet of paper waiting for the user to supply the knowledge. The DSS supplies algorithms and help, but no knowledge of the subject.

An expert system should also not be confused with a database management system (DBMS). There are some similarities between the knowledge base that makes up a significant portion of an expert system and a database. But the differences are more stark. A knowledge base can be executed. It is an active participant in the inference process that is at the heart of an expert system. A database, however, is a passive repository of data. A database doesn't "do" anything, it just "is." However, a knowledge base consists of facts and rules that are used actively by the inference engine in drawing its conclusions. Beyond this fundamental difference, it should be obvious that the way DBMSs are used differs radically from the way expert systems are used. A database supplies raw data, albeit reconfigured, formatted, and even calculated. An expert system interprets data and tells the user what course of action to follow as a consequence of certain knowledge. As we get further into this book we will see how the differences between an expert system and a DBMS can be exploited to make them work together to accomplish our goals.

Types of Expert Systems

With a working definition of an expert system fixed in place, we are ready to begin examining expert systems more specifically. There have been almost as many attempts to classify expert systems as there have been to define artificial intelligence. None has succeeded better than that shown in Table 1-1. It originated with Dr. Donald A. Waterman of Rand Corp. and has appeared in several books on expert systems, including Waterman's *A Guide to Expert Systems* (Reading, MA: Addison-Wesley, 1986).

Table 1-1. Categories of Expert System Applications

Category	Problem(s) Addressed
Interpretation	Inferring data describing a situation, using sensors and other input devices
Prediction	Inferring likely consequences of given combinations of circumstances and situations
Diagnosis	Inferring malfunctions in various kinds of systems based on observable and reportable data
Design	Configuring objects and systems within sets of constraints
Planning	Creating plans of action from goals
Monitoring	Comparing observations of actual events to expected scenarios and values
Debugging	Prescribing remedies for malfunctions (perhaps diagnosed by a diagnostic expert system)
Repair	Executing plans to carry out remedies for malfunctions
Instruction	Diagnosing, debugging, and repairing a student's learning process and behavior patterns
Control	Governing the behavior of a total system

The expert systems we will build fall into a new category: the intelligent interface. This class of expert systems combines some of the elements of diagnosis, design, debugging, and control, with occasional dashes of instruction thrown in for good measure. All of this will become clearer as we progress.

Problems Expert Systems Can Address

Business problems can for our purposes be thought of as falling into three categories in terms of their amenability to solution by an expert system:

- Those that are or appear to be too complex or demanding to be susceptible to expert system solution given the current state of the art

- Those that are too simple to justify the expenditure of time and resources necessary to build an expert system solution

- Those that are of sufficient complexity to warrant the expert system approach and that do not place unrealistic demands or expectations on the AI technology

Some problems require a level of sophistication that does not yet exist in expert system tools. For example, expert systems can't apply real creativity to problems. If a problem requires a novel solution that does not rely particularly on what has been done before, an expert system is not likely to be of much use in resolving it. (We might, though, design an expert system that would "help" a human to sort through the alternatives and stimulate some new thinking. There, the expert system would be a partner to the human user.) Similarly, problems that require a system to "learn" from its interaction and experiences with the user and with the data or knowledge it possesses are beyond the reach of expert system technology today. (Actually, I have argued that the fact that one can update a database via an expert system is itself a rudimentary form of learning. After all, the system's behavior the next time it is run may be altered by the new information. But learning in the classic sense implies a motivation on the part of the system that an expert system does not yet have.)

Many problems are best dealt with through a database program or spreadsheet macro; they just don't need the power of an expert system. This does not mean that you can't use an expert system to approach them or even to solve them. But it does mean that you should understand at the outset that you may be using a more powerful tool than is necessary. There may be other reasons that dictate the selection of an expert system approach where a more conventional solution would appear to be as workable. For example, the elegance of the interface, an issue with which we will be continually concerned, may provide such a justification. Spreadsheets at their best are viewed by many users as ugly and difficult to fathom. A user-friendly front end that asks questions and helps with answers may remove barriers to the effective and efficient use of a spreadsheet that no amount of macro programming is going to address.

In the broad context, deciding if and when to use an expert system to solve a problem is a challenging task. When we concentrate our thinking on the issue of intelligent interfaces, the problems become much simpler. We may choose to use expert system technology to design a front end for a spreadsheet or database application for either or both of these reasons:

- The person entering information into the application or attempting to make good use of it is inexperienced or uncomfortable with computers. Some form of dialogue with the computer will be more "friendly" to such a user than simply being presented with a principally blank screen that seems to say to such a user, "Go ahead! Fill me out! I dare you!"

- The application may be designed in such a way that interdependence of data makes it possible for entry errors to go undetected, perhaps until considerable damage has been done. Inappropriate data entry may not be immediately caught by proofreaders. The spreadsheet or database can't deal with the issue because some data needed to resolve the question of appropriateness of the data may be missing when the user makes the invalid entry.

Knowledge Representation

Having decided that an expert system can help you with a particular business problem now using database or spreadsheet technology, you will be faced with a tool-selection problem (see Chapter 2). But one issue is of broader interest than simple tool selection and is appropriate for us to address before we talk about the specific steps involved in expert system construction.

The knowledge that will be embodied in an expert system can be stored in any of several ways. Databases generally store information either as records (in flat-file systems) or tables of rows and columns (in relational systems). Spreadsheets store information as individually addressable elements of data called cells. The two types of data representation — records or tables and cells — are not entirely mutually exclusive. But each has its strengths and weaknesses.

You might implement a small database within a spreadsheet, particularly if you are using a spreadsheet that provides some built-in facilities for managing such data. However, if your problem is primarily or exclusively a database issue or if the data management task is large, then you are probably going to select a database.

The same is true of expert systems. There are many ways of representing the knowledge embodied in an expert system. None of them is necessarily always the best solution. There is probably little or no knowledge in the world that can't be represented in all of the various knowledge representation schemes. But some of these approaches are better than others for certain kinds of knowledge.

We will briefly examine three knowledge representation techniques: rules (also called production rules), frames, and hypertext.

Rules

If you talk to experts in a particular subject area and try to find out how they make decisions, you will probably find a large number of rules being uttered. For example, ask a chess player how a decision was reached to make a certain move and the response might be "I knew that if my opponent moved the King's Rook to my third rank, I was going to be in trouble, so I blocked that move." More generally, you might ask the chess master, "How do you generally look for moves on the board?" The reply might be: "If I have a piece subject to capture, I first look to see if the capture is logical on the part of my opponent and what it would do to my total position. If the capture would be too costly for my opponent or if the damage would be minimal compared to advantages to be gained by some other move, I ignore it." And so it would go.

Note that experts couch their knowledge in terms of "if-then" groups. This is a natural way to express many kinds of expertise. Common-sense decisions such as "If it's raining or seems like it will rain, then take your umbrella" demonstrate such methods of thinking.

Rules — more properly referred to as production rules — are patterned after such decision-making processes. Their general form is:

> **IF**   some conditions are TRUE
>
> **THEN**   take some actions

The part of the rule that begins with the word "IF" and ends with the word "THEN" is called the *rule premise*. The rest of the rule, beginning with the word "THEN," is called the *rule conclusion*.

Reading production rules is straightforward. IF conditions contained in its premise are true, THEN the actions listed in the conclusion are taken. The following rule about umbrellas is an example of how a rule would be stated in a production rule-based expert system. (We will be using rules extensively in the examples in Chapters 7-10.)

> **IF**   it is raining OR
> it is likely to rain
>
> **THEN**   take your umbrella

Frames

Knowledge that can be expressed procedurally can be represented in production rules. However, it is difficult to embody in a rule a description of an object or of its relationship to other objects. To to so, knowledge engineers often turn to *frames*. A frame is a knowledge representation scheme in which a piece of knowledge is represented as a collection of slots, each of which can have one or more values.

For example, if you were constructing an expert system to help you allocate office equipment and space, you might want a frame that describes the various kinds of desks you have available. You could design a frame called "DESK" that would contain basic information about the most common kind of desk you have. Such a frame might look like Figure 1-2. All desks will have a top surface 4 feet deep by

DESK

Slot Name	Slot Value
Depth_of_Top	4
Width_of_Top	8
Composition	Wood
Center_Drawer	No
Return	No

Figure 1-2. A Standard DESK Frame

8 feet wide, be made of wood, have no center drawer, and no type-writer return, so we create slots for all of these traits and supply values to be assumed for them.

All desks can now be described in terms of how they differ from this "default" or "ideal" desk. Technically, each new frame describing a DESK is a descendant of this parent desk. As such, each desk inherits all of the traits of its parent except for those you choose to specifically override. Each desk may also have some traits that are missing from the parent desk. Figure 1-3 describes two desks in terms of this frame structure. Notice that the desk called EXEC_DESK has a larger top than the normal desk and is made of chrome and glass. The desk called COMPUTER_DESK has a return on which the computer can be placed and adds built-in electrical outlets for safety reasons.

Some expert system tools allow you to combine frame and rule representation of knowledge, selecting in the case of each bit of knowledge that form which will most efficiently represent it.

We will be looking briefly at Personal Consultant Series expert system tools from Texas Instruments in Chapter 12 and Appendix B. This series relies heavily on frame technology for its knowledge representation.

EXEC_DESK

Slot Name	Slot Value
Depth_of_Top	6
Width_of_Top	10
Composition	Glass, Chrome

COMPUTER_DESK

Slot Name	Slot Value
Return	No
Electric_Box	Yes

Figure 1-3. Two "Descendant" Desks

Hypertext

A relatively recent arrival on the AI scene is the use of *hypertext* in conjunction with other approaches to expert system knowledge representation. Hypertext is not, strictly speaking, a knowledge representation scheme. Rather, it is a method by which knowledge that has been represented other ways can be logically connected to other knowledge in the knowledge base or outside of it.

Hypertext derives from two root words "hyper" meaning beyond and "text" meaning, well..., text. Hypertext allows us to connect text in ways that go beyond the normal, linear handling of textual material.

In an expert system sense, hypertext can be used to represent or deal with knowledge that is layered. Much knowledge has this characteristic; some cognitive scientists believe that all knowledge is in fact layered. By "layered," I mean that the knowledge has several levels. For example, let's say you are a Saturday-afternoon mechanic, and you are using a computerized expert system to help you diagnose a problem with your car so you can fix it yourself. You answer a bunch of questions about how the car is behaving and the expert system thinks for a moment before displaying its conclusion: "The ramifratz needs replacing."

If you don't know what a ramifratz is, where it is located, what tool you need to remove it, or how to replace it, you're in trouble. The expert system hasn't been very helpful. An experienced mechanic might look at the message and reach instinctively for the right tool — undoubtedly a ramifratz wrench — to remove the broken part.

The problem is that the knowledge about the problem and its solution has several layers. If the system spent a long time explaining all of this in detail, the experienced mechanic, who might otherwise find the system quite helpful, would discard it. You, however, need more help than the system is providing.

Enter hypertext. The expert system designer simply designs the system so that if you want more information about a ramifratz, you just click on the word with a mouse pointer, hit a function key, or some other way indicate your interest. The system then links you to some text that explains what a ramifratz is and where it's located. If it's under the gizwidget, and you don't know where that is, just tell the system you need more information on gizwidgets, and off it goes.

Chapter 11 covers the issue of using hypertext to extend the intelligence of expert system-based front ends to business applications.

What to Use?

Choosing the right knowledge representation schema or combination is not an easy task. It takes some study of the nature of the underlying knowledge, an understanding of the user's needs and capabilities, and other systems analysis strategies.

In this book, we will keep things pretty simple by sticking largely to production rules. I have chosen to do this because:

- Production rule systems are by far the most widely available and the least expensive of all the expert system tools

- Production rules are easier to deal with for most people than other, more robust methods of representing knowledge

- Production rules, while not entirely standardized, at least follow a predictable pattern. This means that if you choose a different tool from those used in the book, you won't find yourself spending a lot of time trying to translate from my program listings to your shell's capabilities.

Summary

In this chapter, we have gotten our feet onto solid ground vis-à-vis the terms and concepts with which we will work through the rest of the book. We have worked out definitions for artificial intelligence and expert systems that are adequate to our present consideration. We have seen that AI has failed to live up to much of its promise but that expert systems alone are perhaps enough commercial reason to continue the investigations it undertakes.

We have looked at the components of an expert system, focusing particularly on the inference engine and how it uses forward- and backward-chaining strategies to obtain results.

Finally, we have examined various forms of knowledge representation, including the production rules that form the bulk of our interest in this book but also pausing to consider frames and hypertext.

Chapter 2 focuses attention on key design issues in expert systems and acts as a prelude to the hands-on work that will occupy most of our attention for the rest of this exploration.

CHAPTER 2
Expert System Design Issues

In this chapter, we will explore the basic steps and issues involved in designing and constructing an expert system of any kind. These principles apply to expert systems of almost any size or complexity.

More specifically, we will discuss five steps in designing and building an expert system. We will learn two means of classifying expert system tools (shells) for evaluation purposes and will cover key criteria in evaluating expert system tools and the means by which expert system tools interact with the world outside their boundaries. We will discuss how you may define and understand the end user of your application and alter your design appropriately. The chapter will close with a presentation of the concept of "rapid prototyping" and how it can make an expert system project more successful.

Some of the material in this chapter could be useful in designing any kind of software (expert systems are, after all, software). Other steps or suggestions are unique to expert systems design.

Defining the Problem Domain

In most of what we undertake in this book, problem domain definition is straightforward: you have an existing or contemplated database or spreadsheet application that you believe will benefit from the application of expert system techniques. Even in this seemingly narrow context, though, you must focus on narrowing the problem domain. At the very least, you will want to satisfy yourself that your definition of the problem domain is sufficiently focused to ensure a reasonable chance of success for the project once it's undertaken.

For example, if you set out to write an intelligent front end to a complex spreadsheet application, you might want to focus on just one or two areas of data entry that pose particular pitfalls for people entering data into the system. When those tricky data entry tasks are made more intelligent by the application of expert system technology, you can then turn your attention to other aspects of the worksheet that could benefit from the same technology.

Defining the problem domain almost always involves a process of narrowing, of focusing your attention on a subset of what appears to be a monolithic problem. Do you remember in school when your English instructor gave you an essay assignment and you asked how long it was supposed to be? Chances are (if you had English teachers trained in the same schools mine were) you got an answer like, "Long enough to cover the subject." Not much help, right?

Well, you can't expect much better from a discussion of how to define and narrow the problem domain for an expert system application. Unfortunately, the process simply doesn't lend itself well to precise quantification. However, I can offer some general advice on the subject. The basic principles are:

1. The narrower, the better

2. Concentrate on mission-critical problem

3. Be sure there's enough expertise

4. Be realistic about budget and time constraint

The Narrower, the Better

As a principle, the more you can narrow the problem domain, the more likely you will be able to create a successful solution. In the extreme case, you may have one worksheet cell whose value is tricky to explain or validate. A one-rule expert system might do the trick; or it might take a small handful of rules to ensure the user understands what's being asked and that the data entered is valid. A one-cell problem is not likely to crop up, but it is not entirely impossible, either.

If you are looking at a possible intelligent front end to a spreadsheet application and you can break the data entry process into a half-dozen steps, focus on the one or two steps that are most likely to be troublesome or where an error is most significant.

This is not to say that you won't ultimately apply expert system technology to the entire worksheet, or to substantial parts of it. Indeed, there are occasions when the reason for adopting expert system technology for spreadsheet and database applications is simply the "user-friendly" face they present to the user. But it is important, particularly at the early stage of adopting expert system technology, to make the project manageable so that its chances of success are increased.

Mission-Critical Focus

As you examine a potential use of expert system technology in conjunction with a spreadsheet, think about the problems that are most likely to cause a problem if there is a mistake in their understanding or entry. Initially, you want to concentrate on those aspects of the problem that are viewed by management as the most critical to the mission of the organization.

For example, if you were in the business of tracking securities transactions for clients, you might find that you could use an expert system to help the user identify the stock to be tracked in case the spelling or company symbol was difficult to remember. Or you might be able to apply some expert system technology to an analysis of buying trends. However, what if you had a place in your spreadsheet application where the prices of stocks being entered in a way that was probably erroneous (e.g., too far out of phase with previous prices and with market trends) could result in lost business? That would be the logical place to begin applying expert systems.

Again, the message you should get is not that you won't ultimately use an expert system for many aspects of the problem. But at the outset, if you focus on mission-critical areas of interest, you will more likely be able to gain management's support for the project, demonstrate a bottom-line impact, and gain more visibility for yourself and the project.

Being Sure of the Expertise

In many of the cases with which we will be dealing, you are the expert. Or you may be working with a small organization where the owner or manager is knowledgeable about the application on which expert systems are to be brought to bear. In larger organizations, the expertise may reside in manuals, in automated documentation, in programming notes, or in the heads of one or more department staff members. It may, in fact, be scattered among all these sources.

What you want to do at this stage of expert system development is to be sure you are not attempting to tackle a problem, in which the expertise is not available to you for some reason. For example, if the worksheet was developed by an outside consultant and that consultant is no longer available, you may have a difficult time applying an expert system to a natty problem presented by the design. Even if you are conversant with the macro language or the underlying programming issues in the spreadsheet being used, you may have a tough time deciphering someone else's cryptic programming. For the most part, of course, spreadsheet macro programs are fairly straightforward, so assuming you have access to the code and to a copy of the worksheet (without which you can't very well proceed at all), outside expertise may well never become an issue in these kinds of projects.

We'll deal shortly with the process of identifying and securing the services of the required expertise. That is not so crucial at this early stage. But it is crucial that you be sure you are tackling a problem for which appropriate expertise is accessible to you.

Don't Get In Over Your Head

In any organization, the application of new technology should be approached with some trepidation. New technology often generates more problems than it solves. Adapting existing systems to new approaches is quite often psychologically painful. As a result, it is almost always going to be true that the first few expert systems projects approved and undertaken by an organization will be faced with some budgetary and time constraints.

As you focus on the problem subset to be dealt with by an expert system approach, you must be cognizant of these limits. Even if your prior analysis indicates that a particular aspect of the problem is most susceptible to your approach and is narrow enough to be dealt with intelligently, if you can't carry it out within the budgetary and schedule limits, you must go back and attempt to narrow the focus more. It may be necessary for you to focus on a secondary choice of mission-critical need so that you can stay within these constraints.

Nothing will kill a new technology's acceptance by an organization faster than the delays and cost overruns that everyone expects but nobody really wants to deal with.

Finding an Expert

Once you've defined the problem domain on which to focus your expert system development, you must find an expert who can give you the knowledge you must put into the expert system. Or, more accurately, you must locate the source of the expertise. Though this is most often a human person or group, it sometimes involves written and machine-readable documentation. Table 2-1 summarizes some of the more fruitful sources of such expertise to examine as you begin your project.

Locating an expert — or another source of expertise — is one problem; getting the expert's cooperation is another. This is not to say that experts in any field are by nature recalcitrant. What it does mean is that expertise embodied in human beings is often difficult to obtain for projects such as those we are describing. Some of the primary reasons for this difficulty are:

- **Ego involvement**. Experts have spent many years building up expertise in a particular subject area. Their expertise is often a major component of their identity, self-image, and self-worth. Asking them to transfer that knowledge to someone else — or to make it widely available through a computer program — can be viewed as threatening.

- **Sublimation of knowledge**. One problem with knowledge acquisition strategies (the subject of the next section) is that they often rely on experts being able to articulate what they know. But a great deal of what experts know is sublimated knowledge. This is knowledge that the experts no longer realize they know. It appears to be "automatic" or "obvious."

- **Priorities and commitments**. The expert who can provide the best information about the problem is often one of the busiest people in the organization. The expert's expertise is in constant demand.

- **Proprietary secretiveness**. In the business world, knowledge is often a major competitive advantage. If you are an outside consultant, there may be a certain amount of wariness associated with allowing you access to expertise even when no other problems could intervene. This "outsider" status can include employees of the company who work in different departments from the experts. Frequently this protective, secretive attitude cannot really be justified. However, it is part of the reality with which you must deal.

Table 2-1. Possible Sources of Expertise

Source	Comments
Designer/ Programmer	Often knowledgeable about how application should work. May or may not be familiar with its actual day-to-day usage.
Manager/ Supervisor	Probably knows a great deal about (and then spends much time solving) problems and pitfalls. Probably doesn't know details of usage.
User	Can fill you in on daily operational details and point out where problems are often encountered. Particularly knowledgeable about unclear data entry issues. Probably doesn't understand underlying design.
Documentation	Generally sparse to nonexistent in database and spreadsheet applications. Look for comments in code or macro listings, possibly posted notes using third-party commercial program.
Books	Subject-matter expertise can often come at least partially from books written by the designer or others. Find out if anyone has written a magazine article describing how the system was built.

It is essential, then, that you have top-level management support for your project. This will reduce or eliminate the conscious barriers to your success.

Acquiring the Expert's Knowledge

The unconscious barriers to the successful transfer of expertise from its current human-stored form to a computer-usable representation are not so easy to overcome. No amount of top-level management support or even browbeating and threats is likely to jog the faulty memory of an expert who simply can't recall why or how something is done.

The process of *knowledge acquisition*, then, is a delicate balance of three functions: skillful interviewing, effective tool utilization, and good pupil.

To be a successful knowledge engineer, assuming you are handling the tasks alone, you will have to be a good listener, programmer (of sorts), and learner. (Again, some of this knowledge acquisition material may turn out to be moot if you are dealing with straightforward worksheets and database files. If available, however, it won't hurt for you to rely on the expert's background and understanding. Such an approach can not only make your job easier, it might also reveal other fertile ground for application of the expert system that might escape you from the user's perspective.)

Interviewing Techniques

Extracting the knowledge from the expert requires you to be adept at interviewing techniques that are more common in investigative journalists and clinical psychologists than in computer programmers. In addition, you must have a logical, curious mind.

Here are some tips for conducting effective interviews that grow out of years of experience as a journalist and knowledge engineer:

1. **Do your homework**. Know something about the expert. Has he written any major books on the subject of the interview? How long has he been with the company? How recent is his experience with the problem? You should also know as much as you can about the underlying application and the problem set. If possible, you should read whatever documentation exists, run the program a few times, and talk to some users.

2. **Ask mostly open-ended questions**. There are two types of questions you can ask: yes-no and open-ended. A yes-no question might be, "Does this program require that the user enter a decimal value at that point?" An open-ended question that would elicit the same information — and perhaps more — would be, "What kind of data does the program require at this point?" A one-word answer does not provide your interviewee/expert with an opportunity to expand on something that may or may not be related but which your question might trigger. Also, framing open-ended questions presumes less domain knowledge on your part, and this becomes less threatening to the expert if he has a predisposition to feeling threatened.

3. **Faithfully record the interview**. A few people can take accurate notes while listening to someone speak. Most people, though, will be better off using a tape recorder and having the tapes transcribed later. I frequently use both, taking as detailed notes as I can while still participating in the dialogue but falling back on the tape recorder when my notes are unclear.

4. **Follow branches in the discussion**. The toughest part of the interviewing process is differentiating an important branch in the discussion from a distracting tangent. If the expert says something like, "The spreadsheet does a few calculations and then comes back to this cell with an answer that summarizes the gizmos," don't be afraid to ask about those calculations.

5. **Be persistent**. Because the expert's knowledge is sometimes sublimated and often involves his ego, you may encounter resistance at various points in the interview. If the barrier doesn't yield to one or two direct attempts to deal with it, set it aside for the moment. But make a note that you have to resolve the problem later. Perhaps another opportunity will arise naturally in the discussion. If not, you must create one.

6. **Be sensitive**. This tip clashes with the previous one. It is difficult to be persistent and sensitively patient at the same time.

But you must come as close as you can to this ideal. This is the expert's domain of experience. You are a guest in the territory. If several attempts to extract knowledge you believe to be important have failed, don't keep at it. You must maintain friendly relations with the expert. You may later have to go through other channels or try fresh approaches to get the information if it turns out to be essential to your task.

7. **Be interested**. Even if you have to fake interest on occasion, you should make every effort to be both interested in the subject and in the expert's grasp of it and appear to be interested. Submerged interest is as harmful to the process as lack of interest masquerading as overenthusiasm.

In addition to simply acquiring the subject matter expertise, you should catalog and organize it. After each interview session, review your notes and structure the knowledge into subtopics. You may find an outlining or hypertext tool useful for such tasks. This process of bringing some structure to the knowledge will also be useful in transferring the knowledge you acquire into a computer-usable form.

Choosing a Design Methodology

The process of selecting a design methodology is often the most difficult and time-consuming aspect of the design process. In our case, this step is relatively trivial, since the nature of the problems involved narrows the design methodology choices considerably.

For the sake of completeness, though, let's briefly look at this issue. Essentially, the design methodologies available for developing an expert system for any purpose can be reduced to those shown and discussed briefly in Table 2-2.

As you can probably tell, this book will focus exclusively on the third methodology — expert system shells. It is possible to write intelligent interfaces to spreadsheet and database applications using Pascal, C, BASIC, or an AI language such as LISP or Prolog. However, the few benefits these approaches offer are outweighed by the substantial drawbacks they embody. Writing an expert system from scratch would be like writing your own spreadsheet program. There

Table 2-2. Expert System Design

Methodology	Pros	Cons
AI Language	Adapted to special use Efficient Design process Rapid prototyping	Difficult to interface to other programs Programming talent not plentiful Often slow, memory intensive Mostly interpreted
Conventional language	Large programmer pool often compiled, fast Somewhat easier to interface other progrms	Useful data types absent Reinventing inference, other AI techniques Poor or nonexistent "hooks" to spreadsheets and databases
Expert System Shell	"Programming" often easier than languages Integration can be nearly seamless User interface comes almost free Incremental development possible, encouraged	New technology Validation can be hard Variety makes selection difficult

may even be some spreadsheet or database applications where the actions of an inference engine (see Chapter 1) are not necessary to the task and where a program written in a more conventional language would seem to do just as well. There, however, you deal with the fact that conventional languages, on the whole, lack appropriate and easily accessible interface routines to access and manipulate spreadsheet and database files.

Encoding the Knowledge

Once you have defined the problem by narrowing the domain, located an expert, and extracted the appropriate knowledge, you are ready for the actual construction of an expert system. We will be spending most of the rest of the book in the construction process, so we won't devote much attention to the issue here.

It is, however, important to say one thing at the outset. There has been much mystique surrounding AI and expert system technologies during the past few years. Knowledge engineers, researchers, and expert system designers have placed an aura of nearly impenetrable jargon and concept around the AI field. As a result, a myth has been perpetuated that designing expert systems is so fundamentally and radically different from any other kind of software engineering tasks that none of the rules apply.

Nothing could be further from the truth. To be sure, there are some interesting and important differences in the design process. I hope I have pointed out the major ones already. More will become evident as we work through the case studies. However, the basic principles of systems analysis, program management, revision control, and debugging apply equally to expert system development as they do to any other software task.

Encoding knowledge is conceptually different from embodying database records in a program. There is less certainty of the accuracy and validity of our knowledge than of a database. We must be able to deal with multiple outcomes, but we are still dealing with inputs, interactions with the user, and outputs. And the proper design of these components is an essential ingredient in the construction of successful expert systems.

Classifying the Tools

There are a great many ways to cut the stack of expert system shells available for microcomputers today. For our purposes, we can examine shells from two perspectives: user orientation and robustness.

User Orientation of Shells

From the viewpoint of user orientation, expert system shells can be divided roughly into two groups: those that are programmer oriented and appear to be much more like programming languages than anything else; and those that are knowledge-engineer-oriented and contain more templates, forms, and other design aids to mask the programming process. This division is not 100 percent precise; some shells have a foot in each camp. Nonetheless it is a good way to approach the issue of tool classification.

The mere fact that a shell is programmer oriented does not necessarily mean you must be an experienced programmer to use it. Conversely, it does not follow from a shell's knowledge-engineer orientation that anyone can use it regardless of their computer or programming knowledge.

There is a certain amount of programming thinking that goes into the design and construction of any expert system. An expert system is, after all, a computer program. Publishers of expert system tools who try to convince you that anyone can use them and that they are aimed at the "real end user" or the "domain expert" rather than programmers do you something of a disservice. Still, some tools are more usable than others by people with little or no programming background. In general, shells that take the knowledge-engineering approach of "walking you through" the process of building an expert system are more accessible than those that expect you to start with what amounts to a blank sheet of paper and begin developing the system.

Figure 2-1 shows a sample screen from an expert system shell that takes a strong knowledge-engineering approach to shell design. The product is Instant-Expert Plus, which has versions for both the Macintosh and the IBM PC and compatibles. Notice that you are presented with a "template" — a blank form into which you can enter the elements of a rule. Even without a background in expert systems or production rules, you can look at Figure 2-1 and know what is involved in building a production rule.

Clearly some elements of the screen in Figure 2-1 are obtuse to a beginner in expert systems design. However, with all such products that take a knowledge-engineering, fill-in-the-blank approach to designing production rules, documentation and a little experience quickly makes the user relatively comfortable with the environment.

Contrast this approach with that taken by VP-Expert (Figure 2-2) on the IBM PC and compatibles. VP-Expert takes a very programmerlike approach to expert system design. As a designer, you simply type in commands, statements, and rules in a relatively free-form way. VP-Expert then compiles your edited files into knowledge bases it can use during a consultation session with an end user.

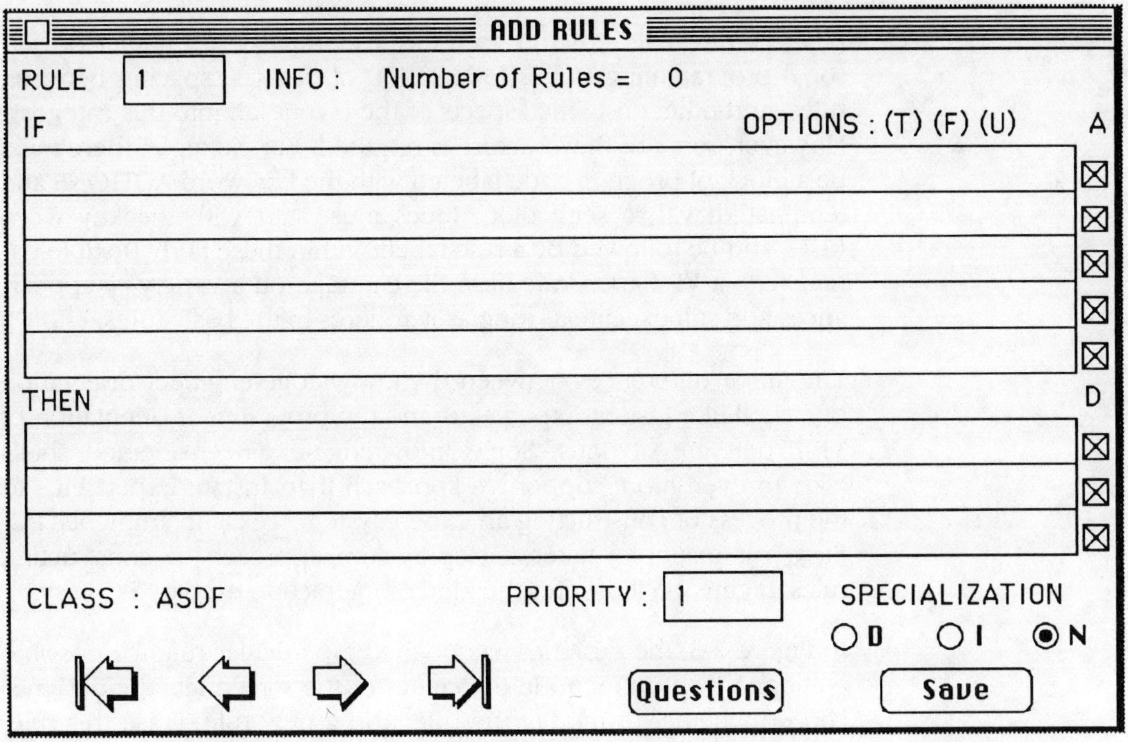

Figure 2-1. Sample Instant-Expert Plus Screen

```
FIND done◄
RESET done◄
END;◄
◄
! Rules Section◄
◄
RULE 1◄
IF          choice=Done◄
THEN        done=Yes;◄
◄
RULE 2◄
IF          choice=Sales_Slips AND◄
            product<>UNKNOWN AND◄
            quantity<>UNKNOWN◄
THEN        WKS data,ROW = (product),inventr1◄
            data[5] = ((data[5]) - (quantity))◄
            data[7] = (data[7] + (quantity))◄
            PWKS data,ROW = (product),inventr1◄
```

Figure 2-2. Sample VP-Expert Screen

Figure 2-2 reveals structure to the rules (some of it a matter of personal programming style). Indentation of clauses, spacing between rules, and other aesthetic aspects of the layout fall into this category. However, some of the structure is required. For example, there must be a block of program code labeled with the key word ACTIONS and terminated with a semicolon. Rules must start with the key word RULE and be followed by a rule label. Within these fairly flexible parameters, a VP-Expert rule base file can take on a variety of appearances and still execute as long as it adheres to the basic rules.

The major differences between the knowledge-engineer orientation of a shell like Instant-Expert Plus and the programmer orientation of VP-Expert are obvious. Some knowledge-engineer-oriented shells take an even more supportive approach than Instant-Expert Plus to the process of constructing an expert system. Texas Instruments' PC-Easy, for example, takes a step-by-step approach to constructing rules. Figure 2-3 illustrates the kind of interaction used by PC-Easy.

In Figure 2-3, the designer has opened a particular rule for possible editing. A pop-up menu in the center of the screen lets the designer choose whether to modify the rule, add a new rule, erase this rule, make a copy of it so another similar rule can be created, translate it (discussed below), or quit working on this part of a rule.

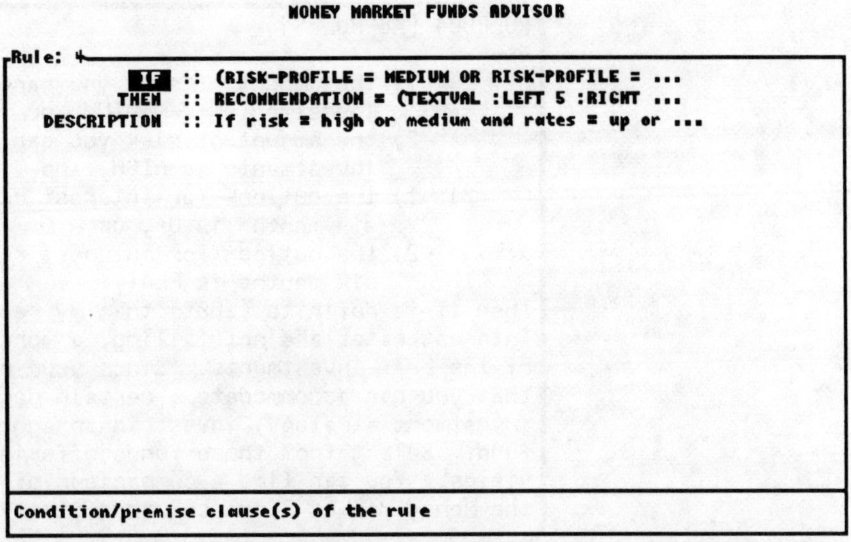

MONEY MARKET FUNDS ADVISOR

```
┌Rule: 4──────────────────────────────────────────────────────────────┐
│              IF  :: (RISK-PROFILE = MEDIUM OR RISK-PROFILE = ...      │
│            THEN  :: RECOMMENDATION = (TEXTUAL :LEFT 5 :RIGHT ...      │
│     DESCRIPTION  :: If risk = high or medium and rates = up or ...    │
│                                                                      │
│                                                                      │
│                                                                      │
│                                                                      │
│                                                                      │
│                                                                      │
│                                                                      │
│                                                                      │
│                                                                      │
│                                                                      │
├──────────────────────────────────────────────────────────────────────┤
│ Condition/premise clause(s) of the rule                              │
└──────────────────────────────────────────────────────────────────────┘
```

Figure 2-3. Rule Editing Screen in PC-Easy

To modify the IF part of the rule in Figure 2-3, a screen like Figure 2-4 appears. PC-Easy, however, may translate the rule into a more English-like presentation, as Figure 2-5 shows. Part of the contents of this English translation of the rule is supplied by the designer, but the structure and the style of presentation are defined by PC-Easy.

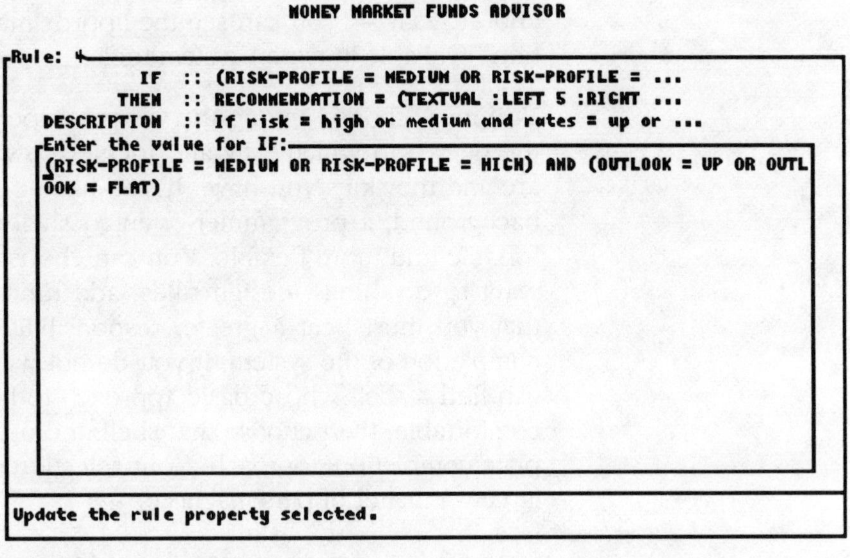

MONEY MARKET FUNDS ADVISOR

```
┌Rule: 4──────────────────────────────────────────────────────────────┐
│                IF  :: (RISK-PROFILE = MEDIUM OR RISK-PROFILE = ...    │
│              THEN  :: RECOMMENDATION = (TEXTUAL :LEFT 5 :RIGHT ...    │
│      DESCRIPTION  :: If risk = high or medium and rates = up or ...   │
├Enter the value for IF:────────────────────────────────────────────────┤
│ (RISK-PROFILE = MEDIUM OR RISK-PROFILE = HIGH) AND (OUTLOOK = UP OR OUTL│
│ OOK = FLAT)                                                           │
│                                                                      │
│                                                                      │
│                                                                      │
│                                                                      │
│                                                                      │
│                                                                      │
│                                                                      │
├──────────────────────────────────────────────────────────────────────┤
│ Update the rule property selected.                                   │
└──────────────────────────────────────────────────────────────────────┘
```

Figure 2-4. Editing the IF Part of a Rule in PC-Easy

```
RULE004 [KB-RULES]
--------
If  1)  1) the amount of risk you can accommodate in your
           investments is MEDIUM, or
        2) the amount of risk you can accommodate in your
           investments is HIGH, and
    2)  1) the outlook for interest rates for the next
           six months is UP, or
        2) the outlook for interest rates for the next
           six months is FLAT,
Then it is definite (100%) that my recommendation is When
interest rates are not falling, a money market fund is one
of the best investments.  Since your risk profile indicates
that you can accommodate a certain degree of risk in your
investment strategy, invest in an aggressive money market
fund.  Select from those funds offering the highest
yields.  You can find a comparison of current yields in
the Money Market Funds column of the Wall Street Journal.
```

Figure 2-5. The PC-Easy TRANSLATE Operation at Work

As you can tell from this necessarily brief discussion of PC-Easy, it takes an even more knowledge-engineer-oriented approach to rule set design and construction than the template approach of Instant-Expert Plus.

Among the three of these shells — Instant-Expert Plus, VP-Expert, and PC-Easy — you can see the approximate range of user orientations available in expert system tools.

You must choose among the various expert system shells based on the degree to which they are oriented toward the kind of user you are and the skills you have. If you have a reasonable programming background, a programmer-oriented shell will be both more comfortable and more flexible. You can choose the order in which you want to do things, design rules, add functionality. Note, however, that you must bear a greater responsibility for the debugging and completion of the system. If you do not want to program and if you can find a shell whose basic approach to knowledge engineering is comfortable, then choose that shell and use its step-by-step or template completion approach. Your selection of expert system shells is largely a matter of personal taste.

Figure 2-6 summarizes graphically the user orientation of some of the shells we discuss here and elsewhere in this book.

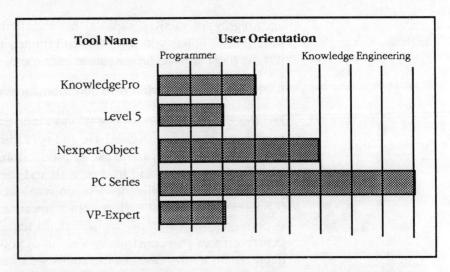

Figure 2-6. User Orientation of Representative Expert System Shells

Robustness

The second basis on which we can categorize expert system tools relates to their robustness. Robustness includes four basic ideas:

- Variety of knowledge representation approaches
- Interface to the outside world
- Ability to use graphics
- Ability to deal with large and complex knowledge bases

It is untrue, though logical, that the more robust a shell is, the less knowledge-engineer-oriented it is likely to be.

Level 5 and VP-Expert are shells we discuss in this book that are strictly production-rule-based systems. Yet both fall strongly at the programmer end of the user-orientation scale in Figure 2-6. Both of these shells have good interfaces to other programs (particularly database and spreadsheet applications, our primary focus). VP-Expert has excellent graphic capability while Level 5's graphic capability is nonexistent on IBM PCs and fairly limited on the Macintosh.

By way of contrast, Personal Consultant Plus is one of the most flexible systems we looked at. It supports (via an optional add-on package) highly interactive graphics, has excellent interfaces to external programs, and lets you use rules and frames as your orientation. Yet it is the most knowledge-engineer-oriented of the shells we focus on.

So there is no correlation between robustness and user orientation.

For our purposes, robustness is important especially where it concerns user interfaces (in database and spreadsheet applications). Our discussion will focus on the use of production rules because they are easier to understand and to deal with and they are always sufficient when designing intelligent front ends. Similarly, only one chapter (Chapter 12) will deal with graphics because their use is quite tool dependent. Most systems we will build together — and the intelligent interfaces you construct as a result of your study — will be relatively small; in any case, all the shells we examine in this discussion will nicely handle the demands of such an application.

Choosing a Tool

Some of the effort involved in choosing a tool is taken care of by the classification process just described. If you want a tool that is robust, deals well with interactive graphics, and is programmer oriented, for example, you can narrow the search considerably by eliminating shells that don't match those criteria.

Once you've narrowed the list of prospects, though, on what basis can you make a final selection of an expert system tool? The answer depends on the job you want the shell to do.

Since we are building expert systems to serve as intelligent front ends to spreadsheet and database applications, we can focus our thinking on those aspects of a shell's design that are relevant to our general needs. (If you were selecting a shell for a more complex application, you might well want to take other, more technical criteria into account.)

Additional nontechnical criteria to consider when you evaluate tools for creating intelligent front ends for business applications include:

- Experience
- Platform support
- Execution speed
- Customer support
- Price

Let's take a quick look at each of these subjects.

Experience

Your application is one that is important to the operation of your business (or your client's business). It's not a good place for on-the-job training or predelivery testing new products. If you have experience with a particular shell, it meets the criteria, and you are comfortable using it that may be sufficient reason to choose it. No shell is perfect.

If you are able to do so, talk to other users of the product. A reputable publisher of expert system tool will give you names of a few users. Call or write them and ask about their experience. Focus your questions on the other criteria covered in this discussion. If you get consistently high marks from users who have needs similar to yours or who run similar businesses, you can be fairly certain the shell has stood the acid test of user evaluation.

Platform Support

Obviously the shell you choose must be able to run on the computer equipment you plan to use. However, you may want to select a tool that will enable you to deliver on more than one hardware platform. If you are developing a product with somewhat broad potential for use, or if the company has a similar or identical spreadsheet or database application running on more than one computer, you should be sure your expert system shell choice takes this into account.

Most shells run on only one platform. Exceptions in our group are Level 5 and VP-Expert (which support both Macintosh and IBM PC), as well as Nexpert-Object (which runs on most major hardware platforms from microcomputers to mainframes). For multiple-platform support, choose a tool that gives it to you without much headache. For example, it is possible to transfer generic production rules from one shell to another. You can simply re-enter them into the second shell or transfer them by some other means. But that won't mean they will run correctly, that the inference engines will match up at crucial points, or that you won't end up doing more work than if you simply rewrote the system from scratch on the second platform.

Execution Speed

In most expert systems, speed of execution is relatively insignificant, at least within broad tolerances — because they are infrequently used, generally address a complex problem, and produce a result that's worth waiting for. This is not the case with intelligent front ends, which are interactive by nature and probably frequently used.

When you talk to other users of the shells you are evaluating, be sure to ask about execution speed. Even if this is not an important issue for the users you are interviewing, it may well turn out to be the criterion that makes the final selection obvious for you.

In that regard, all the shells we are considering fall within acceptable limits. Useful benchmark tests do not yet exist for expert system shells, but Table 2-3 is a rough ranking of these shells with regard to execution speed across several kinds of applications. Don't rely on this table for your final determination, though, since some of the shells do better at some kinds of things than others.

Customer Support

Depending on your experience with expert systems and with the shell you choose, you will need an unpredictable amount of technical support from the publisher during development and perhaps even after delivery of your finished product.

Table 2-3. Relative Speed Ratings of Representative Tools

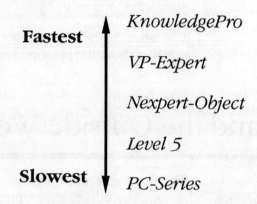

Fastest — *KnowledgePro*

VP-Expert

Nexpert-Object

Level 5

Slowest — *PC-Series*

Evaluating customer support is one of the most difficult aspects of choosing any software. Expert system tools are no exception. You can read magazine and journal reviews of the tools and still not know much, because support ratings in such places are often distorted. If the shell publisher knows or suspects that the caller is writing a review of the product, the reaction the caller receives may be different from the way more routine calls are handled, for example.

Here is where interviewing current users of the expert system shells under consideration is essential. If you get a sense from talking to two or three users that they have had a difficult time getting support, do not use that shell no matter how good it is unless you have enough experience with it to all but eliminate the need for customer support.

Price

Price is the least important of all the considerations. This may sound strange, but think about it for a moment. If you are going to build an expert system with some return-on-investment expectation, your payback will almost certainly exceed the cost of the shell, even if you pick a tool that costs several thousand dollars. Additionally, it is almost always true that the price of the tool is the least significant portion of the project's budget; people and equipment are far more significant influences.

Use price as the final arbiter or tie breaker; all other things being equal, go with the price-performance winner.

Tools and the Outside World

There are essentially two ways an expert system shell (or, for that matter, any other kind of program) can interact with programs outside its boundaries:

- Intermediate file or data transfer
- Direct file manipulation and compatibility

Virtually all expert system tools use one or both of these modes of interacting with external programs. For our purposes, however, only the second mode, that of direct file access, makes any real sense. It is possible to build intelligent front ends using shells that don't have this level of integration and interaction with other programs, but the process is more painful than it needs to be.

Table 2-4 summarizes the shells we are considering and the kinds of external programs with which they are directly compatible. It also indicates whether the tool features the generalized ability to call external routines written in other programming languages. This latter indication can be an important concern if you want to use a spreadsheet or database that is not on the list of those with which the shell has built-in compatibility. It also has other implications that are beyond the scope of this discussion.

You, of course, may choose to evaluate tools other than those under discussion here. In that case, be sure to determine whether the shell has a "built-in" interface to the database and/or spreadsheet program(s) with which you want to use it. Again, it may be a good idea to interview people who have experience using the tool.

Table 2-4. Interfaces of Representative Expert System Tools

Tool Name	Compatibility	General?
KnowledgePro	dBASE, Lotus 1-2-3	Yes
Level 5	dBASE	DOS[1]
Nexpert-Object	dBASE, ORACLE, SQL, DB2[2]	Yes
PC Series	dBASE, Lotus 1-2-3[3]	DOS[1]
VP-Expert	dBASE, Lotus 1-2-3 VP-Info, VP-Planner[4]	DOS[1]

Notes

1. "DOS" here means tool can invoke other programs with calls to DOS but cannot directly execute external procedures written in other languages without going through the DOS level.
2. Nexpert-Object uses its own proprietary intermediate database format to facilitate links to many mainframe, microcomputer, and minicomputer database files.
3. Lotus 1-2-3 interface available only with PC-Plus.
4. VP-Info is dBASE compatible and VP-Planner is Lotus 1-2-3 compatible. Both products are manufactured by Paperback Software, which also publishes VP-Expert.

Defining and Describing the User

Once a tool is chosen, the real work of expert system design can begin. A software project should include at an early stage a description of the end user of the product. For an expert system, this is definitely the case; if anything, it is more important than with other kinds of software. This is because of the intensive ego involvement of the domain expert in the knowledge base and because the end user must ultimately feel comfortable with the system or mission-critical decisions will not be made as efficiently and effectively as they can be.

Obviously, knowing your end user's needs, desires, prejudices, and tendencies is crucial when you are developing interfaces — front ends — as we are in this book.

You need to ask yourself several questions about your end user early in the process of designing an expert system:

1. What does the end user know, both about the computer's use and about the subject of the expert system?

2. What does the end user expect to get out of the system?

3. What does the end user want, but doesn't yet know he wants, to get out of using the system? (Sometimes this question is better stated as, "What does management want the user to get out of the system that the end user is probably unaware of at this moment?")

(We should note at the outset of this discussion that if "you" are the end user of the system, this material hardly applies to you directly. Still, you may find out some things about your own perceptions that are useful. The primary audience for the following sections, though, is the consultant designing an interface for a client.)

What the User Knows

How well the user knows the computer, the underlying program (spreadsheet or database), and the application itself are major factors in designing an intelligent front end for the application.

If the user is a relative neophyte when it comes to the computer system, for example, you might opt to implement an intelligent interface that handles even operating system-level functions such as file management. If, however, the user is a fairly experienced operator of the system, you can leave a great deal of such ancillary processing to the user. Similarly, if the user is comfortable with a keyboard but would be put off by a pointing device such as a mouse or track ball, stick with what the user knows.

It is likely that the end user of a spreadsheet application is not going to be the same person who designed that application. At least that is the case when the possibility of designing an intelligent front end is being discussed. After all, the original designer of a spreadsheet application probably doesn't need much handholding when using it. This fact generally means that the end user is not terribly knowledgeable about the underlying spreadsheet or database management program itself. Such users can probably not create their own spreadsheet templates, for example.

The design implications of this are wide-reaching. If you design an interactive type of interface, for example, you should avoid using program-specific jargon such as "cell," "field," or "template." You should design the interface so that the end user never even sees the underlying program. We will see in Chapters 7-11 how to do so.

The end user of the intelligent interface you are designing will generally have some experience with the application for which the interface is being constructed. That person has probably been frustrated, made a number of data entry mistakes caused by the unfamiliarity of the environment, or complained about how difficult the application is to use. This is in all likelihood why an intelligent interface design is being evaluated or undertaken. It is, of course, possible that you will design intelligent interfaces for new applications. This will become more likely after you have built one or two such products and you or your customer has seen the real value in the approach.

If the end user is familiar with the application, the design job is simplified. You can observe the user interacting with the application, spot areas of difficulty, and note places where the interface might be merely an added layer of interference between the user and the task at hand. This familiarity will also allow you to use terms and rely on concepts with which the user is already comfortable, even if they are program-specific or jargonlike.

A key design rule is to begin with what you are sure the user knows. Users can sometimes become comfortable with the mechanics of an operation without understanding its structure or meaning. For example, a clerical worker might daily enter hundreds of numbers into a spreadsheet application without the foggiest notion of what the numbers mean. The clerical worker might not even be familiar with the idea of a "cell," depending on how transparently the system has been designed and presented during the clerk's orientation.

End-User Expectations

By now you realize that you should not design an intelligent interface without talking to the end user. The user is crucial to the design and to the ultimate successful use of the interface.

One important question to ask the user during your design phase is, "What could the system do to make this application easier to use?" It may take a little probing to find the user's real expectations. It may also require you to do a little education: end users may see computers as capable of doing all things. They must be disabused of this if they are going to be satisfied with the finished interface product.

The end user may not think he will have any impact on the design — an attitude that may reflect his feeling that the original application was simply dumped on him without consultation (which it was, in all probability). In this event, you must take a more proactive approach, asking, "Would it be helpful if the system did this?" rather than eliciting open-ended responses from the user.

One thing is certain. If the end user's expectations, voiced or silent, are not met by your finished product, the user's experience with it will not be as productive and positive as you are trying to achieve.

Invisible Expectations

Experienced computer consultants and software designers will identify with this scenario. You are called by a prospective customer, who wants a "little database application" designed and built. You meet with the customer, get a handle on what is wanted, propose the project, and build the program. Along the way, you have several meetings with the client. There are frequent exchanges that sound something like this:

YOU   We should really make the system flexible enough to handle the next three steps in processing your inventory. I know you're going to want that someday and--

CLIENT   No. I know what I want the computer to do. It can't do those other steps and I don't want to spend that much money to get that done. Just give me what I am asking for.

You finally deliver what the customer "says" and "believes" he wants. Three months later, the phone rings:

CLIENT   Could this computer system you designed for me handle the next three steps in inventory processing for me? It's taking me a lot of time and as I think about it, it seems to me we ought to be able to get the computer to do some of this work.

YOU   (Heavy sighing.)

An intelligent interface to a spreadsheet or database application is no different in this respect from other software you've built. Here's a good rule of thumb: if you feel strongly that the user will want to automate and make intelligent some aspect of the interface later, prototype it and see how the client reacts. (We'll have more to say on the subject of this kind of rapid prototyping later in the chapter.)

In designing intelligent interfaces, there is another aspect to the issue of invisible user expectations. The end user is often unaware of certain aspects of the design that management mandates. The end user may feel, for example, the entry of new employee information into the company database is going along quite well, while the company's managers note a pattern of errors they think your interface can solve. Obviously, the end user's managers are paying your fee, so you design what they want. Still, if you sense that they are imposing something unreasonable, you might try taking the end user's viewpoint and arguing against it. This is thin ice, though, so tread carefully. If you win a point here, you may win a badly needed ally in the end user. If you lose, you could be looking for another contract.

Rapid Prototyping

When AI emerged from academic computer science labs into commercial use, there was a fair amount of resistance on the part of businesspeople to the adoption of this new technology. Those who are responsible for the design of new technology often forget that the person who must "buy off" on this new power sees hidden in it numerous pitfalls and traps for the unsuspecting user. The end user often applies the engineering aphorism, "If it isn't broken, don't fix it."

To overcome these technological objections, early AI developers adopted a development strategy that came to be known as "rapid prototyping." This approach takes the position that the best way to get a reluctant user to accept new technology is to give him something as soon as possible after he agrees to try it. Then to involve him intimately in the design process, which takes on an iterative style. Figure 2-7 summarizes the the process of rapid prototyping.

A properly chosen and designed expert system tool facilitates rapid prototyping by:

- Requiring a minimal amount of overhead, control, administrative, and other support code

- Including an inference engine that is capable of dealing well with unknown data so that early "blind allies" caused by rapid prototyping are transparent at least to the user if not to the designer

- Allowing the designer to implement a single line of reasoning so that it runs properly from beginning to end, yet integrates well with the finished product when multiple lines of reasoning are involved

Many intelligent front ends you build will be small and rapid prototyping will seem unnecessary. In some cases, it may well be unnecessary. Be certain, however, it is not helpful before discarding it. It is difficult to overstate the importance of getting the user involved early in the process, and nothing does that so well as rapid prototyping.

Unconsidered Issues

This discussion is not exhaustive. If we were interested in building large-scale expert systems dealing with complex problems across many subsystems, we would also have to discuss such subjects as:

- Partitioning or subdividing knowledge into manageable chunks to work with individually

- Cost justifying the expert system project

- Validation of the final design

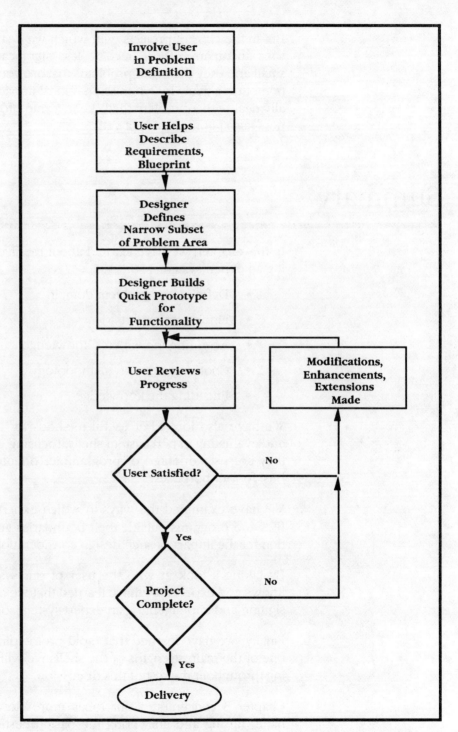

Figure 2-7. Rapid Prototyping Process

But in the class of projects with which we deal in this book, these issues and many others become less significant. These projects are small and they deal with problems that are generally high in aggravation but relatively low in mission-critical impact. After all, they generally deal with a problem that's been around for a while and the business hasn't gone bankrupt yet!

Summary

In this chapter, we have learned about the five basic steps in designing an expert system:

- Defining the problem domain
- Finding an expert
- Acquiring the expert's knowledge
- Choosing a design methodology
- Encoding the knowledge

We have also looked at useful methods for comparing, classifying, and evaluating expert system shells, focusing on the degree to which they are user oriented or programmer oriented and sufficiently robust for our purposes.

We have examined the ways in which expert systems interact with files and programs outside their boundaries and gained an appreciation for the impact of such design considerations on our projects.

By taking a look at who the user of our system is, what the user knows and expects, we have learned that we can make the job of designing and implementing an expert system solution easier.

Finally, we have learned that rapid prototyping of expert systems is one of the main strengths of the shells we will be examining and using throughout the rest of this discussion.

Chapter 3 concentrates our focus more closely on the projects at hand, raising and answering the basic question of how to select a problem that is appropriate in all ways to expert system resolution.

CHAPTER 3
Problem Selection and Definition

In this chapter, we will examine the first step in the process of expert system design and construction: selecting a problem appropriate to an expert system solution. To some degree, we have discussed this subject in Chapters 1 and 2. But in this discussion, we will focus our attention on practical rather than theoretical issues. Specifically, we will look at how the following factors should influence the problem-selection process: the size and nature of the problem, the nature of the user, hardware platforms, and marketing questions.

At the end of this chapter, you will be able to describe a problem by containment, that is, by "putting a fence" around the problem and defining it with enough precision that success is likely.

Size of Problem

An expert system that tries to do too much is a candidate for failure of execution; an expert system that tries to do too little is a candidate for failure of acceptance. You must become adept at determining when a problem is just big enough. The size of the problem is easier to deal with than the scope. Size in a spreadsheet or database situation generally comes down to the number of functions it must automate or support. A spreadsheet that assists an accounting manager in cash management tasks, for example, might involve several steps in processing, as shown in Table 3-1.

Expert system technology can be applied to such a set of tasks at several different points. Since we are examining intelligent interfaces, we will focus on the first two steps. At first glance, it might seem that we should focus on the second step: entering bank policy information into the system. (This information relates to interest rate levels, minimum balance requirements, and other factors that influence how much interest the company can earn on its liquid cash.) This process is one with which a casual system user might be least comfortable, and where an error during entry could result in bad decisions being made later.

Table 3-1. Cash Management Spreadsheet Tasks

Step	Description
1.	Entering checks and other transactions
2.	Entering bank policy information regarding checking account and savings deposits
3.	Reconciling checking account transactions
4.	Entering departmental budget information
5.	Analyzing near-term cash needs
6.	Printing reports for manual analysis

But don't dismiss the routine entry of transactions without thinking about it. What if the user didn't have to think about whether to enter deposits as negative numbers and withdrawals as positive or vice versa? How much efficiency could be gained by allowing the user simply to select the type of transaction and enter an amount rather than trying to figure out which of several columns to enter it in?

There is another reason for choosing step 1 over step 2. The size of the problem in step 1 is manageable and predictable. Transactions will consist of a description, some indication of type of transaction, and an amount. Therefore, the interface can deal with a small number of elements and be sure that they are working together correctly.

This is not, however, to suggest that only a trivial problem should be considered a candidate for an intelligent interface. First, it is not clear that even this relatively simple problem is trivial. For example, you might have a company policy that says certain kinds of transactions have upper limits on their amounts (e.g., petty cash expenditures can't exceed $25, expense account reimbursements can't be more than $1,000, etc.). Programming a macro in a spreadsheet to deal even with this level of complexity can become a daunting task and the feedback you can give the user in such situations can be fairly limited. However, using even a fairly rudimentary expert system approach, we can create meaningful error messages that will help even inexperienced users find their way through the process without a real understanding of the company's policies.

Trying in one step to build an expert system-based approach to dealing with steps 1, 2, 4, and 5 in Table 3-1 would be a mistake. The resulting expert system would be so multifunctioned and intertwined that debugging and validation of the system's operation and results would become a problem. More importantly, the system might take a much longer time to complete than can be justified by the savings.

There are no neat rules for deciding when a problem is big enough to justify the time it takes to write an expert system and small enough to be manageable. I've seen a system that dealt with only two pieces of data being entered into a large spreadsheet pay for itself in a few days. I've also seen very large-scale systems built using dozens of rules and interface techniques that turned out to be too small to solve the real problem in the system. It just takes experience. But if you are aware of the fact that experience is a major consideration in problem-selection, you may at least be able to avoid the more common mistake of picking too big a problem and then becoming bogged down in attempting to solve it.

Nature of Problem

In this book, we are interested only in one kind of problem: those affecting the correct entry of information into spreadsheets and databases. We have essentially predetermined that such problems are appropriate for expert systems solutions in many instances. But that doesn't mean we can ignore the question of the nature of the problem. It simply narrows our focus.

In examining the nature of a problem for possible intelligent interface design, we will be concerned with two issues: its importance and the degree to which it is interrelated with the rest of the system.

Importance

As a general rule, you will want to design intelligent interfaces only for those data-entry components of spreadsheet and database applications that are important to the total system. If the spreadsheet already deals with possible data entry errors or if such errors are of minor importance, you are probably not going to find that applying expert system technology is appropriate.

Returning to our example in Table 3-1, step 4 might well drop from consideration as a possible intelligent interface application based on this issue. If budgets are being entered once a year, consist entirely of numbers, and don't have any particularly tricky parameters associated with them, they are not a good candidate.

In the long run, it will take longer to set up the interface, test it, and teach people to use it than any possible savings. We would reach a similar conclusion about entering text descriptions or labels (which in any case are probably not subject to much intelligence during data entry).

More importantly, in both cases, if a budget is entered incorrectly, the error can probably be easily caught and fixed. Its impact on the total cash management strategy of the company is probably minimal. It is simply not important enough to warrant special treatment. Routine algorithmic procedures (such as checking cross-totals) can be used to verify data accuracy. A typographical error in a department name is not likely to result in an erroneous conclusion being drawn from data in the spreadsheet or database.

Focus your energies in developing intelligent interfaces to segments of the system (such as correct entry of checks against company policy limits and bank policy information which play a crucial role in decision-making) that are important.

Ask yourself, "If I made a mistake entering information into this part of the database, how serious would the consequences be?" If the answer comes out, "Not very serious," then move on to some other area of the application.

Degree of Interconnection

The more interconnected a particular subset of information is with the rest of the system, the more likely a candidate it is for an intelligent interface design. If the question of whether a particular entry is valid depends on entries in other parts of the system, it represents a particularly good candidate for expert system implementation.

For example, let's say that the validity of a particular type of withdrawal transaction in our application depends partly on the size of a departmental budget. When entering a money market fund transfer, the system may need to examine the department's budget and, if there appears to be a discrepancy in the logic or the size of the transfer, alert the user to the possible problem. This is a perfect candidate for an intelligent interface. It might be possible to program such a data validation check in the spreadsheet macro, but if the departmental budget has not yet been entered and the system is therefore dealing with missing data, the process becomes tricky or impossible. Expert systems can be designed to deal placidly with missing data.

Nature of User

The less experienced the operator of the system, the more likely an intelligent interface is to be helpful. The less accurate a typist or data entry operator the user is, the more likely such an interface is to catch mistakes that might otherwise result in bad business decisions.

This principle cuts two ways. If the user of the system is a clerical person who has not been involved in policy setting and is unaware of the implications of such issues as money market fund transfers compared to departmental budget levels, that user cannot be expected to catch such potential discrepancies. An intelligent interface can be quite helpful in such a situation.

However, a manager who could easily catch such a discrepancy, probably without even explicitly looking up the departmental budget, might be a terrible typist and be prone to make data entry errors that could prove disastrous when decisions must be made later.

In cases where both types of user might be involved at different points, you may well want to design more than one intelligent interface to accommodate their needs. For the clerical person, a policy-oriented interface that verifies the probable validity of data based on an analysis of other areas of the system is appropriate. For the manager, a data-validation routine that simply checks the likelihood of errors in data entries might be sufficient. Depending on the degree of complexity involved, you might combine both kinds of interfaces in one package.

Consider the nature of your user in the context of the database or spreadsheet. The less experienced, policy aware, procedure knowledgeable, or expert in the underlying application, the greater the likelihood that an intelligent interface will have a real payoff.

Hardware Platforms

At the present state of expert system art, you would be well-advised not to try to develop an intelligent interface to a spreadsheet or database that runs on more than one hardware platform. (This is not to say you shouldn't tackle projects that run on networks, though. What we mean is different types of hardware: IBM PCs, Macintoshes, DEC VAXs, mainframes, workstations, etc.)

There are relatively few expert system tools that can migrate across these hardware boundaries. Those that do are not particularly strong in their support of multiple spreadsheet or database formats.

Aside from the pure limitation of the tools available to you, you will almost certainly find that the problems of entry and interface vary considerably from one platform to another. This makes your job of providing a consistent interface that everyone will find comfortable using doubly difficult.

Macintosh users, for example, expect a highly graphic interface to their programs. A menu-driven approach will work with them. If you require them to do more typing rather than less to take advantage of your intelligent interface, you will likely make them feel that the interface knows less than they do.

However, people accustomed to a command-line interface like an MS-DOS or UNIX system may feel that a sudden shift to pull-down menus, dialog boxes, and icons is too abrupt a change. They may feel that the interface is now in the way of solving the problem.

For your first few projects, at least, if you have a choice, stay with problems that appear on one platform.

Marketing Questions

Even spreadsheet or database applications designed for your organization have a marketing side to the interface issue. Unless you are a one-person organization, you will have to convince someone else to fund the interface development or to use it, or both. Intelligent interface design involves three marketing considerations:

- Prioritization of needs

- Speed of first delivery

- Payoff (return on investment)

Priorities

Related to the nature of the problem (discussed above), the question of prioritization becomes an issue when you are sorting through a number of candidates for an intelligent interface. If your resources permit you to develop only one or a small number of a large field of potential candidates, you need to prioritize.

Books have been written on how to set priorities, sell them in an organization, and plan their implementation. We're not going to learn how to prioritize here. But we should examine the issue from the perspective of a need to sell management on the adoption of a specific intelligent interface design. This process may be quite political and involve a need to balance various managers' conflicting views of what is most important to the organization's success.

You can help sort out these conflicting priorities by pointing out the need to focus on mission-critical aspects of the spreadsheets and databases under consideration. You can also help by directing management's attention to the design issues discussed in Chapters 1 and 2.

Ultimately, though, prioritization is undoubtedly going to involve a mixture of proper problem selection and political savvy. This will be particularly true if you plan to implement more than one intelligent interface solution and therefore need broad, ongoing management support from a certain level of the organization.

If the product on which you are working is destined for external delivery, whether by sale or by movement to other divisions that may not be involved in the initial decisions, prioritization will probably ultimately focus on pay-off and profit issues, which are discussed later in this chapter. Bringing a product to market to meet an already-expressed customer need is far easier and usually more immediately profitable than trying to make a market for a technology in which you believe but which your customers have yet to acknowledge.

Speed of First Delivery

A consideration that often helps in prioritizing conflicting priorities is the issue of the time lag between project approval and first delivery of technology. If you are weighing the three competing intelligent interface applications depicted in Table 3-2, for example, you should probably express a strong preference for Project A. The sooner you can deliver a working, contributing product, the sooner you will obtain the management backing you need ultimately to make all of your projects successful.

About a month after you receive approval to proceed with it, Project A will be in place and returning benefits. You now have a showcase project with which you can attract other managers' interest. In addition, you will have had the experience of designing, building, deploying, and supporting a real application. The lessons you learn from this experience will make the other projects you undertake go more smoothly. Your estimates of time, cost, and user acceptance will be more refined.

Table 3-2. Three Hypothetical Projects

Project A
    Mission-Critical Level: High
    Return on Investment Projection: 2.3:1
    Time to Complete: 4.2 weeks

Project B
    Mission-Critical Level: High
    Return on Investment Projection: 5.5:1
    Time to Complete: 18 weeks

Project C
    Mission-Critical Level: High
    Return on Investment Projection: 9:1
    Time to Complete: 22 weeks

Management, meanwhile, can see the benefits. One or more users will be able to indicate whether day-to-day realities match your projections and promises. The entire issue of intelligent interfaces will take on a tangibility it could not have achieved for some time if one of the other projects had been adopted first.

Payoff

The return on investment of a project like an intelligent interface can present problems. These projects are like preventive maintenance: The benefits are hard to see until you neglect them for a while.

Still, many management groups require payoff projection before approving new projects, particularly those that involve applying what may be perceived as esoteric technology. Even if you are producing a product for sale to others, a projection of potential sales requires you to analyze the economic benefit of your proposed product.

Table 3-3 summarizes some of the main ways an intelligent interface can be seen to produce savings or generate revenue. There is nothing magical about the list. In your situation, you may find other possibilities that we haven't considered. But the broad categories of areas to research for possible savings or revenue should prove helpful as you plan your intelligent interface project.

Table 3-3. Possible Benefits of Intelligent Interfaces

Reducing Errors
> Reducing need for proofreading of reports
> Cutting down on remakes and reruns
> Improving quality of decision-making the first time

Capitalizing on Previously Missed Opportunities
> Earning interest, income previously overlooked because of errors and omissions
> Taking advantage of supplier policies

Saving Time
> Eliminate data-validation checking in many cases
> Timelier decisions may lead to less need for "recovery" from errors

---

Describing the Problem by Containment

If your experience parallels that of other people who have adopted intelligent interface technology to solve database and spreadsheet management problems, you will find yourself with more projects than you can handle. In fact, you may even start out in that situation.

When you must decide among several potentially useful intelligent interfaces for a company's projects or products, you should adopt a process of "decision by containment." This implies that you surround the problem and possible solutions with parameters to keep them from becoming so big or numerous that dealing with them becomes a more time-consuming task than implementing them.

The principle of containment is simple: narrow the focus, narrow the scope, and narrow the extent of the problem. By using the techniques discussed earlier in this chapter, you will be able to get a handle on the issues in intelligent interface design for your organization. Don't let the problem get too big to solve or the solutions too numerous to implement well. This injection of new technology, like any other, is subject to enough resistance without you — its champion — adding to the problem by being too ambitious at the outset.

Summary

In this chapter, we have examined the major factors in the problem-selection phase of intelligent interface design. Those factors, as we have seen, include:

- Size of problem (big enough to be interesting and useful, small enough to be manageable)

- Nature of problem (complex and interrelated are better than simple and isolated)

- Nature of user (both clerical and managerial people can have problems getting the right data into a system, but their problems differ)

- Hardware platforms (stay away from multiple-system problems, at least until you have more experience and until more tools become available)

- Marketing questions (critical issues include prioritization, speed of first delivery, and profit or return on investment)

We have seen that the best strategy for making a decision among several competing prospects for intelligent interface design is containment, and that this strategy is also best for defining the problem once it has been selected.

Chapter 4 focuses on the types of interaction processes that intelligent interface design can help deal with, and presents some concrete examples of programs to support users of such systems.

CHAPTER 4
Interface Design: The Old and the New

This chapter looks at how people usually interact with spreadsheet and database programs and at how software could be designed to assist them in that interaction. It will also discuss how to deal with user input errors. How a program might be designed to "learn" from the user how he interacts with it.

The Usual Interaction Process

Users interact with spreadsheets somewhat differently than they interact with databases. The designer can make the user's use of either kind of program easier or harder. There are some general observations we can make about each kind of interaction and where potential problems arise. These observations will come in handy later when we are deciding where an expert system-based front end might be most useful.

Spreadsheet Interaction

Spreadsheet users usually find themselves in one of two situations when they are entering data:

- Bare-bones entry with perhaps some written instructions
- Macro-driven entry with more structure and guidance

In the first instance, the user is simply told, "Enter the sales figure in the appropriate column opposite the label that says 'Sales.'" Perhaps the user isn't even given that much information, since the person who built the spreadsheet might feel that the user can figure out that April's sales ought to go under the column headed "April" and in the row labeled "Sales" without much additional help.

The problem with this approach is that nobody but the user can control to any degree of usefulness what the user enters in a given cell. Most spreadsheets will handle with little or no macro programming validation of the right type of data being entered (i.e., text vs. numeric). Without some programming, however, it is impossible to ensure that a value entered by the user falls within a certain range or meets certain formatting or other conditions required by the application. Even a very experienced user accustomed to a particular worksheet can make a mistake during entry that can have serious consequences when the formulas are calculated and the results passed on to the next level of organization for a decision.

In a one-person operation — with one person designing the spreadsheet, entering the data, analyzing it, and making the decision — a bare-bones approach to spreadsheet data entry may be acceptable. Even in the bare-bones approach, however, the user can forget between uses of the program what kind of information is expected or what the ultimate use of the data is. In a work group — whether a small departmental team or a large corporate finance office — the potential for error and damaging consequences is simply too great.

Recognizing this fact, many organizations' worksheets are designed to use macro programs. These programs are created either by a keystroke method in which the program observes the user's actions and records them for later playback or by programming in a macro language that comes with the spreadsheet. The programs attempt to deal with some of the pitfalls of unguided and unsupervised data entry in a spreadsheet and they work with varying degrees of success. Macros can be designed to force the user through the process of entering data in a certain sequence, examine information after it is entered into a cell to see if it falls within predefined acceptable ranges, and the like.

Macro programs are certainly a significant improvement over bare-bones data entry approaches but are by no means the final answer. They cannot, for example, examine a value entered in a specific cell of a spreadsheet to see if that value "makes sense" when related to other cells. This is particularly true if one or more of the related cells may not yet contain data. Dealing with the unknown or uncertainty of real-world business situations is not something spreadsheets are designed to do. Expert systems are.

Another shortcoming of macro programs as data entry guides is that they are, on the whole, fairly easy to break. Macro programming languages lack control structures and other language components that make it possible to prevent the user from breaking in to the executing macro and essentially overriding it. Such interruptions are not necessarily intentional. An employee entering information into a sales analysis worksheet whose boss needs a letter typed "right now" or who needs to check on a value in another program must be able to leave the spreadsheet task and return to it later. That's how the real world works, however, spreadsheet macro programs are not easy to build so that they have this kind of resilience. In some spreadsheets' macro programming languages, such an approach would not even be feasible.

Spreadsheet applications have inherent limitations in terms of such things as user prompts (where the size of a string is limited and windows are generally not available to support the environment), menu size (resulting in cryptic and less-than-helpful menus), and other interface components. This means that even a first-class macro programmer who understands the user and the problem thoroughly may be unable to create the kind of elegant, help-laden user interface that we can build fairly easily in an expert system environment.

Finally, macro programming is still programming. So, to some extent, is expert system construction. On the one hand, macro languages are generally terse, filled with arcane abbreviations and terms, and syntactically brittle. Expert systems tools, on the other hand, are generally rich (though not robust in the usual programming language sense), fairly English-like, and syntactically supportive or soft. This means that the typical spreadsheet user who does not consider programming to be a main strength or interest will find designing simple IF-THEN rules for an expert system far less difficult and time-consuming than building spreadsheet macros. Combine this with the fact that the expert system can do more things, more effectively and efficiently, and you begin to understand where an expert system can fill in for a macro and bring users significant improvements.

Database Interaction

To some degree, database designs are less prone to the kinds of data entry errors and problems outlined in the preceding section. Databases have a kind of intermediate "middle ground" of interaction class. The user can interact with a database in one of three ways:

- Bare-bones data entry, largely unprompted and unsupported

- Fill-in-the-form designs in which it is at least somewhat clear what information is needed

- Program-driven, interactive data entry

The first and third approaches are virtually identical, conceptually, to the two spreadsheet techniques discussed in the previous section. The middle one, however, deserves examination.

Early microcomputer database products like dBASE II from Ashton-Tate provided for almost no screen-level support. Laying out input screens that users could feel comfortable with if they were unfamiliar with database ideas was a formidable task. Over time, this has changed somewhat. There is a very significant range of database products available for desktop computers and their range of capabilities in terms of user interface design are also quite varied.

Experience has shown that users can deal with forms-based data entry to the extent that the form design either:

- Follows the flow of information users are accustomed to dealing with in their jobs

- Matches some real-world printed form to which users have become accustomed

- Becomes so routine through constant use, even if first exposure was confusing

One problem with forms-based data entry is that not everyone who works with the form and the data it represents approaches things the same way. Similarly, the user's experience when not using the computer may or may not match the screen display, particularly if the database product runs on a computer system whose graphics are limited and whose ability therefore to "map" to reality is limited.

Another problem is that forms-based data entry is in some ways similar to spreadsheet data entry. For the most part, screen-based forms are designed so that intercepting the user's data entry is difficult or impossible. This means the process of data entry cannot usually call attention to errors until the user finishes filling out the form and returns control to the program. (There are exceptions to this, but they typically require more programming ability on the part of the original database designer than most power users have.)

Database management systems' built-in programming languages are often rich, robust, and approachable — though far more complex than the easier IF-THEN production rules of an expert system.

Helping the User

Intelligent interfaces to worksheets and databases can help end users interact with the systems. We've identified some problems with existing approaches and can now define ways our expert systems approach can help. Three ideas are worth further exploration:

- Context-sensitive help

- Intelligent assistance

- Guided data entry

Let's look at each of these approaches briefly.

Context-Sensitive Help

When a person entering information into a worksheet or database file does not understand what is expected at a given point or how to enter some anomalous information (such as a negative number or a very large or very small value that may not have been encountered before), help is needed. However, the help received from most applications is fairly general and simplistic. This is because the help routines are written for the underlying spreadsheet or database management system, not for the particular application.

The user wants help with this specific problem. What is received is a general message, perhaps along the lines of "Enter a numeric value and press the Return or Tab key." That's not really much help. The content of ontext-sensitive help depends on what the user is doing, where the user is in the system, and what difficulty is being encountered. In other words, it is help that is sensitive to the context in which it is sought.

Expert systems can be brought to bear on this problem. By moving the entire data-entry process away from the spreadsheet or database — as we will see in the next few chapters — we can put the user into a situation where the expert system can be programmed to deal specifically with the kinds of issues and problems that might arise during the running of the application.

Intelligent Assistance

At first, intelligent assistance might sound like another way of saying context-sensitive help. But it's not. Intelligent assistance doesn't wait for a user invitation but jumps in and offers itself.

An expert system can be designed so that if the user enters some invalid or inappropriate information into a spreadsheet cell via the expert system and after several attempts is unable to correct the problem, help is offered or presented. We will see examples of this in the case studies in Chapters 7-11. A carefully worded message to the effect that "You seem to be having trouble with this entry. Would you like some help?" can make the user heave a sigh of relief. The problem with most help systems, even if context-sensitive, is that the user has to know a problem exists before help can be called. Frequently a user won't know that the system can help with a problem.

Guided Data Entry

Clearly the most widely applicable area for an expert system is that of guided data entry. We can design and write expert systems that will provide a screen between the user and the application (see Figure 4-1). This screen acts as a filter through which the user interacts

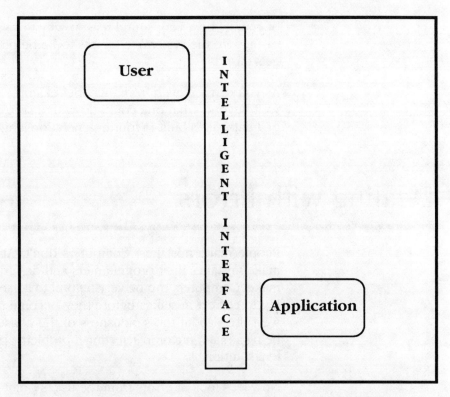

Figure 4-1. Expert System as a Filter for Guided Data Entry

with an application. The screen can be written in such a way that it "talks" to the user in an understandable language rather than in the jargon of the application area, or of the underlying tool.

Most of our work in this book focuses on guided data entry, with sprinklings of context-sensitive help and intelligent assistance.

The biggest advantage of guided data entry is that it can be set up so that it simulates a dialogue between the application and the user. The user is asked a question. The user answers it. The system stores the answer and based on it might change the course of questioning. After 15 questions, the system might detect that the user is working with data that appears to be in conflict with itself. For example, the user might enter three consecutive months of declining sales and then show profits higher. The system can be designed to probe the user: "Are you sure your profit and sales figures are right?" it might gently ask. "They seem inconsistent with each other." There might, of course, be a very sound reason why this situation arises. The user can ignore the system's attempts to be helpful. But at least the issue gets raised.

As you can see even from this brief example, guided data entry goes well beyond what one could do with a spreadsheet macro language or a database's built-in fourth-generation language.

Dealing with Errors

People make mistakes. Computers don't. At least, computers don't make mistakes their programmers and designers don't cause them to make. Computers can be very helpful to a user in detecting and helping to correct mistakes before they become problems. In Chapter 3, we talked about the seriousness of the consequences of an error as being a major factor in selecting a problem appropriate to expert system solution.

Now let's look at errors from the user's point of view. From that perspective, errors can be:

- Obvious

- Probable

- Possible

- Contextual

If the user enters a positive number into a cell designed to deal only with negative numbers, that's an obvious mistake. The expert system needs no great amount of intelligence to diagnose the problem or to explain it. The user will immediately see it (if the system has been designed correctly) and know how to fix it or to recover.

Probable errors are those that appear to be out of conformance with an expectation. Our earlier example of declining sales and rising profits is such an error. It is a probable error because the system would be designed to flag the mistake as one to call to the user's attention but the user would be permitted to override it and say, in effect, "I'm smarter than you, machine, and I know this value is correct in spite of what it seems to be." It follows naturally, then, that a possible error is something akin to a probable error, only with less certainty on the part of the system. This kind of error is one which might either be an error or an anomaly.

Finally, contextual errors are those mistakes that can only be spotted in a context. They are neither probable nor possible taken alone, but in a context with other entries, perhaps even with knowledge that exists outside the program, they are errors of one of the other three kinds: obvious, probable, or possible. For example, if you were designing an intelligent interface to a spreadsheet designed to track stock prices and the system had been previously given the information that the stock market was sharply lower on a particular date but you signaled that a stock was up, this is a possible error that can only be spotted in context.

Each of these types of errors must be dealt with somewhat differently in terms of how the user is notified and what the user is expected or permitted to do in response. Table 4-1 depicts these types of errors and describes the system and user responses.

Table 4-1. Errors and System-User Response Groups

Error Class	System Response	User Response
Obvious	Alert user, explain reason for error, correction needed	Must correct before proceeding, not permitted to override
Probable	Ask user if error exists, explaining rationale only on demand	Must either correct or take some deliberate action to override
Possible	Ask user if error exists, explaining rationale only on demand	May ignore by a simple action (e.g., carriage return)

Learning from the User

There are as yet no expert systems that can truly be said to "learn" from their users or their "experiences." But it is possible to simulate learning in some ways that turn out to be helpful in designing intelligent interfaces to business applications.

The learning process (we'll stop putting quotations around the word *learning* but you should understand that we know that what we are describing isn't true machine learning) can be simple and direct. Figure 4-2 depicts the process and an example will clarify it.

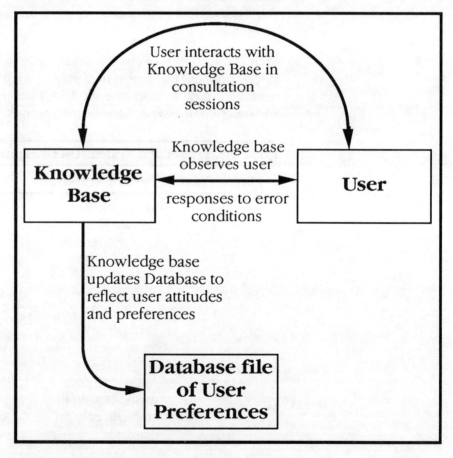

Figure 4-2. Simulating Expert System Learning

Assume we built a stock market tracking expert system into which our user enters closing prices of stocks each day. We've connected the system to a spreadsheet where the calculations take place, and to a database where an automatic monitoring process updates key market conditions and indicators regularly. We've built a rule into the expert system that says something like this:

```
IF      Dow-Jones = "Down" AND
        Dow-Jones-Delta > 35 AND
        User-Stock-Current > User-Stock Recent
THEN    Probable-Error="Trend line not followed"
        Display "Are you sure?  Your price is out of
        line with trend!"
        (* and some other actions we want to take in
        this event *)
```

Let's further assume the user is running this system, enters a stock with a price increase in a down market, and the error is flagged with the message shown above. The user says, "It's OK. Proceed." In that case, we might well want to design a database file or text file to record the fact that the user, in a market that was down by more than 35 points, recorded a price increase for WidgeCo and overrode our error. If this pattern occurs a few more times, we might want to treat the situation either not as an error at all (i.e., not flag it) or downgrade it to a possible error to call to the user's attention later or more subtly. That might require a different rule that looks like this:

```
IF      Probable-Error = "Trend line not followed" AND
        Stock-Name = Override-File-Stock-Name
THEN    (* ignore the error or change its status)
```

(Note that neither of these is a complete rule; they are simply framework examples of what such a rule might look like in principle. We will build some rules with this specific behavior later in the book.)

Now when the error condition in the first rule is established by the user's entry, a subsequent rule examines a database file, brings in the names of stocks on a list of those for which the user regularly overrides the error, and takes some other action when the two stock names match. In a sense, the system has adapted to a behavior exhibited by the user.

Summary

In this chapter, we have learned that:

- The usual interaction processes of users with worksheets and databases leaves room for error and user confusion.

- Even macro and fourth-generation language programming cannot deal with as wide a variety of errors and user needs as an expert system can.

- We can design expert-system-based intelligent front ends to business applications that assist the user through context-sensitive help, intelligent (unprompted) assistance, and guided data entry.

- There are several classes of errors, including obvious, probable, possible, and contextual, and each must be dealt with differently both by the system and by the user.

- It is possible to design an expert system so that it simulates learning from the user's behavior in interacting with it.

In Chapter 5, we will turn our attention to guided data entry strategies and techniques, including how to attain the goal of making the interaction between user and system more human.

CHAPTER 5
Guided Data Entry Strategies and Techniques

In this chapter, we will compare and contrast two approaches to the use of a small prototype spreadsheet application. First we will describe the application. Then we will see how a user would enter information into the spreadsheet using bare-bones data entry processes. After taking a look at how a spreadsheet macro program could help make that interface somewhat more useful, we conclude by describing a small expert system that serves as an intelligent, guided data entry gateway for the user's interaction with the spreadsheet. This example also forms the basis for the discussion of data validation techniques in Chapter 6, so those issues are not dealt with in this chapter, which focuses only on the user interaction issues.

The Application

This worksheet represents a small part of a larger inventory management system. The entire contents of this worksheet are shown in Figure 5-1. As you can see, this part of the total system tracks the inventory flow of 3.5-inch floppy disks as they are purchased from four different vendors. The disks come in single- and double-density formats and the price per unit varies with the density and the vendor.

The worksheet columns hold product codes, descriptions, vendor name, cost per unit, reorder point (below which inventory should not be allowed to fall), quantity on hand (QOH), ceiling (above which inventory should not be allowed to rise), and year-to-date orders for the item. Each row except the last represents one product entry. The last row displays the calculated totals of reorder points, quantities on hand, ceiling levels, and year-to-date quantity sales.

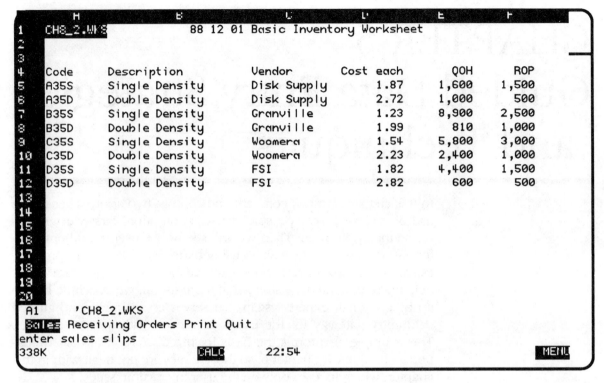

Figure 5-1. Basic Inventory Worksheet

As spreadsheet applications go, this one is trivial but nonetheless typical of the types of data and manipulation that are often included in worksheets.

Data Entry

The person responsible for maintaining the inventory of 3.5-inch floppy disks would typically be concerned with entering each day's sales and shipments received, and with determining when to reorder a product from a particular vendor.

We'll first look at how this process would be handled in a spreadsheet with no assistance from a macro program. Then we'll demonstrate and briefly describe a set of macros that will make the interface somewhat more automatic and menu-driven. This will set the stage for an evaluation of how much easier and more straightforward an expert system solution to the same problem will be.

Manual Entry

In a purely manual, bare-bones data entry situation without even the use of formulas, this user would probably follow a procedure similar to the tasks described in the following list.

1.   Arrange the day's sales orders by product code

2.   Position the cursor at the first row (Disk Supply's single-sided disks) under the QOH label

3.   Type (or copy) the current quantity on hand, then a minus sign, then the new order volume (e.g., if the sales slip indicated a sale of 20 disks and the quantity on hand was 500, the user might type 500 - 20 to change that cell's value to 480)

4.   Move the cursor to the YTD column and type in the quantity in that column, a plus sign, and the size of the order (e.g., 32767 + 20 to change that cell's value to 32787)

5.   Repeat steps 2 through 4 for each of the sales slips

6.   Examine the REORD and QOH columns for each product to ensure that no product had fallen below reorder point as a result of the day's sales

7.   Place orders for any products that had fallen below that point

Macro-Driven Entry

No sizable business establishment would be likely to set up and handle its inventory in such a completely manual way. It is likely that the manager or owner would have programmed a somewhat more elegant way for data to be entered. (Though we've seen worksheets where a bare-bones data entry process like the one described above

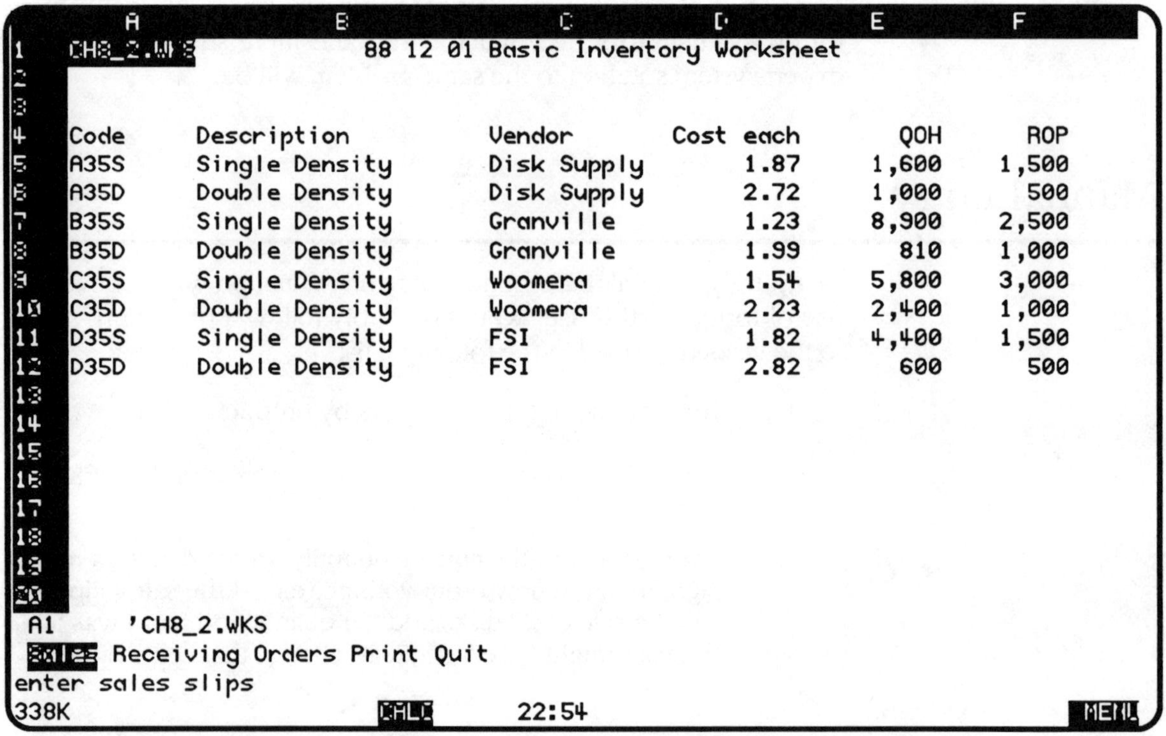

```
        A              B              C           D           E          F
1   CH8_2.WKS            88 12 01 Basic Inventory Worksheet
2
3
4   Code       Description      Vendor      Cost each      QOH        ROP
5   A35S       Single Density   Disk Supply     1.87      1,600      1,500
6   A35D       Double Density   Disk Supply     2.72      1,000        500
7   B35S       Single Density   Granville       1.23      8,900      2,500
8   B35D       Double Density   Granville       1.99        810      1,000
9   C35S       Single Density   Woomera         1.54      5,800      3,000
10  C35D       Double Density   Woomera         2.23      2,400      1,000
11  D35S       Single Density   FSI             1.82      4,400      1,500
12  D35D       Double Density   FSI             2.82        600        500
13
14
15
16
17
18
19
20

A1        'CH8_2.WKS
Sales Receiving Orders Print Quit
enter sales slips
338K                      CALC        22:54                              MENU
```

Figure 5-2. Menu Line for Sample Worksheet

has been in use for some time. This is particularly true where the user is also the owner or manager, who knows the process well and doesn't see a need for prompting and help.)

More likely, this worksheet would include a menu interface that would look something like Figure 5-2. The user would indicate what was needed, such as enter sales slips, receive orders, check for reorder requirements, print worksheet data, or quit the spreadsheet.

If the user wanted to enter sales slips, a prompt would appear stating that a product code be selected (Figure 5-3). The user would then be asked to enter the quantity ordered and, when entered, the macro would update the values in the appropriate cells.

	AB	AC	AC·	AE	AF	AG	AH
3		Unit		Original	New	Original	New
4	code	Sales	Sales $	QOH	QOH	YTD Units	YTD Units
5	A35S			1,600	1,600	32,760	32,760
6	A35D			1,000	1,000	7,865	7,865
7	B35S			8,900	8,900	39,325	39,325
8	B35D			810	810	15,730	15,730
9	C35S			5,800	5,800	47,190	47,190
10	C35D			2,400	2,400	15,730	15,730
11	D35S			4,400	4,400	23,595	23,595
12	D35D			600	600	7,865	7,865
13							
14							

AB3

A35S A35D B35S B35D C35S C35D D35S D35D Main Menu
Disk Supply SD
338K   8:57   MENU

Figure 5-3. Menu Prompt for Unit Sales

We will not walk through that process here since our focus is on expert systems and not on spreadsheet macro programming. An experienced macro programmer might not find them difficult to design but most users, even those with a great deal of experience, would probably find the task of designing, building, and testing such a macro too daunting to attempt. If you wanted to design help for the user to access along the way, the task would become even more formidable. Appendix C provides a full-blown, working example of what we mean — which you are welcome to copy and experiment with

Even though not very approachable from a programming perspective, this menu-driven interface constitutes a significant improvement from the user's perspective over the bare-bones data entry method described earlier. However, neither offers the kind of interface and support that even a fairly rudimentary expert system can provide.

Using the Expert System

Figure 5-4 shows the beginning of what is clearly a more friendly, understandable way to interact with the inventory worksheet. As we will see in a moment, the user's entire use of the worksheet can be handled this way — through a series of menus and question-and-answer dialogues rather than tedious data entry.

One obvious difference between the expert system style interaction of Figure 5-4 and the worksheet style interaction in Figure 5-3 is that the user need not even see the worksheet when an expert system front end is used. From the viewpoint of the user, particularly the unsophisticated or untrained, using the spreadsheet is more like being interviewed than being expected to know where to put information and how to enter it. There is less of a sense of using a program and more of a flavor of cooperating with the machine to solve a problem.

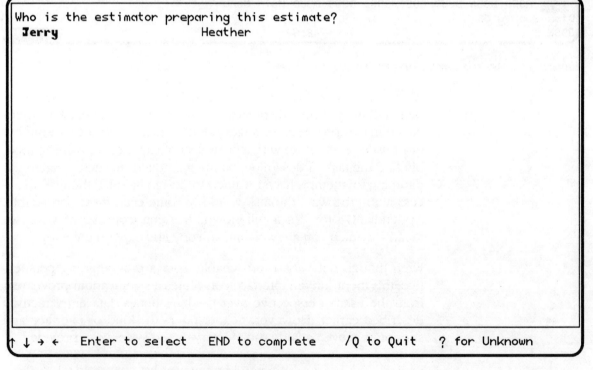

Figure 5-4. Beginning of Expert System Dialogue

```
If you want to enter today's sales slips into the inventory system,
then you should choose the 'Sales Slips' option.  Before you do this,
you should have sorted the sales slips by product code.  Product
codes need not be in a particular order but grouping all of the orders
for one product code together makes entering the information more
efficient.

If you want to ask the system to give you a list of all product codes
where the quantity on hand is lower than the reorder point, you should
choose the 'Reorder Check' option.

                      PRESS ANY KEY TO CONTINUE.
```

Figure 5-5. Help Screen in Expert System Interface

For example, when the user of the expert system interface needs help with an operation, the designer can include an option for such assistance in one of several ways:

- In the case of a menu-driven response, by supplying a help option that displays assistance

- In the case of a dialogue, by designing rules to look for the word help (or some other signal) and displaying appropriate information

- Broadly, by taking advantage of the F1 key when the expert system tool being used provides for this

Figure 5-5 shows what a help screen might look like for the first question in the expert system interface. Notice that it is possible to supply more than one line of prompting help, to which a spreadsheet application is typically limited.

In this design, the expert system handles the entire interface between the user and the worksheet. When the user has answered all of the

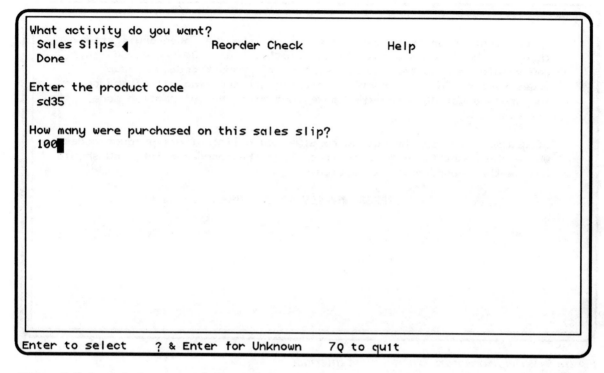

Figure 5-6. Sample Session with Expert System Interface

questions and entered all the information, the expert system updates the contents of the worksheet so that the user never even sees the worksheet on the display. (Of course, if the user wants or needs to the worksheet can be opened using the spreadsheet program, but the point is the worksheet need not be opened to accomplish the desired tasks.)

Figure 5-6 shows a somewhat abbreviated session of interaction with the expert system. Besides the general flow, notice how little typing the user is required to do to enter sales slip information into the worksheet. Compare this with the number of keystrokes that would be required if the user were working with the spreadsheet alone and you get a glimpse of the increased efficiency offered by an expert system acting as a simple interface to a worksheet.

Listing 5-1 is the expert system written in VP-Expert that handles the spreadsheet interface depicted in Figures 5-1 through 5-8. We will discuss some specific segments of the listing in the next section.

Listing 5-1

```
! (c) 1989, Dan Shafer

! This knowledge base first appeared in "Designing,
! Intelligent Front Ends for Business Software,"
! published by John Wiley & Sons, Inc., 1989.

! Procedural control section

ENDOFF;
ACTIONS
WHILETRUE choice<>Done THEN
FIND done
RESET done
END;

! Rules Section

RULE 1
IF          choice=Done
THEN        done=Yes;

RULE 2
IF          choice=Sales_Slips AND
            product<>UNKNOWN AND
            quantity<>UNKNOWN
THEN        WKS data,ROW = (product),inventr1
            data[5] = ((data[5]) - (quantity))
            data[7] = (data[7] + (quantity))
            PWKS data,ROW = (product),inventr1
            RESET choice
            done=No;

RULE 3
IF          choice=Help
THEN        CLS
            DISPLAY "
If you want to enter today's sales slips into the
inventory system, then you should choose the 'Sales
Slips' option.  Before you do this, you should have
sorted the sales slips by product code.  They need
not be in a particular order but grouping all of
the orders for one product code together makes
entering the information more efficient.

If you want to ask the system to give you a list of
all product codes where the quantity on hand is
lower than the reorder point, you should choose the
'Reorder Check' option.

                        PRESS ANY KEY TO CONTINUE.~"
```

```
          RESET choice
          done=No;

RULE 4
IF        choice = Reorder_Check
THEN      WKSprodcode,COLUMN=CODE,inventr1
          WKS onhand,COLUMN=QOH,inventr1
          WKSreorderpoint,COLUMN=REORD,inventr1
          X=1
          WHILEKNOWN prodcode[X]
                  FIND level
                  X = (X + 1)
                  RESET level
          END
          RESET choice
          done=No;

RULE 5
IF        onhand[X] < (reorderpoint[X])
THEN      DISPLAY "You should reorder {prodcode[X]}."
          level = low
ELSE      level = ok;

! User interface and housekeeping section

ASK choice:"What activity do you want?";
CHOICES choice:Sales_Slips,Reorder_Check,Help,Done;

ASK product:"Enter the product code";

ASK quantity:"How many were purchased on this sales
   slip?";
```

This is our first real VP-Expert code, so let's take a look at some portions of it in depth.

Writing the Expert System

This VP-Expert knowledge base is divided into three main areas:

- An ACTIONS block, or *procedural control section*

- A rules section

- A user interface and housekeeping section

This is the structure we will typically use in presenting and discussing VP-Expert system listings in this book.

Let's look first at the rules, since they are the most generic part of the program.

The Rules

The expert system known as INVEN1.KBS and shown in Listing 5-1 consists of only five rules. Four of these rules correspond directly to one of the menu choices presented to the user when the system begins to run and at the end of each processing step. This menu is typical of menu-driven interfaces: it asks the user what action is desired and offers a list of alternatives from which a choice is made.

RULE 1 deals with the choice labeled Done in the menu. It is quite simple, merely assigning the value Yes to a variable called done. We'll see in a moment why this has the desired effect of ending processing in the system.

RULE 2 addresses the processing to take place if the user chooses the Sales Slips option from the menu. Notice that unlike RULE 1, this rule has three conditions, all of which must be true for the rule to fire. The first ensures that the user has indeed indicated that sales slips are to be processed. The second and third conditions demonstrate a technique of forcing the system to ask the user for a value. By checking the variables called product and quantity to be sure they have a value (i.e., their value is not represented by the special system value UNKNOWN), we force the system to look for their values. Since these variables will typically not have a value when this rule is first examined (because the user has not yet told us what product code is to be worked with), the system follows its usual procedure for finding a value. That procedure consists of two steps.

First, it looks for a rule whose conclusion includes the assignment of a value to the variable in question. When VP-Expert's inference engine encounters the line

```
IF product<>UNKNOWN
```

it looks for a rule that assigns a value to the variable `product` as one of its conclusions. In this case, it won't find one.

Second, it looks for an `ASK` statement (or one of several other statements we will encounter later) that permits it to ask the user for the value of the variable. If it finds such a statement — as it does here — it simply asks the question and assigns the user's response to the variable.

The effect of RULE 2, then, is that the user will be asked to enter the product code to be worked with, and then enter the number of units of that product code sold on the sales slip being processed. With that information in hand, all of the rule's conditions are met and the conclusions can be processed.

The first conclusion in RULE 2 uses VP-Expert's WKS clause (see Figure 5-7) to access data stored in a spreadsheet. The WKS clause requires three arguments: a VP-Expert variable to which the results of the worksheet read are to be assigned, a worksheet location, and the name of the worksheet file (without the ubiquitous .WKS extension).

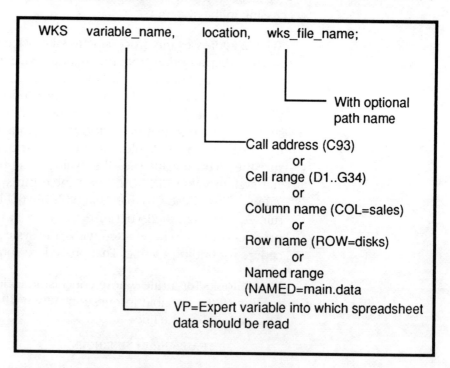

Figure 5-7. Syntax of VP-Expert's WKS Clause

The first conclusion clause in RULE 2 instructs VP-Expert to open a worksheet file called INVENTR1.WKS, and to read the row whose first entry corresponds to the product code entered by the user. The result is assigned to the variable data. Because the row has more than one value (or column), VP-Expert automatically makes data a *dimensioned variable*. This means the variable consists of a series of compartments, each of which contains a value.

In RULE 2, the second and third clauses in the conclusion assign new values to two of the columns read into VP-Expert with the WKS clause. Individual compartments of the dimensioned variable data are accessed by a method known as sub-scripting. The first column entry, which holds the product description, is referenced as data [1]. The brackets enclose the number of the column you want to access. (The first column, in our case the product code, is not referenced directly since it is viewed by VP-Expert as a label. It is used to locate rows and columns, but its value is not directly accessible.)

The second and third lines update quantity on hand (data [5]) and year-to-date sales (data[7]) by respectively subtracting the quantity sold from to its current value and adding the quantity sold to its current values.

You can deduce that the next line, beginning with the VP-Expert PWKS clause, updates the worksheet. (Think of PWKS as meaning "Put into WKS file.") It updates the entire row just read by replacing its contents. The syntax of the PWKS clause is shown in Figure 5-8.

Next, we use the RESET command to give the variable choice the value UNKNOWN again. Then we assign the value No to the variable done. Both of these actions have implications for the control procedure, which we'll discuss in a few moments.

RULE 3 is much more straightforward than RULE 2. If the user selects the option labeled Help from the menu presented, this rule fires. It simply clears the screen (with the CLS command) and then displays some text. The tilde character (~) at the end of the text causes the system to pause for the user to press a key before it continues. (VP-Expert can actually open windows with different background colors to handle help text and other messages.)

Again, at the end of RULE 3, we RESET the variable choice and assign the value No to the variable done.

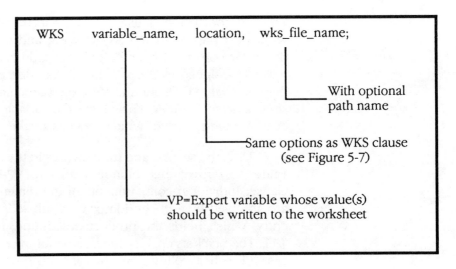

Figure 5-8. Syntax of VP-Expert's PWKS Clause

The rules labeled RULE 4 and RULE 5 work together to deal with the processing required when the user wants to examine the inventory file to see if any products need reordering. Much of what is in these rules is already familiar.

RULE 4 is the main rule. It fires when the user picks the Reorder Check option from the menu we create. This is followed by the conclusion section of the rule, which begins with three WKS clauses. These clauses read, in turn, the CODE, QOH, and REORD columns from the worksheet into the variables prodcode, onhand, and reorderpoint, respectively. When these three statements have been executed, three new dimensioned variables exist, with the contents shown in Table 5-1. Note that these values correspond to the column entries in the worksheet shown in Figure 5-1.

Table 5-1. Three Variables' Values After Worksheet Is Read

Compartment	procode	onhand	reorderpoint
[1]	FD31D	985	500
[2]	FD31T	333	250
[3]	FD31W	275	500
[4]	FD31A	75	50
[5]	FD32D	720	700
[6]	FD32T	500	500
[7]	FD32W	809	500
[8]	FD32A	1200	1000

The next six lines of the conclusion of RULE 4 constitute a loop using VP-Expert's WHILEKNOWN clause.

First, we establish a beginning value for a counter variable called X. Then we use the WHILEKNOWN loop to look at each entry in the variable called prodcode, where the product codes are stored. The WHILEKNOWN loop is designed so that it continues to execute all of the instructions between its opening command and the requisite END statement as long as there is a known value for its argument (in this case, prodcode[X]). In other words, it will loop as many times as there are values in the dimensioned variable prodcode.

For each loop, we do three simple things:

- Tell the inference engine to find a value for yet another variable, this one labeled level

- Increment the counter X we are using to control which element of the dimensioned variables prodcode, onhand, and reorderpoint we wish to examine

- RESET the value of the variable level.

The reason for the third step is that if we don't reset its value, the WHILEKNOWN loop will read only the first element of the variable prodcode. The second time through the loop, the FIND command will not execute because the variable already has a value from the last time the inference engine sought one.

Each time the WHILEKNOWN loop is carried out, the FIND command instructs VP-Expert to locate a value for the variable whose name is supplied as an argument (in this case, level).

To do so, the inference engine follows its usual procedure of looking first for a rule with the variable in a conclusion assignment statement. This time, it finds such a rule, RULE 5, so it attempts to determine if it can fire the rule. To do so, it compares the value of the entries in the variables onhand and reorderpoint that correspond to the location of the variable prodcode with which it is working.

If the quantity on hand is lower than the reorder point, it tells the user that the part should be reordered. If not, it simply assigns a value to the variable level, which satisfies the FIND command.

ACTIONS Block

Every VP-Expert program must have an ACTIONS block. This section
of a knowledge base will typically contain a reasonably large amount
of code. This section of the system is the place you can control the
actions of the consultation and the inference engine with great precision. We will deal with it only cursorily here, but in later chapters it
takes on an increasing significance.

The first lines in the procedural section actually precede the keyword
ACTIONS. These are the commands ENDOFF and RUNTIME. (Note
that in Listing 5-1 each is followed by a semicolon, which is the
clause-ending punctuation mark in VP-Expert.) Both of these commands affect what the user sees and how the user interacts with the
system during a consultation. We will discuss them in greater detail
later in this chapter.

The ACTIONS block itself begins with the keyword and ends with a
semicolon. In our case, we want to process the user's menu choices
repeatedly, so we simply set up a small loop using the WHILETRUE
command. It says, in essence, "As long as the user hasn't chosen the
Done option from the menu, see if you can find a value for the variable done. When you do, reset it." This creates a loop that will run
forever until the user chooses the Done option from our menu.

User Interface Section

The final section of our knowledge base consists of three ASK statements, one of which has an accompanying CHOICES statement. The
ASK statement is used to provide VP-Expert the question you wish to
ask when the value of its variable is needed and VP-Expert cannot
find a rule that will assign it a value.

Notice that the syntax of the ASK command is quite simple. The keyword is followed by the name of the variable whose value is being
sought. Then a colon is used as a delimiter and the question itself is
supplied, enclosed in quotation marks. The by-now-familiar semicolon indicates the end of the command.

The CHOICES command is far more powerful than it appears. It has essentially the same syntax as the ASK command except that its second argument is a list of alternatives that can be chosen by the user to be assigned to the variable. In the CHOICES line in Listing 5-1 (third line from the bottom of the listing), we indicate that the variable choice can have any of four values: Sales Slips, Reorder Check, Help, or Done. Note that the two two-word choices must be entered as one word, joined by an underscore, because the space is an illegal character in a VP-Expert label. They will display as two words, with the underscore omitted, but when you are testing for the value of the variable, you must remember the one-word syntax rule.

The mere fact that the CHOICES command is present is all that is required to generate the menu we saw that initiates the dialogue with the user when this expert system is run.

Summary

In this chapter, we have seen that the normal methods of interaction between a user and a worksheet consist of either bare-bones data entry directly into cells of the spreadsheet or a one-line menu-driven interface created within the worksheet. We have seen the pitfalls and usage problems with such an approach.

We have also seen how a simple expert system can make this interaction much cleaner, easier, more elegant, and more efficient for the user. The expert system approach does this by reducing keystroke requirements, by hiding the worksheet's cells and complexities from the user, and by making extensive help accessible during the data entry process.

We have examined our first VP-Expert program listing in some detail, gaining our first exposure to the tool in real-world use.

In Chapter 6, we will augment this expert system with some data validation rules that will help ensure the accuracy of the information the user supplies.

CHAPTER 6
Data Validation Techniques

This chapter continues to build on the expert system we began designing in Chapter 5. The emphasis, in this chapter, shifts from pure data entry to data validation: ensuring that the information entered by the user is correct and that it conforms to certain "reality checks" we might wish to perform on it.

Data Entry Pitfalls

In our sample worksheet, particularly in data entry mode, a user can make any of several kinds of mistakes while entering information:

- Positioning mistakes (i.e., entering information into the wrong cell, either by choosing the wrong row for the product or by choosing the wrong column for the information)

- Typing mistakes (transposing numbers, and others)

- Reality mistakes (e.g., selling more product than is available)

The first two types of mistakes are similar to each other from the user's viewpoint, though their consequences and the means of dealing with them can be quite different. In both cases, as seen by the user, a typographical error has been committed.

For an expert system, or any other method we might conceive, to assist the user in the data entry process by validating entries, an approach must include the ability to:

- Detect the fact that an error has occurred

- If possible, determine what might be done to correct it

- Alert the user, hopefully suggesting what action to take

- Apply the correction

Types of Data That Can Be Validated

Data validation applies almost exclusively to numeric data. It is at least theoretically possible to validate character and string entries, but for the most part in spreadsheet and database applications we do this by limiting the choices the user can make to those entries that are valid. This will generally take the shape of a menu from which the user makes choices. Free-form text entry data validation is generally a difficult process to encode in an expert system.

Not all numeric data can be validated either. The number being examined must be subject to some kind of rule statement before an expert system can be expected to help us determine whether a particular entry constitutes an error or not. Generally, this means the numeric data must have one of two characteristics:

- Logical or absolute boundary values that constitute a range of minimum and maximum values within which the data is valid or likely to be so and outside of which it is invalid or likely (or even certain) to be so

- Relationships with other data in the application so that its validity can only be determined by examining other entries and seeing whether its value makes sense in view of their content

Infrequently, data will have both characteristics so that a value must fall within a range dependent on other values in the worksheet or database. The technical term for these characteristics is "constraints."

Validation Strategies

To validate data being entered into an application via an expert system interface, we can adopt any combination of several strategies. Although you will encounter situations in which one of these strategies is clearly adequate to the task without mixing with other strategies, that will not often be the case. Generally, you will combine two or more of the following strategies:

- Managing the user's interaction with the system to prevent some kinds of data entry errors

- Comparing entered values against known boundaries, either stored in the knowledge base itself or present in the worksheet or database application

- Evaluating relationships among data according to established rules in the knowledge base to spot logical entry errors

- Suggesting or supplying missing or apparently incorrect information for the user

Data validation can also take place as each piece of information is entered or after some isolated portion of the data entry process is complete, in a batch.

We'll take a look at each of these strategies in the remainder of this section.

Managing the Interaction

Chapter 5 was devoted entirely to this particular kind of data validation, but in that chapter the emphasis was on ease of use and user understanding. An interactive data entry process contributes to the validity of the data in several ways, however.

First and foremost, the kind of error that results in the user putting information into the wrong cell of a spreadsheet or the wrong field of a database can be all but eliminated using an intelligent interface. The user is essentially buffered from the underlying application; the expert system places the data into the application. The user simply answers questions and the system determines where to place the data.

Second, by using menus of choices, the system can and should be designed so that easy-to-make typographical errors are reduced or eliminated. In the sample worksheet in Chapter 5, for example, the user could be presented with a menu list of product codes from which to choose the one for which a sale is to be entered. We chose not to do that because we wanted to keep the example brief and clear, but in later examples, you will see that we use this approach quite often. With VP-Expert, this is particularly easy to do with database applications. The language includes the ability to generate a menu listing of valid options dynamically from the contents of a database file.

Third, by adopting a dialogue process for data entry, it is (or should be) always clear to the user what information is expected or required at each step. Guesswork is eliminated.

Finally, the use of context-sensitive help, of which we saw the rudimentary beginnings in Chapter 5, enables the user to obtain specific assistance when there is doubt about the kind of information needed in a particular cell or field.

As you can see, simply designing a well-thought-out user interaction with the application can go a long way toward assuring as close to error-free data entry as possible. But there are other strategies that can also be employed to deal with the need.

Comparing Boundaries

Boundaries defining a valid range of values for a particular piece of data can exist in one of two places: within the worksheet or database application itself, or in the "outside world." In the latter case, the boundaries are encoded in one or more rules in the knowledge base.

Regardless of where boundaries are found, the rule-based approach to checking them is generally the same. It involves these steps:

1. Define a variable whose value will be set to True or Yes (or any other arbitrary value, for that matter, so long as you know what it means) if the data falls within the appropriate boundary range, and False or No if it doesn't

2. Make the variable's value being true a condition in a rule

3. Define a rule (or rules) to set the value of the variable depending on the range checking you do with comparison operators

A small example of this kind of data validation is displayed in Listing 6-1. We assume a situation in which we have a value that must fall between 1 and 100; no other value is allowed. The variable being checked is called `score`. (Notice that we do not supply the entire knowledge base or rule set here. This is a fragment that will not work as listed; its purpose is only to provide the framework for an approach.)

Listing 6-1

```
! Not a complete knowledge base; do not attempt to run.

RULE 1
IF        score<>UNKNOWN AND
          scorevalid=Yes
THEN      PWKS score,C8,test1;
RULE 2
IF        scorevalid=No
THEN      DISPLAY "Sorry, but the score must be between
                1 and 100.  Please try again.~";
RULE 3
IF        score >= 1 AND
          score <= 100
THEN      scorevalid=Yes
ELSE      scorevalid=No;
```

If your expert system shell does not include the ELSE clause, you'll need a fourth rule that looks like Listing 6-2.

Listing 6-2

```
RULE 4
IF        score < 1 OR
          score > 100
THEN      scorevalid=No;
```

VP-Expert, however, does include the ELSE construct, so the three-rule set will work correctly.

The rules are probably self-explanatory, but let's describe the function of each briefly.

RULE 1 ensures that we have a value for the variable `score` (i.e., that it is not `UNKNOWN`), and that the variable `scorevalid` has a value of `Yes`. To find out the value of `scorevalid`, it will have to use RULE 3, which we'll examine in a moment. If both of those conditions are true, RULE 1 uses VP-Expert's PWKS command to write the score into cell C8 of the worksheet called TEST1.WKS.

RULE 2 looks at the value of the variable `scorevalid` and, if it is No, displays an error message that not only tells the user an error has been made but tells how to correct it.

RULE 3, of course, performs the boundary condition check on the entered value for the variable `score`, setting the value of the variable `scorevalid` as a consequence of its findings.

Later in this chapter we will see how we handle boundary conditions when they are contained in the worksheet or database application — the process is similar.

Spotting Logical Mistakes

In some respects, spotting logical mistakes by examining relationships among data is similar to boundary checking. The primary difference lies in the fact that we are generally not concerned so much with absolute values of the entered data as we are with its likely accuracy in light of related data.

For example, assume we have designed a worksheet in which we are tracking stock prices against certain economic and market indicators. Further assume that today's trends indicate that the Dow-Jones Industrial Average is down and volume is above average.

Now the user enters a new price for a stock showing a significant increase in its price over yesterday. The expert system looks at all the data and concludes there's at least a high degree of probability that this is a mistake. Perhaps the user was looking at the wrong stock price or perhaps a double-hit was made on a key (e.g., entering 111.5 instead of 11.5).

The expert system, analyzing all of this information, can step in and at least suggest that the user re-examine the entry.

Dealing with Missing Data

One of the real strengths of an expert system in designing interfaces is its ability to deal nonchalantly with missing information that would trip a less sophisticated program. This means that one way of dealing with missing information is to simply ignore it. If a rule requires a certain variable to have a specific value before it can fire and that variable has no value and there is no way for the system to obtain or determine a value, the rule simply does not fire. No error message is generated. No system crash occurs. The rule just gets ignored.

If that's not the behavior you want, then you have to program a rule to deal with the situation of the data being missing or undetermined (by using the IF variable=UNKNOWN approach, for example).

Continuing with our stock market example, if the Dow-Jones averages had not yet been entered when the user began putting today's stock prices into the worksheet, the expert system could be programmed to object, to "ask" the user for the data, or to go blithely on its way, depending on what action is appropriate to the situation.

When to Perform Data Validation

The primary factor involved in determining whether to perform data validation as each entry is made or after all of the entries are complete and the worksheet is ready to be updated is the nature of the data. We might, for example, look at the inventory example of Chapter 5 and see that if we accumulate all of the orders for a particular product code until the user is finished making all of the entries, we might become more efficient in the program's interaction with the worksheet. However, what if a problem arises because of an overordering situation? If you've entered 35 orders and the 28th one runs the product out of stock, how are you going to recover?

If the worksheet is updated and the data validated after each entry, however, you will be able to alert the user to an out-of-stock situation the instant it arises rather than some time later. This data is ordered; it flows from one minute to the next, from one sales slip to the next, each affecting inventory cumulatively.

But our stock market tracker might well be a candidate for postponing data validation until all of the user's entries for the day have been made. If one of them seems erroneous or causes a problem, that does not impact on any of the other entries, which can be processed exactly as if no such anomaly had arisen. The impact is not cumulative, so batch data validation is probably appropriate.

Validating Inventory Entries

With this background, let's return to our example expert system from Chapter 5 and see if we can add useful data validation routines to it.

If we think about the data entry process as we've refined it with the expert system rules already built in Chapter 5, there are only two pieces of information the user enters: the product code and the quantity. The product code presents an opportunity for a typographical error sort of entry; the user could enter a nonexistent code or a wrong code. From the standpoint of the seriousness of such an error (see the discussion of this general topic in this chapter), this ranks fairly high: a sale either does not get added to the system at all or is added to the wrong product code. Out-of-inventory situations, bad sales tracking, unpaid commissions, and a number of other problems can result.

In entering a sale, the user can also make a typographical error. In our hypothetical store, it is unusual for anyone to buy very large quantities of disks at one time, so we may wish to check for any sale larger than some value (e.g., 500 disks) and confirm that the user means 500 and not 50. Also, a particular sale may result in an out-of-stock situation of a particular disk (i.e., the sales slip represents a sale of more of the product than the inventory system indicates is on-hand). This can be caused by either a typographical error in the quantity sold or in the entry of a valid but incorrect product code.

Let's take a look at the rules it would take to deal with each of these kinds of data entry problems.

Product Code Validation

What happens when users enter an invalid product code? If you've built the expert system in Chapter 5, you can easily find out by entering an illegal code and seeing how the system reacts. If you do, you'll find that the system gives you no indication at all that it can't find the product code. When VP-Expert attempts to read a row of a worksheet file and that row doesn't exist, it simply doesn't perform the read operation. In essence, then, nothing happens, even though if you watch your system during the processing of your erroneous request, it will activate the disk and appear to be doing something.

To set up a trap that will catch such invalid product code entries, we must modify one of the existing rules in the INVEN1 knowledge base of Chapter 5 and add two new rules. Modify RULE 2 to check for a valid product code by creating a new variable whose value is to be checked. When you are done, RULE 2 should look something like Listing 6-3.

Listing 6-3

```
RULE 2
IF      choice=Sales_Slips AND
        product<>UNKNOWN AND
! new lines for data validation
        productvalid=Yes AND
        quantity<>UNKNOWN AND
        quantityvalid=Yes
THEN    data[5] = ((data[5] - (quantity))
        data[7] = ((data[7] + (quantity))
        PWKS data,ROW = (product),inventr1
        RESET choice
        done=No;
```

Notice we added two lines to the conditional part of the rule. (It only takes one of those statements to work with the issue of product code validity, but since we know we'll need to account for invalid quantity entries at some point, we might as well make all the edits at once.) We also deleted the WKS clause that reads the worksheet file. This is because we cannot use an IF clause in the conclusion of a rule (the programming equivalent of nested IF statements is not permitted in most expert system shells, including VP-Expert). So we must perform the read in another rule and then check its result. This means we must write not one but two new rules to confirm valid quantity entries. They are RULE 6 and RULE 7, shown in Listing 6-4.

Listing 6-4

```
RULE 6
IF        productvalid=UNKNOWN
THEN      WKSdata,ROW=(product),inventr1
          dataread=Yes;

RULE 7
IF        dataread=Yes AND
          data[1]=UNKNOWN
THEN      DISPLAY"
     Sorry, but that product code is nonexistent!
          PRESS ANY KEY TO GO ON~"
          productvalid=No
          RESET choice
          done=No
ELSE
          productvalid=Yes
          RESET choice
          done=No;
```

You can see the basic purpose of the rules by examining them. RULE 6 determines if the value of the `productvalid` variable must still be found. If so, it reads the spreadsheet row we have identified and then sets the variable `dataread` to Yes. Rule 7 uses this variable in turn to ensure that we've attempted to read valid data from the worksheet. If so, we check the value of the first data element of the row. If still UNKNOWN, it means that the read did not work, no data was retrieved because the row name supplied by the user in response to the request for a product code is invalid. RULE 7 then assigns the appropriate value to the variable `productvalid` and performs the housekeeping RESET and assignment to the variable done.

Quantity Validation

With this pattern established, we can quickly examine how to define new rules to validate the user's quantity entries. Recall that we have already shown and explained the modification to RULE 2. We now add the following new rules to the knowledge base to deal with the possible errors involving:

- Entry of quantities greater than 500 units; or

- An attempt to order more disks of a particular type than the system believes are on-hand

We will check these conditions in the above order. Recall that our objective is to give the variable quantityvalid a value of Yes or No. Also note that by this time we will already have read the worksheet row and determined that it contains valid data, since we have validated the product code. There is no need to repeat that process, as you can see from Listing 6-5.

Listing 6-5

```
RULE 8
IF        quantity <= 500
THEN      quantityOK=OKsofar
ELSE      quantityOK=NotOK
FIND      verifybigorder;


RULE 9
IF        verifybigorder=Yes
THEN      quantityOK=OKsofar
ELSE      quantityvalid=No
          RESET choice
          done=No;


RULE 10
IF        quantityOK=OKsofar AND
          quantity <= data[5]
THEN      quantityvalid=Yes
          RESET choice
          done=No
ELSE      quantityvalid=No
          DISPLAY"
          Sorry, but that can't be right.  I show
          only {data[5]} units on hand!

          PRESS ANY KEY TO CONTINUE~"
          RESET choice
          done=No;
```

As you can see, we have defined three more new rules, bringing our knowledge base to 10 rules.

We must also add an ASK statement to the last portion of the knowledge base so that the FIND command in RULE 8 can ask the user to confirm that an unusually large order has been placed.

RULE 8 checks to be sure the order is not 500 or more units. If not, it assigns the value OKsofar to the newly defined variable quantit-yOK. This rule can't use the variable quantityvalid because the inference engine would find a value for it here and stop without assessing the second issue — whether sufficient parts on-hand exist to fill the order. If the quantity is larger than 500, we ask the user to verify that it is what was intended by forcing the inference engine to ask for the value of the new variable, verifybigorder. This FIND command results in the newly defined question, "Are you sure this order is that large?" being asked with a Yes-No menu choice.

RULE 9 looks at the value of verifybigorder to see if the user has confirmed the order larger than 500 units. If confirmed, we assign the value OKsofar to the variable quantityOK. Again, note that we cannot yet assign a value to the final variable for which RULE 8 is waiting because we still must confirm the quantity on-hand.

RULE 10 compares the quantity, which has now been confirmed to be either in range (i.e., not larger than 500) or acceptable even though out of range, to the quantity on-hand, which is already stored in the fifth element of the dimensioned variable data as a result of the earlier WKS command. If it passes this test, then quantityval-id is assigned the value Yes. This means RULE 2 can fire and continue the process by updating the worksheet's values.

Listing 6-6 is the entire INVEN2.KBS knowledge base in VP-Expert, incorporating all of the above changes.

Listing 6-6

```
!Procedural control section

ENDOFF;
ACTIONS
WHILETRUE choice<>Done THEN
FIND     done
RESET    done
END;

! Rules Section

RULE 1
IF       choice=Done
THEN     done=Yes;
```

```
RULE 2
IF        choice=Sales_Slips AND
          product<>UNKNOWN AND
          ! new lines for data validation
          productvalid=Yes AND
          quantity<>UNKNOWN AND
          quantityvalid=Yes
THEN      data[5] = ((data[5] - (quantity))
          data[7] = ((data[7] + (quantity))
          PWKS data,ROW = (product),inventr1
          RESET choice
          done=No;


RULE 3
IF        choice=Help
THEN      CLS
          DISPLAY "
If you want to enter today's sales slips into the
inventory system, then you should choose the 'Sales
Slips' option.  Before you do this, you should have
sorted the sales slips by product code. Product codes
need not be in a particular order but grouping all of
the orders for one product code together makes entering
the information more efficient. If you want to ask the
system to give you a list of all product codes where
the quantity on hand is lower than the reorder point,
you should choose the 'Reorder Check' option.

                          PRESS ANY KEY TO CONTINUE.~"
          RESET choice
          done=No;


RULE 4
IF        choice = Reorder_Check
THEN      WKSprodcode,COLUMN=CODE,inventr1
          WKSonhand,COLUMN=QOH,inventr1
          WKSreorderpoint,COLUMN=REORD,inventr1
          X=1
          WHILEKNOWN prodcode[X]
              FIND level
              X = (X + 1)
              RESET level
          END
          RESET choice
          done=No;


RULE 5
IF        onhand[X] < (reorderpoint[X])
THEN      DISPLAY "You should reorder {prodcode[X]}."
          level = low
ELSE      level = ok;
```

```
RULE 6
IF        productvalid=UNKNOWN
THEN      WKSdata,ROW=(product),inventr1
          dataread=Yes;

RULE 7
IF        dataread=Yes AND
          data[1]=UNKNOWN
THEN      DISPLAY"
              Sorry, but that product code is
              nonexistent!
                  PRESS ANY KEY TO GO ON~"
          productvalid=No
          RESET choice
          done=No
ELSE      productvalid=Yes
          RESET choice
          done=No;

RULE 8
IF        quantity <= 500
THEN      quantityOK=OKsofar
ELSE      quantityOK=NotOK
          FIND verifybigorder;

RULE 9
IF        verifybigorder=Yes
THEN      quantityOK=OKsofar
ELSE      quantityvalid=No
          RESET choice
          done=No;

RULE 10
IF        quantityOK=OKsofar AND
          quantity <= data[5]
THEN      quantityvalid=Yes
          RESET choice
          done=No
ELSE      quantityvalid=No
          DISPLAY"
          Sorry, but that can't be right.  I show
          only {data[5]} units on hand!
             PRESS ANY KEY TO CONTINUE~"
          RESET choice
          done=No;

! User interface and housekeeping section

ASK choice:"What activity do you want?";
CHOICES  choice:Sales_Slips,Reorder_Check,Help,Done;

ASK product:"Enter the product code";

ASK quantity:"How many purchased on this sales slip?";
```

Summary

In this chapter, we have examined several kinds of errors that can take place during data entry and we've seen how an expert system can be used to approach dealing with them for the user. We have also studied an example of how to add data validation to our inventory management worksheet by defining new rules that:

- Confirm that the product code entered is valid

- Confirm that the quantity ordered is within normal ranges

- Confirm that the quantity ordered is not more than the quantity on hand

In Chapter 7, we will walk through a more typical worksheet application, keeping the size of the application small enough to be manageable, and extend our understanding of the various user interface strategies available in expert systems like VP-Expert.

CHAPTER 7
A Small Spreadsheet
Example

In this chapter, we will take a step-by-step approach to building a small example of using an expert system to create an intelligent front end to a spreadsheet application. The worksheet will be relatively small so that we can focus attention on the expert system. The principles, procedures, and methods outlined in this chapter, however, are applicable regardless of the size of the worksheet. This application is typical of the things spreadsheets are often called on to do.

The Approach

In the remaining chapters of this book, we will be building worksheets and database applications and then designing and constructing expert system based front ends for them. We take a strongly procedural approach to the problem, presenting each step in the process. If you are a relative newcomer to spreadsheets, databases, or expert systems, you will find all you need in each chapter to construct and understand the example.

This necessarily leads to overly detailed explanations of some steps for the experienced reader. Whether you are an experienced spreadsheet creator, database designer, expert system builder, or some combination of the three, we want you to be able to avoid wading through a great deal of needless detail. To accomplish the dual goal of providing enough detail for the beginner and a brisk enough pace for the experienced reader, we have adopted a convention.

Each step in the process is listed and, if necessary, briefly explained, in a box. If any explanatory figures are needed or helpful, they are referred to in this box, even though they may not follow until some distance later in the text. After each step has been stated as simply as possible, a complete explanation of the step is provided. As we explain spreadsheet and database procedures, we provide the detailed steps required to accomplish the task listed in the step under discussion. We do not, however, intend this to be a tutorial on spreadsheets or databases. As a result, we do not discuss in detail the reasons behind the step, how it fits into the overall nature of the worksheet, or other similar items.

We explain the expert system steps as thoroughly as necessary. We intend this to be a tutorial in the use of expert systems.

A final preliminary word is in order. We have chosen to use VP-Planner Plus Version 2 as the spreadsheet in this chapter and in Chapter 10 where we discuss a more detailed worksheet. We have done so because VP-Planner Plus is a Lotus 1-2-3 workalike that wins rave reviews from editors and users and because everything we say about VP-Planner Plus can be substituted to apply equally to Lotus 1-2-3 and other 1-2-3 workalikes, including Quattro. We have also chosen VP-Planner Plus because it is the spreadsheet program we use when we build products for customers and for internal use, so we are comfortable with it. In the database chapters, we use dBASE III Plus from Ashton-Tate. It is clear that dBASE III Plus is the standard database on the IBM PC and clones, with millions of users. The equivalent Paperback Software product, VP-Info, has not caught on as quickly as VP-Planner has and it features enough differences that explaining them would occupy an unnecessarily large piece of our attention.

As we have from the outset, we use VP-Expert to build the expert system rules. In keeping with our policy of making the book as product-independent as possible, we try to stay with constructs that are as generic as possible so that if you are using some other expert system shell, following along will not be difficult. (Appendix B explains how some of the more popular shells differ from VP-Expert to assist you in creating the example applications in the remainder of the book.)

The Application

You are the owner of Jerry's Tile & Flooring. For the past two years, you have handled all of the estimating of jobs for the company, but business has grown so quickly that it is no longer feasible for you to do so. You have trained a new estimator, who is not very experienced in the use of computers or spreadsheets, to use the spreadsheet you've set up for this purpose. Errors can be costly. If you give a customer a low estimate and it is accepted, you lose money on the job. If you give a customer a high estimate, you may not get the job. You really want to ensure that your estimates are within reason.

You've decided to hire a consultant to design an easier to user interface for the spreadsheet so that your new estimator can answer a few English-language questions and print an estimate.

The spreadsheet is simple in appearance (see Figure 7-1). It requires, however, that the user have some knowledge of the tile business. The estimator and customer's name must be entered as well as the following five basic pieces of numeric information:

- Per tile cost

- Room length

- Room width

- "Fudge factor" for irregularly shaped objects in the room

- Additional factor to be applied if the customer wants the job done faster than your normal lead time

The spreadsheet then takes all of these factors into account and produces a total estimate, which the estimator gives the customer on the telephone and stores or prints for later retrieval.

Although both the room length and width are straightforward entries, the other three values needed have a significant amount of variability. Each of these factors is discussed briefly below.

```
                          ╔ A              ║  B        ║  C       ║  D       ║  E  ║
 1  Estimating Form
 2  Jerry's Tile & Flooring
 3
 4  Prepared by:
 5
 6  Prepared for:
 7
 8
 9               Per Tile Cost:
10               Room Length:
11               Room Width:
12   Adjustment for Irregularity:
13               Rush Charge:
14     Total Charge/Square Foot:
15          Area to be Covered:
16
17            Estimated Total:
18
19
20
    B11    (F2) 10
```

Figure 7-1. The Sample Spreadsheet

Per Tile Cost

The price per tile depends on the type of tile the customer selects. A tile company has dozens of tyle types, each carrying a different price. For our example, we are assuming only three types are available: asphalt, no-wax, and custom Italian marble. The estimator must determine which tile the customer wants to use and then look up the current price for that type of tile and enter it into cell B9.

Irregularity Adjustment

If a room is rectangular and has no fixtures in the floor, the tiling job goes quickly. However, any objects protruding from the floor must be tiled around requiring more time, resulting in a higher estimate.

Your experience indicates that in a bathroom, for example, the toilet and the sink cabinet will generally add about 25 percent to the cost of the job in time lost by the installer, since pieces must be hand trimmed to fit around the fixtures. If protrusions consist only of a water pipe or two, as in a typical utility room, the factor is about 5 percent. Other kinds of protrusions fall between these two extremes but are not particularly predictable.

Rush Charge

You charge a rush fee of 50 percent of the total price of the job for customers who are in a hurry. But the question of what constitutes a customer being in a rush varies depending on your company's workload. You have a lead time that is subject to change but which forms the basis of this rush charge determination.

If, for example, you are presently quoting jobs that you expect to start 22 days after the customer places the order, any customer who wants the job done sooner than that must pay the rush charge.

Building the Worksheet

Let's construct the worksheet needed to carry out this relatively simple estimating task.

STEP 1. Create a new worksheet

After starting your spreadsheet program, you will see an empty worksheet like that shown in Figure 7-2. (Note: Some spreadsheet programs have some preliminary screens or menus before you get to the point where you can define a new worksheet.)

STEP 2. Widen column A to 32 characters

We plan to have some fairly long labels in the final worksheet, so we must set up column A to be as wide as necessary so the user can see them. To widen a column, be sure the cursor is placed within the column you want to resize and then type:

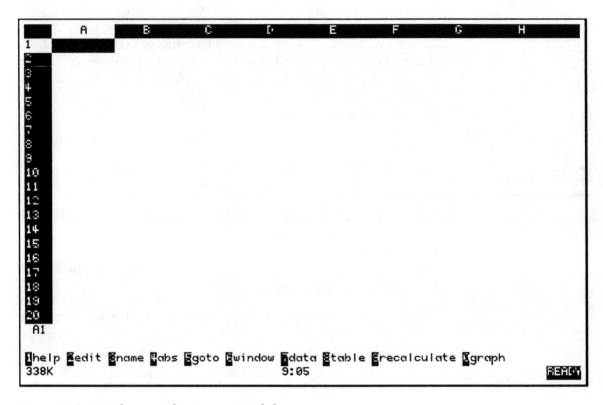

Figure 7-2. VP-Planner Plus Empty Worksheet

/WCS

(for Worksheet Column-width Set). Respond to the resulting prompt by telling the spreadsheet program how wide you want the column (see Figure 7-3). In this case, we answer by typing the number 32 and pressing Return. The column is automatically widened.

STEP 3. Enter the labels in column A as shown in Figure 7-1

To type labels into a worksheet just position the cursor in the cell where the label will go and begin typing. The application assumes you want to use the text you are typing as a label (provided you don't make the first character of the label a number or another special symbol that the spreadsheet interprets as a formula indicator).

STEP 4. Realign cells A9 through A17 so they are right aligned in the column

---

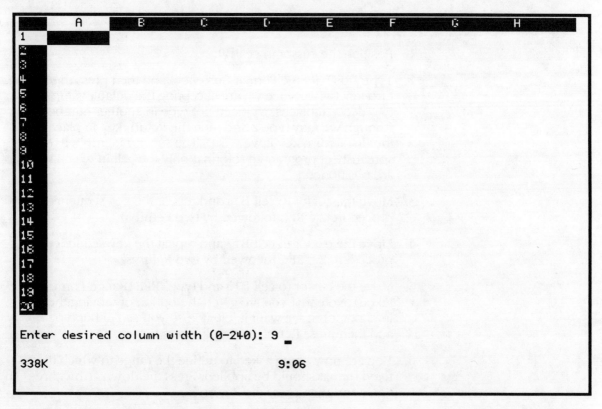

Figure 7-3. Widening a Column

The labels in cells A9 through A17 are prompts for the user to follow in entering information into the spreadsheet. It will be easier for the user to see the line being worked on and what is entered if we move the labels on these lines so they are closer to cell B, where the entries themselves will appear. Position the cursor at cell A9 and then type:

/RLR

(for Range Label-Prefix Right). Now select the range of cells to be affected by the realignment by pressing the down-arrow key eight times and then press the Return key. All of the labels in cells A9 through A17 will shift to the right.

STEP 5. Format the cells in column B so that B9, B14, and B17 are currency cells with two decimal places and the others are fixed cells with two decimal places

---

The following procedures will achieve this objective:

1. Position the cursor in cell B9.

2. Type /RFC (Range Format Currency) and then press the Return key twice. Since we are accepting the default value of two decimal places, we need not type in another number (though we may type 2 and then the Return key in place of the first Return key if we wish). The second Return tells the spreadsheet program to reformat only the cell in which we are positioned.

3. Move the cursor to cell B14 and repeat the key sequence in procedure 2 (/RFC followed by two Returns).

4. Move the cursor to cell B17 and repeat the key sequence in procedure 2 (/RFC followed by two Returns).

5. Move the cursor to cell B10 and type /RFF (Range Format Fixed). Note that you are given the option of moving the decimal point but we want it left at 2, so you can either type 2 and then press Return or simply press Return.

6. You are now being asked to define the range to which the fixed format should be applied. Press the down arrow three times and then press the Return key.

7. Move the cursor to cell B15 and repeat procedure 5.

8. Define the range of B15 to B16 by pressing the down arrow key once and then press the Return key.

This completes the cell formatting required in this worksheet.

STEP 6. Save your worksheet

In VP-Planner, the command to save a worksheet is

```
/FS
```

(for File Save) The first time you type this command, you must give the worksheet a name. We call our worksheet TILEJOB. Press return once you've typed the name and the worksheet will be saved.

STEP 7. Enter the formula (B9 * (1+B12) * (1+B13)) into cell B14

Cells B14, B15, and B17 are all calculated cells whose values are determined by the contents of other cells. This is our first formula entry in this worksheet.

Entering a formula is simple. Just position the cursor in the cell where you want the formula and begin typing it exactly as you did with the labels at step 3, above. To be recognized as a formula, the entry must begin with one of several special characters that have meaning only in calculations. These characters include the plus and minus signs, the left parenthesis and the commercial at (@) sign.

Because we are having the user enter the values in cells B12 and B13 as percentages by which to increase the price of the job, we must add 1 to each of them before we multiply. Otherwise, the result of their presence would be to reduce rather than increase the price.

STEP 8. Enter the formula +B9 * B10 into cell B15

The process for entering this formula is identical to that outlined in detail in step 7. Just position the cursor in cell B15 and begin typing it. The formula starts with a plus sign so the spreadsheet application won't think the letter "B" is the beginning of a label.

The formula simply calculates the square footage of the room to be tiled.

STEP 9. Enter the formula +B14 * B15 into cell B17

This formula calculates the total job cost by multiplying the area to be covered by the calculated cost per square foot.

Position the cursor in cell B17 and type the formula as shown.

STEP 10. Save the worksheet

Type:

```
/FS
```

(for File Save) followed by the Return key and then the letter "R." This sequence uses the same name as last time and then confirms that the program should replace the current copy of the worksheet with the new one.

STEP 11. Test the worksheet

Testing the worksheet is always a good idea when you have finished it. The best way to test a worksheet is to enter numbers that will make it easy for you to see if the results are correct by choosing values with which you can work in your head.

Enter the values in Table 7-1 into the indicated cells. If you've built the worksheet correctly and entered the numbers as shown, your screen should look like Figure 7-4 when you are done. If it doesn't, go back through the steps and find out where your mistake is.

Table 7-1. Sample Data for Worksheet

Cell	Value
B9	1
B10	10
B11	10
B12	0
B13	0

(Note: The entries you make in testing a worksheet need not make any sense in the real world. Here, for example, we apply factors of 0 to irregularity and to rush charges, simplifying the testing of our worksheet.)

STEP 12. Clear the sample data from the worksheet

Just enter zeros in cells B9 through B13 so that there is no remaining data to confuse the operator during the next data entry.

STEP 13. Save the worksheet in its final form

Type:

```
/FS
```

(for File Save) followed by the Return key and then the letter "R."

```
                            A              B        C    D      E
 1    Estimating Form
 2    Jerry's Tile & Flooring
 3
 4    Prepared by:
 5
 6    Prepared for:
 7
 8
 9                    Per Tile Cost:      1.00
10                    Room Length:       10.00
11                    Room Width:        10.00
12    Adjustment for Irregularity:        0.00
13                    Rush Charge:        0.00
14    Total Charge/Square Foot:           1.00
15          Area to be Covered:         100.00
16
17               Estimated Total:      $100.00
18
19
20
     B11    (F2) 10


    █help █edit █name █abs █goto █window █data █table █recalculate █graph
    337K                                9:14                              READY
```

Figure 7-4. Test Worksheet Entries

Enhancing the Worksheet

We could now make a number of enhancements and modifications to the worksheet we've just built. For example, we could protect the labels from accidental alteration by locking the user out of them entirely. In fact, we could protect all cells except those where we expect the user to make entries.

We will not take the time to do any of these enhancements now because the creation of polished worksheets is not the focus of our discussion. However, we did not want you to leave this discussion unaware of the fact that a great deal could still be done to make this worksheet more easily usable.

Designing the Expert System

As we examine the description of the worksheet, we can spot several areas where an expert system can be helpful to the user. Remember that the user is someone who is just becoming familiar with the tile business and with your company's operations. Recall, too, that data entry mistakes can be costly to your organization.

Names to Be Furnished

To begin with, we see that two pieces of information need to be inserted into the worksheet we haven't yet accounted for. The name of the estimator and the name of the customer are needed to make the form complete for printing and filing. The customer's name is unpredictable, of course, but not that of the estimator. There are, after all, only two candidates for the estimator's name: you (Jerry) and the newly hired estimator (Heather). Thus we can design a VP-Expert menu to make it easy to answer this question.

Figures to Be Entered

Next we examine the five pieces of numeric information the system needs in order to do its job.

It is logical to ask the customer about the size of the room to be tiled. This gets the discussion started between your estimator and your prospective buyer on ground with which the customer is probably familiar. It is also clear that if the customer doesn't know how big the room is, finishing the estimate won't be possible in any case. Therefore, we'll design the expert system to obtain this information first.

The worksheet needs the per tile cost of the tile chosen by the customer. As we saw, three types of tile are available: asphalt, no-wax, and custom Italian marble. This is also a candidate for a VP-Expert, but we note that the estimator's answer will require us to translate the type of tile into a per tile cost.

Dealing with the irregularity adjustment turns out to be a little trickier than first appeared to be the case. Most jobs don't have any irregularity adjustment, so the first thing we need to do is to ask the customer if there are any objects attached to the floor of the room. If the answer is no, then we can skip the rest of the irregularity probing. However, if there are such protrusions, then we should probably ask the customer if the room is a bathroom, if the protrusions are pipes, or if they are some other kind of protrusion altogether. In the case of the bathroom and the pipes, we can place a figure directly into the worksheet from the expert system. In the case of an answer that there are protrusions but none of the standard ones for which we have supplied a predetermined figure, we must allow the estimator to enter a number after further discussion with the customer. This number should be checked to make sure it doesn't accidentally go lower than 5 percent, since that's our minimum charge for irregularities. Nor should it go higher than about 25 percent, since your experience is that a room seldom has enough complexity to warrant a surcharge higher than that.

To determine if a rush charge is applicable to this estimate, the estimator must know two things: what would constitute "normal" completion time given the firm's current schedule, and when the customer wants the job done. We could design the expert system simply to prompt the estimator to ask the customer when the job is to be completed and then the estimator can determine whether a rush charge is in order. But that would be inefficient. The customer probably wants the job done "as soon as possible," because that's when everyone wants everything done! Also, there's no reason we can't use the expert system itself to keep track of the number of days' lead time needed by the company. We'll set up a variable to hold that information and then edit the expert system listing to update it as necessary. (In a finished system, we'd undoubtedly devise a method by which the estimator or some other user could keep this figure up to date without the necessity of editing the program, but we're trying to keep this system short and manageable, so we'll skip that at this point.)

Once all of this information is obtained from the user and confirmed, we are ready to calculate the estimate amount. We could simply perform the calculation within VP-Expert. However, the expert system has limited math capabilities and the worksheet has already been set up to handle the calculations, so we'll use the worksheet. This necessitates our placing the information into the worksheet once it's obtained, then causing the worksheet to be recalculated before retrieving the estimate from the worksheet and placing it in the expert system. There are several ways this could be accomplished. We could, for example, simply put the information we've obtained directly into the worksheet and then let the user take over.

Dealing with Unknown Data

As we have seen, a strength of expert systems when compared to other types of programs is their ability to deal with unknown or missing information, as well as handling uncertain data. If we were to pursue an estimate for a tiling job even if some information were unavailable at the time the estimate was being prepared, we would have to stay within the expert system and not rely on the spreadsheet program. The reason for this is that missing information in the worksheet results in incorrect answers. For example, if the customer did not know if there were any irregularities in the floor layout of the room, then the worksheet would maintain a zero in that cell. The result would be a no-charge estimate. Granted that no estimator would unquestioningly give such an estimate to a customer, the point is that erroneous estimates could undoubtedly be generated by missing data.

Similarly, we could permit our expert system to be designed to deal with information about which the customer was less than 100 percent confident. This would permit us to attach a confidence factor to the final bid that could be passed along to the customer and recorded. Then if the customer turned out to be wrong about some measurement or other factor, the estimate would have been qualified and conditioned on the possibility of alteration if the facts supplied by the customer were inaccurate.

In Chapters 12 and 13, when we deal with a large-scale application, we will demonstrate how to handle missing and uncertain information when dealing with an underlying spreadsheet or database program. For the moment, keep in mind that you could, if necessary, expand even the simple application in this chapter to accommodate such a demand.

Building the Expert System

We will take a careful, step-by-step approach to building the expert system in this chapter. This method is the best to use in most situations. It calls for building the system modularly, testing each step of the way. Because this is a small system, it may seem unnecessary to build the system so painstakingly. But the discipline and the approach will stand you in good stead when the time comes for you to construct a real-world system with more complexity.

Table 7-2 outlines our approach to constructing this expert system. Each step is the subject of a separate section in the following discussion. Accompanying each step is a listing of the VP-Expert code required to accomplish it. The entire system is reproduced at the end of the chapter so that typing the finished system into your computer is facilitated. As we go along, we will sometimes have to change code previously produced to accommodate new needs, much as we saw in Chapter 6 when we examined rule definitions.

Table 7-2. Construction Steps for Sample Expert System

1. Entry process for names

2. Entry process for room dimensions

3. Data validation techniqes for room dimensions

4. Entry process for per tile cost

5. Entry process for room irregularities
   a. Any irregularities? If so, what kind?
   b. Deal with "other" option

6. Determination of rush charge
   a. Entering and updating current "normal" delivery
   b. Asking customer question and updating charge

7. Updating spreadsheet

8. Retrieving and displaying estimate

Entry Process for Names

We do not need a production rule for the entry of the name information, since no data validation will be performed on these entries. Instead, we can make this part of the up-front housekeeping. In VP-Expert, this means we will place the entire process in the ACTIONS block except for the ASK statement that prepares the menu for the name of the estimator. Listing 7-1 presents the VP-Expert code to ask for the two names and place them into the spreadsheet.

Listing 7-1

```
AUTOQUERY;
ENDOFF;
ACTIONS

FIND  estimator
FIND  customer
PWKS  estimator,A5,tilejob
PWKS  customer,A7,tilejob
DISPLAY "Done!";

ASK estimator:"Who is the estimator preparing this
estimate?";
CHOICES   estimator:Jerry,Heather;
```

There is only one new element in this ACTIONS block and that is the first line, which is really outside the ACTIONS block itself. The AUTOQUERY statement is a very useful development tool in VP-Expert. Most other shells have similar constructions. This statement instructs VP-Expert's inference engine that if it can't find a value for a needed variable and there is no ASK statement with which to frame a question to the user, it should pose its default question. In this case, when the system reaches the point where it needs the name of the customer, it will ask "What is the value of customer?" Not a very user-friendly way to ask the question and we will certainly want to change it for the final system, but during development, the use of AUTOQUERY can make it easier to finish the construction and testing phase. It is also sometimes a good idea to turn the task of writing the questions to be posed to the user over to a writer or communications professional.

Let's finish this step now, though, by removing the AUTOQUERY statement so that testing will look more like the finished product. We just wanted you to know the option is available. We will make periodic use of it throughout the rest of the book.

Listing 7-2 shows the way the first phase of the expert system should be built.

Listing 7-2

```
ENDOFF;
ACTIONS

FIND  estimator
FIND  customer
PWKS  estimator,A5,tilejob
PWKS  customer,A7,tilejob
DISPLAY "Done!";

ASK estimator:"Who is the estimator preparing this
estimate?";
CHOICES   estimator:Jerry,Heather;

ASK customer:"What is the name of the customer for whom
this estimate is being prepared?";
```

Test this phase of the entry process. In VP-Expert, you do this by saving the knowledge base, exiting the editor, and then pressing F4. When the knowledge base has been loaded, press the Return key and the consultation will begin. Select the name of the estimator, then type in the name of a customer.

When you've made these entries and the system has indicated it is done updating the spreadsheet, go to the spreadsheet and examine it. If it has the estimator's name in cell A5 and the customer's name in cell A7 then you've successfully completed this phase of the expert system construction. If there is anything amiss, return to VP-Expert and ensure that you typed everything correctly. A common typographical error is to provide the wrong cell address for the PWKS command. Also be sure that you have given VP-Expert a complete file path name by which to find the worksheet. We keep our worksheets and VP-Expert in the same directory during development for the sake of ease of programming.

Entry Process for Room Dimensions

We will be creating some data validation techniques for the room dimensions being entered, so we must make a choice between a process resembling batch data entry and the more traditional rule-based expert system approach we saw in Chapter 6.

In order to take a batch approach to data entry, we could provide FIND statements for all the variables we want the user to supply and then, after all the data has been entered, verify their validity. If we find any apparent mistakes at that point, we ask the user to confirm or fix them. Generally, this approach is not very efficient because it requires the user to backtrack. When the data has several interrelationships, as it does here, this approach also sometimes means that the user lacks sufficient data to complete the processing. Waiting until the user thinks that all of the needed information has been entered successfully and then stating that a mistake has been made is unfair.

So we typically use the production-rule approach to data entry for any information on which we expect to perform validation. You may encounter situations where the batch mode is more appropriate, however. Don't be afraid to use it when you're certain it's the most efficient way to get the job done.

By now, the method of creating data-validation rules should start looking familiar. The techniques vary only by the content of the data being examined and the number of possible combinations of errors that might arise.

In our example, we've decided that any time an estimator enters a room larger than 50 feet in either dimension, it's probably a mistake. Our firm specializes in residences and few have rooms larger than 50 feet on any one side. However, we don't want to throw out the occasional large job if one arises! So we won't make this error trap one that the user must correct. Rather, we'll ask the user to confirm its accuracy.

Listing 7-3 shows the rules necessary to perform this error checking. As you can see, these rules look a great deal like the rules developed in Chapter 6 for testing the sizes of orders for disks.

Listing 7-3

```
ENDOFF;
ACTIONS

FIND  estimator
FIND  customer
WHILETRUE dimensions_ok <> Yes THEN
        RESET length
        RESET length_ok
        RESET width
        RESET width_ok
        RESET dimensions_ok
        RESET yn
        FIND dimensions_ok
END
PWKS  estimator,A5,tilejob
PWKS  customer,A7,tilejob
PWKS  length,B10,tilejob
PWKS  width,B11,tilejob
DISPLAY "Done!";

RULE Get_length
IF    length<50
THEN  length_ok=Yes
ELSE  confirm_length=Yes;

RULE Get_width
IF    width<50
THEN  width_ok=Yes
ELSE  confirm_width=Yes;

RULE Confirm_Length
IF    confirm_length=Yes AND
yn=Yes
THEN  length_ok=Yes
RESET yn
ELSE  length_ok=No;

RULE Confirm_Width
IF    confirm_width=Yes AND
yn=Yes
THEN  width_ok=Yes
RESET yn
ELSE  width_ok=No;

RULE Sizes_OK
IF    length_ok=Yes
AND   width_ok=Yes
THEN  dimensions_ok=Yes;

ASK estimator:"Who is the estimator preparing this
estimate?";
CHOICES   estimator:Jerry,Heather;
```

```
ASK customer:"What is the name of the customer for whom
this estimate is being prepared?";

ASK length:"What is the length of the room to be
tiled?";

ASK width:"What is the width of the room to be tiled?";

ASK yn:"That's an awfully big room! Are you sure?";
CHOICES yn:Yes,No;
```

Notice that the WHILETRUE loop that we started with in Chapter 6 has become quite a bit larger, with several RESET statements contained in it. This construction is one of the most powerful and useful in VP-Expert because it lets us perform tasks that are procedural in nature without having to resort to creating "dummy rules" to make them happen. In the ACTIONS block, we use the WHILETRUE approach to create a procedural loop that will continue to execute until its condition becomes false. In this case, as long as the value of the goal variable dimensions_ok is anything other than Yes, the program will continue to try to find a value for it. In other words, this program won't let us escape until we've provided acceptable dimensions or confirmed that the ones we are giving it are exceptions of which we approve.

Turn your attention now to the rules themselves. Notice first that we have moved from numbering rules to giving them meaningful names. In a very small expert system, you can get away with calling rules RULE 1, RULE 2, and so forth. However, as the complexity of your systems grows, so too does the need to be able to track what is happening during the expert system's execution. Giving rules names that describe their purpose is a helpful way to support your design and debugging efforts.

The WHILETRUE loop in the ACTIONS block establishes a goal variable of dimensions_ok. When the inference engine looks at the rules, it finds that the only one that sets a value for this goal variable is the rule Sizes_OK. To satisfy this goal, it must find that both length_ok and width_ok have values of Yes. Thus it searches for the first rule in the knowledge base that will satisfy the first goal, namely assigning a value to length_ok. The first of the two rules it finds is Get_length. It examines this rule and determines that it has only one premise, namely that the variable length have a value less than 50. Now it seeks a rule that sets the value of length. It does not find one, so it looks for an ASK statement for the variable. Locating it, the inference engine poses the question, waits for a response, assigns the answer to the variable length, and returns to the rule called Get_length.

If the user enters a value less than 50, then the rule Get_length assigns the value Yes to the variable length_ok. This permits the inference engine to satisfy the first of the two premises of the rule Sizes_OK, which is the one with which it is currently working. The second goal is satisfied in much the same way.

If either of the values for length or width is greater than 50 feet, then one of two secondary rules is invoked to confirm that this value is intentionally large. If the user answers "No" to the confirmation request, then its respective goal variable (e.g., length_ok) is set to "No." This causes the rule Sizes_OK to fail. As a result, the WHILE-TRUE loop resets all the values of the key variables and starts the process over.

Notice that we've added two more PWKS statements to the ACTIONS block in Listing 7-3. These statements record the length and width of the room as entered by the estimator.

You can now test this phase of the expert system interface. Try the combinations of values shown in Table 7-3 as trial data. The results you should see are shown in the table. If things don't happen as expected, go back and look at your code again, compare it carefully to Listing 7-3, correct any errors, and try again.

Table 7-3. Test Data for Room Dimension Entry Validation

Length	Width	Confirm?	Expected Result
10	20	N/A	Done!
10	200	Yes	Done!
10	200	No	Re-enter length
100	NA	Yes	Proceed to width
100	NA	No	Re-enter length
100	200	Yes, both	Done!

After each trial run that ends in the expert system informing you that it has completed the processing, you might want to take a look at the worksheet to see how its contents have been altered.

Note, too, that the calculation should have taken place as the values were placed into the worksheet. If they have not, then you must turn on automatic recalculation.

This is done by typing

```
/WGRA
```

(for Worksheet Global Recalculation Automatic).

Entry Process for Per Tile Cost

To enter a per tile cost, the estimator using your expert system interface is simply going to choose from among the three available alternatives. The system will then assign a value to the price. For the purposes of this limited demonstration, we will store the values for each kind of tile in the expert system program listing. In a real-world situation, you would probably store these values either in a spreadsheet or in a database which you would control with this or another expert system interface.

Since no data validation is needed for this entry, it might appear that we don't need production rules, that we could use a simple FIND statement to locate the values. If we were asking the user to choose from among values rather than from among a list of choices that in turn "lead" to values, that would be the case. However, we need some way to translate the user's selection from this list of tile types into a per tile cost. In an expert system environment, the most efficient way of accomplishing this objective is to use production rules. These rules are simple and straightforward. Listing 7-4 shows only the new rules and the new ASK and CHOICES statements. You must also add to the ACTIONS block, immediately following the END statement that closes the WHILETRUE loop of the previous section, this line:

```
FIND tile_price
```

This will force the inference engine to find a value for the tile price. You must also add a fifth PWKS command:

```
PWKS tile_price,B9,tilejob
```

so that the price you furnish will be placed into the correct worksheet cell for calculations.

Listing 7-4

```
RULE Asphalt_Tile
IF    tile_type=asphalt
THEN  tile_price=.39;

RULE Nowax_Tile
IF    tile_type=no_wax
THEN  tile_price=.79;

RULE Italian_Tile
IF    tile_type=Italian_marble
THEN  tile_price=2.44;

ASK tile_type:"What kind of tile does the customer want
to use?";
CHOICES tile_type:asphalt,no_wax,Italian_marble;
```

There is nothing terribly new about the contents of Listing 7-4. The goal variable set up in the ACTIONS block is tile_price, so the inference engine looks for the first rule that can give it a value for this variable. The rule Asphalt_Tile is the first one it encounters. It turns out that it wouldn't have mattered which rule we'd placed first since the same result would be obtained. The program finds that in order to assign a value to the goal variable tile_price, it must first find out what the tile_type is. It then finds the ASK and CHOICES statements that assist it in this process and executes them.

Again, testing the interface as it stands now is a good idea. Figure 7-5 shows a sample session that takes us to this point in our processing. We have supplied acceptable room sizes to reduce the amount of text in the illustration to a minimum. Figure 7-6 shows what the TILE-JOB.WKS worksheet should look like after you've run the test shown in Figure 7-5.

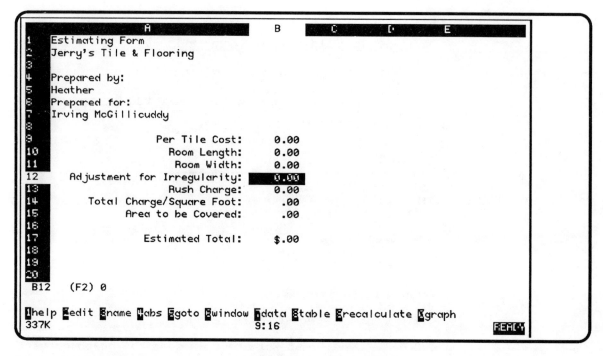

Figure 7-5. Testing in Process on Expert System for Tile Estimating

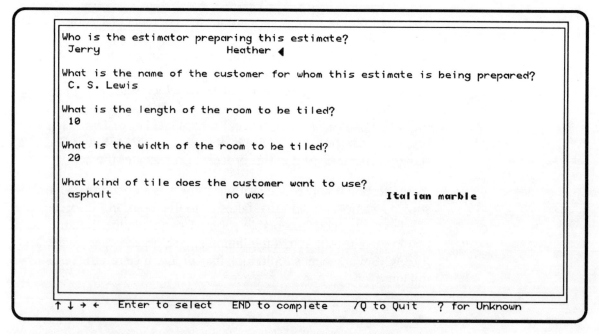

Figure 7-6. Worksheet Contents during Tile Estimating Interface Testing

Entry Process for Room Irregularities

The next step in building our expert system is to provide a means for the estimator using the system to enter irregularities in the floor's shape or content that could affect the price of the tile job. We could approach this by asking two questions:

1. Are there any irregularities? (Yes or No)

2. Are the irregularities best described as those found in:
    a. Bathrooms
    b. Utility rooms
    c. No standard room type

Question 2 would only be asked if the user answered "Yes" to question 1. In this case, since we have so few secondary choices, we're better off combining the two questions into one:

"Describe the irregularities, if any, in this room. Are they like those typically found in a bathroom or utility room, or are they different from either?"

Recall from our earlier discussion that you want the estimator to be able to enter an arbitrary value between 5 and 25 percent for difficulty added by floor protrusions. There are therefore three possible situations. First, the protrusions could be like those found in a typical bathroom, in which case the factor for irregularity adjustment will be 25 percent. Second, they could be more typical of a utility room, with a small number of small pipes involved, in which case the adjustment factor will be 5 percent. Third, they could be somewhere between these extremes, in which case we will ask the user to enter a percentage between 5 and 25 percent by which to adjust the estimate.

We will add a fourth choice: none. This will result in a zero being placed in the appropriate worksheet cell. Since that cell already contains a zero, it might seem redundant to put one there with a PWKS statement. On the contrary, it is always possible that someone has left a previous copy of the worksheet on the disk, with a value other than zero in the cell. To be safe, let's write out the value.

To make this aspect of the expert system work, we will define two new statements in the ACTIONS block:

```
FIND irreg_adjustment
PWKS irreg_adjustment,B12,tilejob
```

The first statement should appear immediately after the FIND tile_price command added in the preceding section. The second can go anywhere in the group of PWKS statements but most logically belongs at the end of the current list there.

Listing 7-5 presents the four new rules and the two new ASK statements along with a CHOICES clause needed to make this part of the interface work.

Listing 7-5

```
RULE   Bath_Irregularities
IF     irregularities=bathroom
THEN   irreg_adjustment=.25;

RULE   Util_Irregularities
IF     irregularities=utility_room
THEN   irreg_adjustment=.05;

RULE   No_Irregularities
IF     irregularities=none
THEN   irreg_adjustment=0;

RULE   Other_Irregularity
IF     irregularities=other
THEN   FIND other_adjust
       irreg_adjustment=(other_adjust);

ASK irregularities:"Describe the irregularities, if
any, in this room.
Are they like those typically found in a bathroom or
utility room, or are they different from either?";
CHOICES  irregularities:bathroom,utility_room,other,
none;

ASK other_adjust:"How much of an adjustment do you want
to include?";
```

There is nothing surprising or new in this listing, so we will move on to the next step in the construction of the expert system.

Dealing with "Other" Option

In the preceding step, we did not perform any data validation on the user's entry if it was indicated that an adjustment was to be made other than the normal ones. But recall that we intend to ensure that no adjustment smaller than 5 percent or larger than 25 percent is entered here. So we need to provide a means for ensuring that the entry is in the acceptable range.

As we have seen before, the way to handle error trapping when we want to force the user to continue to enter responses until one is entered that is acceptable is to use a WHILETRUE loop. In previous situations, we've inserted this loop into the ACTIONS block. However, in VP-Expert, this loop can also be used as a conclusion in a rule. That is how we will approach the problem here.

Listing 7-6 shows the modified rule called `Other_Irregularity` designed to deal with the possible error conditions.

Listing 7-6

```
RULE Other_Irregularity
IF    irregularities=other
THEN  FIND other_adjust
      WHILETRUE other_adjust<.05 OR other_adjust>.25
      THEN
          DISPLAY "Sorry, but this value must be between
          .05 and .25!"
          RESET other_adjust
          FIND other_adjust
      END
      irreg_adjustment=(other_adjust);
```

As you can see, we simply execute a FIND statement, then examine the result of that operation. If it does not fall within the acceptable range, the WHILETRUE statement traps it and forces the user to enter a value that *is* in the acceptable range. (A real-world application, would provide the user with another way out of this loop. Designing such an exit would be a useful exercise for you.)

Note, too, that in the final clause of the new rule we use parentheses to surround the variable name `other_adjust`. This is VP-Expert's way of telling the system to use the current value of that variable and treat it as a number.

Determination of Rush Charge

The last set of rules we must design deal with the question of whether this order is subject to a special charge for rushing its completion ahead of our usual schedule. Recall that we said earlier that we will simply put the current lead time into the VP-Expert program; in a real-world situation, you might want to include this in a different file and provide some means of updating it automatically or manually.

First, let's define a variable called `normal_delivery` that will contain the number of days from the date of the order that Jerry's Tile can normally finish the job. The process of defining such a variable and giving it a value is called initialization. Normally initialization is not required in VP-Expert (or most other shells) but it *is* essential when you want to use its value as a constant in the program. In VP-Expert, this initialization takes place in the ACTIONS block; by convention, we put such "housekeeping" chores at the beginning of the block.

We'll also need to define both a FIND statement and a PWKS command to deal with this new information. These three new lines for the ACTIONS block look like this:

```
normal_delivery=22

FIND rush_charge

PWKS rush_charge,B13,tilejob
```

It will require only a single rule and a single ASK statement to deal with the issue of rush charges. Listing 7-7 presents these new elements of the expert system interface.

Listing 7-7

```
RULE Find_Rush_Charges
IF    days_needed < (normal_delivery)
THEN  DISPLAY "That will require a rush charge."
      rush_charge=.5
ELSE  rush_charge=0;

ASK days_needed:"How many days from now does the
customer want the work done?"
```

We could obviously deal with this rush charge issue in a slightly different way. We could start an estimating session by asking the user what the current lag time is between order and job completion, then use that value instead of a prestored one. However, since this number probably seldom changes, it is better not to interfere with the normal data entry process by asking a question to which the answer will most often be the same as the last time we asked it.

Updating the Spreadsheet

We have been testing our system with the PWKS statements in place to update the spreadsheet. If you listen carefully to your computer as you test this system, you can detect that each PWKS statement results in the disk being activated.

We can, however, reduce this slowdown in processing to a single disk access for the numeric update. (We will still require two other steps for the names of the estimator and the customer, however, since they are not in contiguous cells and therefore cannot be defined as a range.) The process involves three steps:

1. Defining a range in the worksheet where the data will be placed

2. Assigning each bit of information gathered in the expert system to a separate element of a dimensioned variable

3. Writing this dimensioned variable in one step to the range of the worksheet

Let's see how this could be done.

First, if you are working in your expert system environment, leave it and open the worksheet TILEJOB.WKS. We'll define the area B9 through B13 to be a region called "input." To do that, you would follow these steps:

1. Position the cursor in cell B9

2. Type /RNC (for Range Name Create)

3. In response to the system's request for the name of the re-

gion, type "input" (without the quotation marks) and press RE-
TURN

4.   Press the down arrow key four times to select the area B9
     through B13

5.   Press RETURN

6.   Save the worksheet using the /FS command (for File Save),
     and use the Replace option

Next, leave the spreadsheet program and re-open the expert system
TILEEST.KBS with which we have been working. Delete the five numeric PWKS commands and in their place put one command that
looks like this:

```
PWKS data,NAMED=input,tilejob
```

Finally, just before the new PWKS command line, we must assign
each value found by a FIND command or a rule firing to its correct
element in the variable data. Listing 7-8 shows what the ACTIONS
block should look like when all of this is accomplished.

Listing 7-8

```
ENDOFF;
ACTIONS

normal_delivery=22
FIND estimator
FIND customer
WHILETRUE dimensions_ok<> Yes THEN
     RESET length
     RESET length_ok
     RESET width
     RESET width_ok
     RESET dimensions_ok
     RESET yn
     FIND dimensions_ok
END
FIND tile_price
FIND irreg_adjustment
FIND rush_charge
data[1]=(tile_price)
data[2]=(length)
data[3]=(width)
data[4]=(irreg_adjustment)
data[5]=(rush_charge)
PWKS estimator,A5,tilejob
```

```
PWKS customer,A7,tilejob
PWKS data,NAMED=input,tilejob
DISPLAY "Done!";
```

The worksheet having been updated, the estimate has already been calculated for us by the spreadsheet application. We are now left only to retrieve it and display it to the estimator.

Retrieving and Displaying the Estimate

Use the WKS statement to read the estimate from the worksheet file. Place this command immediately after the last PWKS command:

```
WKS estimate,B17,tilejob
```

Now we'll change the DISPLAY statement at the end of the ACTIONS block to be more meaningful than the simple "Done!" used during testing. In so doing, we will take advantage of the fact that VP-Expert will permit us to display the values of variables in a DISPLAY statement. Here is our way of phrasing this statement; you can obviously rewrite it any way you wish, just so it is syntactically correct:

```
DISPLAY"
The estimate is now prepared. Please inform {customer}
that the total bill for the tiling job will be
${estimate}.~";
```

Note the semicolon at the end of the DISPLAY statement. This is required since this is the last statement in the ACTIONS block.

We have included the tilde at the end of this statement even though it is not necessary in the testing environment since the program will automatically leave us at this screen. But as we shall see later, we intend to create a runtime environment in which the program will return us immediately to the main VP-Expert title screen unless we place the tilde in the final DISPLAY command.

Also note that we have referenced two variables' values: `customer` and `estimate`. We have indicated to VP-Expert that we want to display the values of these variables by enclosing them in curly braces. Just to make things a bit neater, let's add a CLS (clear-screen) command just before the DISPLAY command so that the closing message will appear on a screen by itself.

When you run this system through another test, the resulting final screen looks like Figure 7-7.

The formatting of the estimate is not very pretty, so we'll take advantage of another of VP-Expert's features to make it more presentable.

Using the FORMAT command, you can specify how many digits should be displayed in a numeric variable, and how many decimal places you want it to have. Insert the following line before the DISPLAY statement:

```
FORMAT estimate,7.2
```

This command tells VP-Expert to allow a total of seven digits, including two past the decimal point, for the value of the variable `estimate` when it is displayed. This will accommodate values up to $99,999.99; if you anticipate larger orders, change the FORMAT values accordingly.

Rerun the test and the result should look more like Figure 7-8.

A Final Clean-Up

We will now make one final change to our expert system before we consider it ready to deliver to the new estimator. If you are using VP-Expert, you have undoubtedly noticed during your testing of the system that the system is constantly showing us the rules being executed, the current values of variables, and other such helpful information in two small windows at the bottom of the display. You've also noted that we always have to press the RETURN key to start the consultation after the knowledge base is loaded. That's fine during system design and construction, but the user isn't going to find this very friendly.

Let's get rid of these annoyances. We can do this by adding two one-line commands at the beginning of the knowledge base, before the start of the ACTIONS block. These commands are RUNTIME and EXECUTE. The first removes the two small windows, leaving the entire screen for user interaction. The other causes a consultation to begin

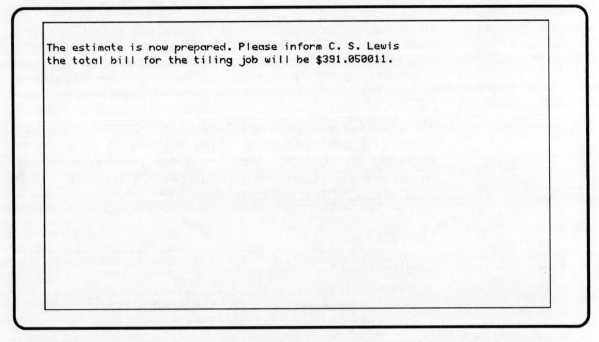

The estimate is now prepared. Please inform C. S. Lewis
the total bill for the tiling job will be $391.050011.

Figure 7-7. Output Screen with Formatting Problem

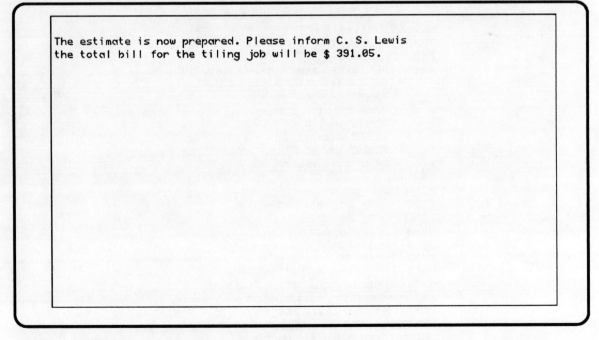

The estimate is now prepared. Please inform C. S. Lewis
the total bill for the tiling job will be $ 391.05.

Figure 7-8. Output Screen, Formatting Problem Solved

automatically when the system is loaded. You should never add these commands to a VP-Expert knowledge base until you are ready to deliver it to your customer. Remember that each of these lines must be followed by a semicolon since each is a command that appears as a separate entry outside the ACTIONS block.

The finished program is shown in Listing 7-9. Note that we have not included comments because we have spent so much of this chapter discussing the contents of the knowledge base. Normally, you should comment your systems liberally. When you need to change them six months later, you'll be glad you did!

Listing 7-9

```
! (c) 1989, Dan Shafer

! This knowledge base first appeared in "Designing
! Intelligent Front Ends for Business Software,"
! published by John Wiley & Sons, Inc., 1989.

RUNTIME;
EXECUTE;
ENDOFF;
ACTIONS

normal_delivery=22
FIND estimator
FIND customer
WHILETRUE dimensions_ok <> Yes THEN
        RESET length
        RESET length_ok
        RESET width
        RESET width_ok
        RESET dimensions_ok
        RESET yn
        FIND dimensions_ok
END
FIND tile_price
FIND irreg_adjustment
FIND rush_charge
data[1]=(tile_price)
data[2]=(length)
data[3]=(width)
data[4]=(irreg_adjustment)
data[5]=(rush_charge)
PWKS estimator,A5,tilejob
PWKS customer,A7,tilejob
PWKS data,NAMED=input,tilejob
WKS estimate,B17,tilejob
CLS
```

```
FORMAT estimate,7.2
DISPLAY "
The estimate is now prepared. Please inform {customer}
the total bill for the tiling job will be
${estimate}.~";

RULE Length
IF     length<50
THEN   length_ok=Yes
ELSE   confirm_length=Yes;

RULE Width
IF     width<50
THEN   width_ok=Yes
ELSE   confirm_width=Yes;

RULE Confirm_Length
IF     confirm_length=Yes AND
yn=Yes
THEN   length_ok=Yes
RESET  yn
ELSE   length_ok=No;

RULE Confirm_Width
IF     confirm_width=Yes AND
yn=Yes
THEN   width_ok=Yes
RESET  yn
ELSE   width_ok=No;

RULE Sizes_OK
IF     length_ok=Yes
AND    width_ok=Yes
THEN   dimensions_ok=Yes;

RULE Asphalt_Tile
IF     tile_type=asphalt
THEN   tile_price=.39;

RULE Nowax_Tile
IF     tile_type=no_wax
THEN   tile_price=.79;

RULE Italian_Tile
IF     tile_type=Italian_marble
THEN   tile_price=2.44;

RULE Bath_Irregularities
IF     irregularities=bathroom
THEN   irreg_adjustment=.25;

RULE Util_Irregularities
IF     irregularities=utility_room
THEN   irreg_adjustment=.05;
```

```
RULE No_Irregularities
IF    irregularities=none
THEN  irreg_adjustment=0;

RULE Other_Irregularity
IF    irregularities=other
THEN  FIND other_adjust
      WHILETRUE other_adjust<.05 OR other_adjust>.25
      THEN
      DISPLAY "Sorry, but this value must be between .05
      and .25!"
      RESET other_adjust
      FIND other_adjust
      END
      irreg_adjustment=(other_adjust);

RULE Find_Rush_Charges
IF    days_needed < (normal_delivery)
THEN  DISPLAY "That will require a rush charge."
      rush_charge=.5
ELSE  rush_charge=0;

ASK estimator:"Who is the estimator preparing this
estimate?";
CHOICES estimator:Jerry,Heather;

ASK customer:"What is the name of the customer for whom
this estimate is being prepared?";

ASK length:"What is the length of the room to be
tiled?";

ASK width:"What is the width of the room to be tiled?";

ASK yn:"That's an awfully big room!  Are you sure?";
CHOICES yn:Yes,No;

ASK tile_type:"What kind of tile does the customer want
to use?";
CHOICES tile_type:asphalt,no_wax,Italian_marble;

ASK irregularities:"Describe the irregularities, if
any, in this room.
Are they like those typically found in a bathroom or
utility room, or are they different from others?";
CHOICES irregularities:bathroom,utility_room,other,
none;

ASK other_adjust:"How much of an adjustment do you want
to include?";

ASK days_needed:"How many days from now does the
customer want the work done?";
```

Summary

This has been an extraordinarily long chapter. In it, we have taken a step-by-step approach to building a complete worksheet from the ground up, then designing and building an expert system to act as an intelligent interface to it for a user who is somewhat unfamiliar with the worksheet and the business that needs it used correctly.

In Chapter 8, we will examine this same spreadsheet interface problem from a different perspective, using a different tool, Knowledge-Pro from Knowledge Garden, Inc., to solve the interface problem differently.

CHAPTER 8
Other Spreadsheet Interface Methods

This chapter discusses the design of an intelligent front end to the spreadsheet application of Chapter 7 where the expert system tool does not allow for the direct writing of a worksheet file. We will discuss the use of KnowledgePro and its optional Database Toolkit as a typical tool for this purpose.

This chapter will be of interest to you if you are using any expert system tool which does not afford direct write access to worksheet files. Most systems are in that category. Though we use a specific tool, the steps, principles, and approaches suggested here will be useful regardless of your tool selection.

First, we will describe KnowledgePro and its unique approach to knowledge processing. Then we will look at how it could be used to duplicate the behavior of the interface described in Chapter 7. Finally, we'll examine how to import the text file created with KnowledgePro into one spreadsheet program. This will serve as a model for how to accomplish the same task with other programs whose file import capabilities and details might differ.

KnowledgePro: An Overview

KnowledgePro is different from most expert system tools available on microcomputers. It is strongly language-oriented, which might lead to the conclusion that it is very programmerlike. However, it can be made to create powerful and imaginative knowledge-based systems with relatively little programming knowledge because of the way it is built. The program's authors, widely known industry pundits Bev and Bill Thompson, describe KnowledgePro as "a new kind of communications tool. We have found that what excites people most about expert system technology is not the idea of building intelligent machines, but rather the concept of using the computer to communicate expertise."

By combining the use of lists with the powerful idea of topics, KnowledgePro permits you to design and build intelligent systems, often without using the if-then-else logic of production rules. If production-rule logic is needed, however, KnowledgePro includes that syntax as well.

Basic KnowledgePro Vocabulary

With a basic vocabulary of nine commands, we can create most of the knowledge bases we will want to build as intelligent interfaces in KnowledgePro. These nine commands are:

- SAY
- ASK
- DO
- TOPIC
- END
- IF
- THEN
- VALUE_OF
- IS

It is not our intent to provide a course in KnowledgePro, but to understand the sample knowledge bases with which we will work in this chapter, you need a basic understanding of these terms. Their use will be more easily understood in the context of two small knowledge bases, the first of which is shown in Listing 8-1.

Listing 8-1

```
say('This is a small demonstration system.').
ask('What language do you speak?', language,
    [English,French,Spanish]).
do (value_of(language)).

topic English.
say('Welcome.').
end.
```

```
topic French.
say('Bienvenu.').
end.

topic Spanish.
say('Bienvenido.').
end.
```

The SAY command takes one argument: a string to be displayed on the user's terminal. It is used to convey information to the user when the user is not expected to do anything in response.

The ASK command takes three arguments, the third one of which is optional. The first argument is a string that defines the question to be displayed on the screen. The second argument is the name of the variable (actually a "topic" in KnowledgePro, as discussed below) to which the user's answer to the question is to be assigned. The final, optional, argument is a list of possible answers. If the third argument is supplied, it is enclosed in square brackets. KnowledgePro uses this list to create a pop-up menu from which the user can select an appropriate response. In this respect, it is similar to the VP-Expert CHOICES command.

When KnowledgePro encounters the DO command, it looks at the command's lone argument and searches for a topic of that name. If it finds one, it does whatever that topic tells it to do. (We'll have much more to say about topics and the things they can do in the next section.)

The argument to the DO command is quite often a VALUE_OF parameter. The VALUE_OF command is used so often in Knowledge-Pro that it has a shorthand equivalent: the question mark. Thus the third line in the knowledge base in Listing 8-1 would more usually be written as:

```
do(?language).
```

Whether it is written out as VALUE_OF or abbreviated to a question mark, the function has the same effect in KnowledgePro. It stands for the value of the variable or topic whose name follows it.

The TOPIC and END statements are used to delimit the contents of a KnowledgePro topic. The name of a topic must be one word or enclosed in single quotation marks.

We will look at the remaining four commands in a moment. First, let's examine the knowledge base in Listing 8-1 and see what it does.

The first line displays the message describing what this knowledge base is. The second asks the question, "What language do you speak?" and displays a pop-up menu with three choices in it. When the user selects one of those choices, the third line of the knowledge base looks at the value of the user's response and then finds and executes a topic with that name.

If the user answers "English," the system displays the word "welcome" in English. Similarly, selecting French or Spanish results in the equivalent of "welcome" in that language being displayed.

As you can see, writing this same knowledge base in VP-Expert or any other production rule-based system would require the use of several IF-THEN constructs. Listing 8-2 is a VP-Expert equivalent of the KnowledgePro knowledge base in Listing 8-1.

Listing 8-2

```
ACTIONS
DISPLAY("This is a small demonstration system.")
ASK language:"What language do you speak?"
FIND finished;

RULE English
IF    language=English
THEN  finished=Yes
      DISPLAY("Welcome.");

RULE French
IF    language=French
THEN  finished=Yes
      DISPLAY("Bienvenu.");

RULE Spanish
IF    language=Spanish
THEN  finished=Yes
      DISPLAY("Bienvenido.");

CHOICES language: English,French,Spanish;
```

In KnowledgePro, you would use the IF-THEN logic of production rules primarily when you must check for the presence of two or more conditions. The small demonstration knowledge base in Listing 8-3 depicts this situation. It also shows an alternate approach to knowledge base construction from that shown in Listing 8-1.

Listing 8-3

```
do(get_answer).

topic get_answer.

if ?'number of seats' > 1
and ?mobile is No
then object is couch.

if ?'number of seats' = 1
and ?mobile is No
then object is chair.

if ?'number of seats'=1
and ?mobile is Yes
then object is motorcycle.

if ?'number of seats'> 1
and ?mobile is Yes
then object is automobile.

say('You are describing a ', ?object, '.').

end.

topic 'number of seats'.
ask ('How many people does the object seat?','number of
   seats').
end.

topic mobile.
ask('Is the object mobile or not?',mobile,[Yes,No]).
end.
```

The format of the IF-THEN construct is self-evident and follows the approach used by other production-rule systems. The ELSE form of the production rule design is available in the event it is appropriate.

Notice in Listing 8-3 that we create separate topics for the two variables whose values we need — number of seats and mobile. Rather than simply hard-coding ASK commands in the main topic or as knowledge base-level operations a we did in Listing 8-1, we embed the ASK commands within these topics. The difference might seem unimportant. However, if we later defined a new way of determining the value of one or both of these variables, we could do so simply by changing the topic and not having to alter any of the rest of the programming. The topic 'number of seats,' for example, might be turned into a calculation or it might be inferred from other information obtained by the system or inferred from answers provided by the user.

Topics in KnowledgePro

The most powerful idea in KnowledgePro — and its central building block — is that of the topic. KnowlegePro topics can be viewed as pieces of knowledge. They can:

- Contain commands (like a procedure in Pascal or C)

- Store values (like a variable)

- Return values (like functions)

- Be assigned properties (like frames or objects)

- Inherit values from other topics in a hierarchy

- Act as if they were system commands or extensions to the KnowlegePro language

- Serve as hypertext nodes (see Chapter 11)

We'll encounter several uses of topics even in the simple examples we build in this chapter. If you work with KnowledgePro, you'll come to appreciate the power and significance of this extended idea of knowledge representation.

KnowledgePro Syntax

From the small knowledge bases shown in Listings 8-1 and 8-3, you can see that KnowledgePro has a relatively free-form syntax. In fact, its entire syntax can be expressed in just seven rules:

1. KnowledgePro commands consist of the command name and a set of parentheses enclosing any parameters.

2. All commands end with a period except when they are embedded within other commands.

3. Strings must be enclosed in parentheses if they include any characters other than alphanumeric characters and the underscore character.

4. Lists are surrounded by square brackets and the elements of the list are separated from one another by commas.

5. Topic names must be 80 characters or less in length and must contain no carriage returns.

6. Spaces and blank lines are insignificant and can be used to format knowledge bases unless they are within single quotation marks.

7. Comments can be entered in a knowledge base by enclosing them within the special character combinations (* and *).

A KnowledgePro Interface Routine

Recall that the intelligent front end we designed in Chapter 7 in VP-Expert performs the following tasks:

1. Accept the names of the customer and the estimator

2. Ask for the size of the room

3. Ask for the type of tile to be used and convert this into a per tile cost

4. Make an irregularity adjustment if necessary

5. Find out if a rush charge is required and, if so, apply it

Let's build each of these modules in KnowledgePro and then combine them into one knowledge base to address these issues. We will create separate topics for each of these modules so that it will ultimately be easy to combine them.

Accepting Customer and Estimator Names

The customer's name, of course, is not predictable. However, the name of the estimator will be chosen from a list of people in the company who are authorized to prepare estimates. For our purposes, this list consists of two names: Jerry and Heather.

Listing 8-4 shows one way of handling this in a single topic called "get names."

Listing 8-4

```
topic 'get names'.
ask('Who is the estimator preparing this estimate?',
  estimator,
        [Jerry,Heather]).
ask('What is the name of the customer for whom this
  estimate is being prepared?',customer).
end.
```

There is nothing new or tricky about this topic. Compare it with the VP-Expert approach in Listing 7-2 and you can clearly see the similarities. (The only major missing element in common is the updating of the worksheet, which we deal with later in this chapter.)

Room Size Entry and Validation

The procedural language nature of KnowledgePro makes data validation somewhat more direct than in VP-Expert. We can simply define two topics to obtain values from the user and a generic confirmation routine. The KnowledgePro topics to handle this task are shown in Listing 8-5.

Listing 8-5

```
topic width.
ask('How wide is the room?',width).
if ?width > 50 then do(confirm,width).
end.

topic length.
ask('How long is the room?',length).
if ?length > 50 then do(confirm,width).
end.

topic confirm (dimension).
ask('That''s an awfully big room! Are you sure?', yn,
  [Yes,No]).
if ?yn is No then
  do(?dimension).
end.
```

Notice that when we call the DO command in the topics called "width" and "length" we pass a parameter to the CONFIRM topic. The parameter is the name of the topic being executed. Parameter passing is one of the advantages of a programming-language approach to knowledge system design. Also note that the CONFIRM topic has an argument in parentheses after its name. This is a parameter that the topic can use as it executes. In this case, the name of the topic that called the "confirm" topic is being tracked as the "confirm" topic runs.

We use the VALUE_OF command (abbreviated as "?") to cause the calling topic to re-execute if the user indicates a mistake has been in entering a number larger than 50. Otherwise, we let it go.

Entry Process for Per Tile Cost

We'll demonstrate two approaches to converting the user's answer about the type of tile to be used into a per tile price for the job. The first mimics the production-rule approach used in VP-Expert (see Listing 7-4). The second takes advantage of lists in KnowledgePro to produce a more elegant and efficient solution.

Listing 8-6 shows the production-rule approach to the problem. It is nearly identical to that used in the VP-Expert solution in Chapter 7.

Listing 8-6

```
topic tile_type.
  ask('What kind of tile does the customer want to
  use?',tile_type,
      [asphalt,'no wax','Italian marble']).

  if ?tile_type is asphalt then per_tile_price is 0.39.
  if ?tile_type is 'no wax' then per_tile_price is
      0.79.
  if ?tile_type is 'Italian marble' then per_tile_price
      is 2.44.
end.
```

There is nothing in this listing you haven't seen before, so we'll just move on to Listing 8-7, which gives an example of using lists rather than rules.

Listing 8-7

```
topic find_price.
  tile_type is [asphalt,'no wax','Italian marble'].
  tile_price is [0.39, 0.79, 2.44].
```

```
    ask('What kind of tile does the customer want to
        use?',tile,
        ?tile_type).
 per_tile_price is element (?tile_price, where
     (?tile_type,
         ?tile)).
end.
```

In this sample, we first set up two lists named "tile_type" and
"tile_price" so that their elements are paired: the first item in the list
of tile types corresponds to the correct price as the first element in
the list of tile prices, and so forth. Next, we ask the user what type of
tile the customer wants. Note that we use the value of the list
"tile_type" rather than reproducing it here.

Finally, we use two new commands — ELEMENT and WHERE — to
locate the price of the selected tile type. ELEMENT returns the item at
a specified location in a list. For example, if you executed this command:

```
    tile_name is element (?tile_type,2).
```

the topic "tile_name" would take on the value "no wax" because
that is the second element in the list "tile_type." WHERE finds an
element in a list and returns its position. Reversing the logic of the
previous example:

```
    tile_position is where(?tile_type,'no wax').
```

would result in the topic "tile_position" having the value of 2,
since "no wax" is the second element in the list "tile_type."

   We combine those two commands in the small knowledge base
fragment in Listing 8-7. The user's selection of a tile type is assigned
to the topic "tile". The WHERE command then evaluates to a 2 if the
user chooses "no wax," since that is the second element in the list
"tile_type." Now the ELEMENT command is interpreted as:

```
    element(?tile_price,2).
```

and the second element in the list "tile_price" — in this case,
0.79 — is returned and assigned to the topic "per_tile_price."

In this example, we did not save much code by using lists. But ima-
gine if we had 15 or 20 types of tile from which to choose. The ex-

ample in Listing 8-7 would grow only by the list of types and prices while the example of the production-rule approach in Listing 8-6 would require a separate IF-THEN statement for each combination.

Adjustments for Irregularities

As with VP-Expert (see Listing 7-5), there is nothing unusual or new in our approach to the problem of entering adjustments for irregularities. We could use either the production-rule approach or the list approach as described in the previous section.

Listing 8-8 presents the production-rule approach to this problem. Compare it to Listing 7-5.

Listing 8-8

```
topic irregularities.
  ask('Describe the irregularities, if any, in this
      room. Are they like those typically found in a
      bathroom or utility room, or are they different
      from either?',irreg,[bathroom,'utility room',
      other,none]).
  if ?irreg is bathroom then irreg_adjustment is 0.25.
  if ?irreg is 'utility room' then irreg_adjustment is
      0.05
  if ?irreg is other then
      ask('How much of an adjustment do you want to
      include?',
          irreg_adjustment).
  if ?irreg is none then irreg_adjustment is 0.
end.
```

Determination of Rush Charge

The last step in our KnowledgePro-based intelligent interface, before we deal with spreadsheet interface issues, is to determine whether the job requires a rush charge. Recall that we add a rush charge of 50 percent of the total price if the client needs the job done in fewer days than "normal completion." In Chapter 7, we arbitrarily set the normal completion period at 22 days. We'll stay with that figure here.

The only significant difference between the KnowledgePro approach here and the VP-Expert solution in Listing 7-7 is that we don't have a separate ACTIONS block in KnowledgePro. As a result, we initialize the constant "normal completion" in the topic itself. The Knowledge-Pro version is shown in Listing 8-9.

Listing 8-9

```
topic rush_charge.
  normal_completion is 22.
  ask('How many days from now does the customer want
    the work done?',
            days_needed).
  if ?days_needed < ?normal_completion then rush_charge
    is 0.5 else
            rush_charge is 0.
end.
```

Exporting to the Worksheet

Because KnowledgePro does not provide for the writing of data into a worksheet file, we will use a two-step approach to transferring information from the expert system to the worksheet. First, we'll build an intermediate file containing the data. Then we'll run the spreadsheet and use a macro to read this file into the worksheet.

Once we've done this, we must come back to KnowledgePro, read the worksheet cell containing the calculated estimate, and display the result. This step and the automation of the process will be discussed in the concluding section of this chapter.

File Format

Every spreadsheet program can read one or more external file formats. Some support a wider variety of such files than other programs.

Almost any file format supported by your favorite spreadsheet program can be generated from a KnowledgePro knowledge base; writing text files in flexible formats is one of KnowledgePro's strengths.

We'll opt for a simple, straightforward file format that is supported by VP-Planner Plus Version 2 and Lotus 1-2-3. With minor variations you may find it works for your spreadsheet program as well.

This file format treats each row of a region of the spreadsheet as a line in a text file. Where there should be blank cells, a comma is used. Text is enclosed in quotation marks. Numbers are simply presented as they should be entered into the worksheet.

To read such a file into a worksheet, you just position the cursor at the upper left corner of the region of the worksheet where the data is to be placed, and type:

```
/FIN
```

(for File Import Numbers). You then provide the name of the file to be imported and the spreadsheet application reads the file into the appropriate cells.

To simplify our import task, we will make a minor modification to the spreadsheet as it was designed in Chapter 7. We will move the name of the estimator from cell A5 to cell B4 and the name of the customer from cell A7 to cell B6. This will put these names opposite their labels rather than under them.

This will also enable us to read all the data generated by the KnowledgePro knowledge base into one column of the worksheet. (Since KnowledgePro doesn't do the writing directly, it doesn't understand ranges as VP-Expert does, so this modification is appropriate.)

Creating the File in KnowledgePro

This simple file format can be generated easily by KnowledgePro. Listing 8-10 contains the program that will build the file so that the data shown in Table 8-1 is entered.

Table 8-1. Sample Data File Format

Cell	Contents
B4	Estimator's name
B5	Empty (",")
B6	Customer's name
B7	Empty (",")
B8	Empty (",")
B9	per_tile_price
B10	length
B11	width
B12	irreg_adjustment
B13	rush_charge

Listing 8-10

```
topic makefile.
new_file('tile1.sdf') write('tile1.sdf',?
    estimator,',',
      ?customer,',',',',').
write('tile1.sdf',?price_per_tile,?length,?width,
    ?irreg_adjustment,?rush_charge).
end.
```

The NEW_FILE command in Listing 8-10 ensures that any file called TILE1.SDF will be overwritten. This will be the intermediate transfer file between KnowledgePro and the worksheet when we prepare an estimate. (The .SDF extension is arbitrary, meaning "Structured Delimited Format" but you can choose any extension you want.")

Reading the File into the Worksheet

Once this file has been constructed from the user's answers and the inferences drawn by the knowledge-based system, you must quit KnowledgePro. You should then run your spreadsheet program, opening the tile estimating worksheet TILEJOB.WKS. Then you simply import the newly created file into the worksheet following the steps outlined earlier. In VP-Planner Plus Version 2, you could create a keyboard autostart macro that would handle the entire file import and save process. It would look like this:

```
{goto}B4
/FINtile1.sdf<CR>
/FS<CR>R
```

In VP-Planner Plus Version 2, this macro automatically executes when the worksheet is opened by using the /WAD (for Worksheet Autokey Define) command and assigning the macro to the F10 key.

Reading and Reporting the Estimate

We have now reached the final step in the intelligent interface design process. We must design a KnowledgePro knowledge base that will open the worksheet file into which the SDF file was just imported, and read the estimate as the worksheet has calculated it. KnowledgePro provides a single command to read the value in a single cell or a group of discontiguous cells in a worksheet. Its use is demonstrated in the program in Listing 8-11.

Listing 8-11

```
topic report_estimate.
data is read_spreadsheet('tilejob.wks',B13).
estimate is element(?data,2).
say('The estimate is now prepared. Please inform',
    ?customer, 'that the total bill for the tiling
    job will be $', ?estimate, '.').
end.
```

READ_SPREADSHEET, provided as part of the add-on KnowledgePro Database Toolkit, takes two arguments. The first is the name, including pathname, of a Lotus 1-2-3 compatible worksheet. Users of Lotus 1-2-3 need not supply the file extension, since KnowledgePro assumes an extension of .WK1 unless it is given one. The second argument is a single cell address or a list (enclosed in square brackets) of such cell addresses, from which data is to be read.

We use the second element of values read by the READ_SPREAD-SHEET command because the first value it returns is an error code. Good programming would dictate that we should check that error code before assuming the value is correct (or even present!) but in the interest of time and simplicity, we do not do that in Listing 8-11.

Automating the Connection

Because of the lack of direct writing of the worksheet, this interface requires more work on the part of the user than the VP-Expert interface we built in Chapter 7. We can, however, take advantage of the MS-DOS batch-file facility to create a file that will require the user only to quit KnowledgePro once and then to quit VP-Planner Plus once. Here's the file for my computer; you'll have to edit for the spreadsheet you're using and for the pathnames appropriate to how you have set up your directory.

```
CD \GARDEN
KP0 TILING
COPY TILE1.SDF \VPX\VPP
CD \VPX\VPP
VPP TILEJOB
CD \GARDEN
KPD TELLEST
```

I call my knowledge bases TILING.KB (to prepare the data for the worksheet) and TELLEST.KB (to extract and report the estimate). I keep VP-Planner Plus in my VPX\VPP subdirectory.

Summary

If you are using an expert system tool that does not afford direct write access to worksheet files, you can still create intelligent interfaces to your spreadsheet applications. In this chapter, you saw how we could create an intermediate file with KnowledgePro, then load that file into a worksheet file to create the estimate.

By judicious use of the powers of the expert system tool, the macro capabilities of the spreadsheet program, and the batch-file capabilities of your machine, you can create a nearly seamless interface even though more effort is required on your part to do so.

In Chapter 9, we return to VP-Expert, this time examining its use with database applications.

CHAPTER 9
A Small Database Example

This chapter uses the step-by-step approach introduced in Chapter 7, this time guiding you through the creation of a small database example in dBASE III Plus, the design of an expert system interface for that database example, and the construction of the expert system in VP-Expert.

The Application

The dBASE application we will construct will be used as part of an expense account verification system. Two dBASE III Plus files are involved. The first stores information about various cities to which corporate executives might travel. The second contains basic personnel information that is useful in verifying an expense form. The first file is called EXPLIMIT.DBF. Its structure is shown in Table 9-1. The second file, EXECS.DBF, contains the structured information shown in Table 9-2.

Table 9-1. Structure of File EXPLIMIT.DBF

Field Name	Type	Size	Decimal Places
City	Character	24	0
HOTEL_EXEC	Numeric	3	0
MEALS_EXEC	Numeric	3	0
TRANS_EXEC	Numeric	3	0
HOTEL_MGR	Numeric	3	0
MEALS_MGR	Numeric	3	0
TRANS_MGR	Numeric	3	0
HOTEL_ADM	Numeric	3	0
MEALS_ADM	Numeric	3	0
TRANS_ADM	Numeric	3	0

Table 9-2. Structure of File EXECS.DBF

Field Name	Type	Size	Decimal Place
LASTNAME	Character	18	
FIRSTNAME	Character	18	
GRADE	Numeric	2	0

Our expert system will allow the user to enter new information into these files, update existing information in them, and validate expense accounts submitted by executives against company policies and limits.

At the beginning of this development assignment, the two files contain the information shown in Tables 9-3 and 9-4.

Table 9-3. Initial Contents of File EXPLIMIT.DBF

City	Executive			Manager			Administrator		
	Hotel	Meals	Trans	Hotel	Meals	Trans	Hotel	Meals	Trans
Chicago	125	95	50	125	70	30	100	50	20
Detroit	100	75	50	100	65	30	85	45	30
Milwaukee	90	75	40	90	65	30	90	45	30
San Francisco	225	100	50	195	80	30	140	60	20

Table 9-4. Initial Contents of File EXECS.DBF

Lastname	Firstname	Grade
Alvorsen	Sven	5
Bolton	Susan	9
Evergreen	Barbra	13
Humboldt	Karl	3
Magnusson	Wilbur	8
Smitz	Trevor	7
Zachary	Alain	15

As presently used, the system is quite manual. When an expense voucher is submitted to the finance clerk responsible for handling validation, the employee's grade level is looked up in the EXECS.DBF file or in a printout made from that file.

Brackets are then put around the employee's major title classification according to Table 9-5.

Table 9-5. Grades Equated to Major Title Classification

Grade Range	Title Class
1-5	Administrator
6-10	Manager
11-15	Executive

With that information, the clerk looks at the city in which each expense occurred, the type of expense, and then checks the amount claimed against the company maximums in the EXPLIMIT.DBF file or a printout made from that file. If the expense is no greater than the amount in that file, it is approved. If it exceeds the amount in the file, it is disapproved and the expense form is returned to the traveler.

If the clerk uses the system on-line, that is, by looking up the relevant information in the database files, the clerk must type the traveler's name, note the grade level, manually convert the grade level to a title classification, then go to the EXPLIMIT.DBF file and type in the city and type of expense to see the maximum allowed. Then a comparison is made manually of the maximum to the claimed amount and the proper reaction is given.

Creating the Database Files

We will start this assignment by creating the database files to match Tables 9-1 through 9-4. We will use dBASE III Plus from its "dot prompt" rather than going through the Assistant interface it supplies. The Assistant provides more support for the creation and management of dBASE III Plus files than the bare-bones dot prompt, but it is also somewhat slower to use. Our primary interest is in the expert system rather than in the database management system. Also, all dBASE clones work from a dot prompt but not all include a program equivalent to the Assistant. Approaching the problem with the dot prompt, then, will be more universally useful.

As we did in Chapter 7, we will take a step-by-step approach to constructing these two database files. The steps are listed briefly in boxes, followed with explanatory text for users who are not entirely comfortable with dBASE III Plus. If you are using a dBASE clone, you may need to adjust the instructions accordingly.

STEP 1. Create the file called EXPLIMIT.DBF

From the dot prompt, type

```
create explimit
```

and press Return. You will be taken (in dBASE III Plus) to a screen that looks like Figure 9-1. You will use this screen to define the fields in your database.

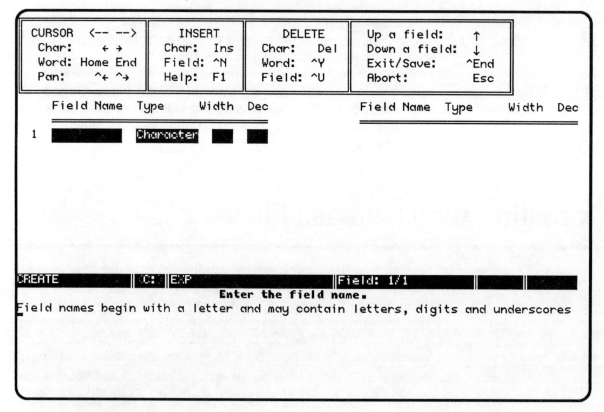

Figure 9-1. Starting Field Definition

STEP 2. Define the field CITY as a character field with a length of 24

Type the field name (CITY) into the first field on the file-design form shown in Figure 9-1. Press Return. You are now positioned in the column of the layout where you enter the type of information to be placed into this field. Since you want to use the suggested default character data type, press Return again. You will now be in the column where you define the field's width. Type 24 and press Return.

You will automatically be positioned at the place to define the second field in the file. Note that dBASE III Plus skips over the field where you define the number of decimal places to use in the field because character-type data fields do not use decimal places. Only numeric data types use decimal places.

STEP 3. Define the field HOTEL_EXEC as a numeric field with a width of 3 and no decimal places

This field will hold the maximum hotel allowance per day for an executive-level traveler in a given city. We always use round dollar amounts in setting maximum levels, so we don't need decimal places. Hotel expenses can run higher than $99 per day, so we need three digits in the number.

Enter the name of the field as HOTEL_EXEC dBASE III Plus will not allow you to enter a space, so use the underscore as punctuation in the field name. You won't have to press Return after entering this field name because it is exactly the right width to fill the field on the layout.

Once you are in the part of the file design layout where you are to enter the the data type, press the Space bar once. The word "Character" changes to the word "Numeric." Press Return and enter the number 3 in the next field. Press Return and enter the number 0 in the next field. The program will position you to enter the next field.

STEP 4. Define the field MEALS_EXEC as a numeric field with a width of 3 and no decimal places

The process is identical to that used in step 3 except the name of the field changes. This field contains maximum allowable expenditure levels for meals by an executive in a given city.

STEP 5. Define the field TRANS_EXEC as a numeric field with a width of 3 and no decimal places

---

The process is identical to that used in step 3 except the name of the field changes. This field contains maximum allowable expenditure levels for local transportation (taxis, buses, trains, helicopters) by an executive in a given city.

If you have followed the instructions correctly, your screen should now look something like Figure 9-2.

STEP 6. Repeat steps 3 through 5, changing the last letters of the field name from EXEC to MGR

You will create three new fields: HOTEL_MGR, MEALS_MGR, and TRANS_MGR. Each will be numeric, three digits wide with no decimal point. These fields will contain maximum allowable expenditures for managers in each city for each category of spending.

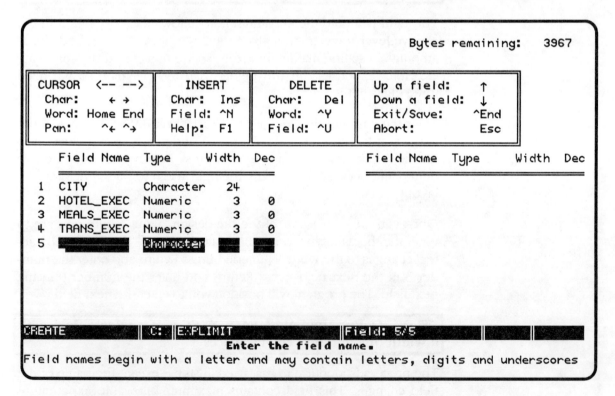

Figure 9-2. File EXPLIMIT.DBF Partially Defined

> **STEP 7. Repeat steps 3 through 5, changing the last letters of the field name from EXEC to ADM**

You will create three new fields: HOTEL_ADM, MEALS_ADM, and TRANS_ADM. Each will be numeric, three digits wide with no decimal point. These fields will contain maximum allowable expenditures for administrators in each city for each category of spending.

You are now finished defining the structure for the file EXPLIM-IT.DBF. Your screen should look like Figure 9-3. Double check all your entries against those in Figure 9-3 before proceeding.

> **STEP 8. End your database file definition and save the database structure**

In dBASE III Plus, do this by pressing Control-End. You will then be asked to press Return to confirm that you have designed the entire file. Press Return. Any other key will return you to file definition.

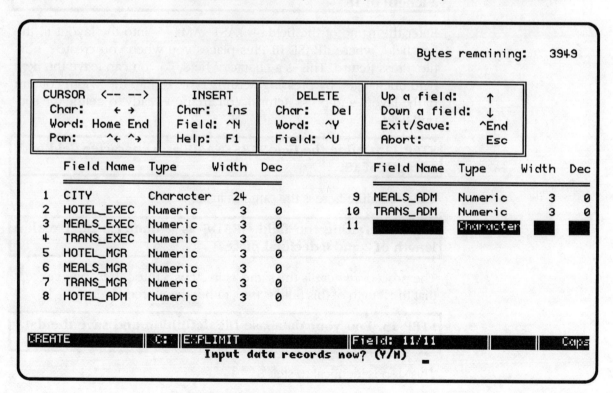

Figure 9-3. File EXPLIMIT.DBF Correctly Defined

You will now be asked (in dBASE III Plus) whether you wish to begin entering data records now. Type "N" and you will find yourself back at the dBASE III Plus dot prompt. The file structure has been defined and saved.

STEP 9. Create the second database file, naming it EXECS

From the dBASE III Plus dot prompt, just type

```
create execs
```

as you did to create the first file at step 1.

This file has only three fields. We'll define the first one in detail and assume that by now you are able to define new fields with some facility.

STEP 10. Define the field LASTNAME as a character field with a length of 18

Enter the name of the field — LASTNAME — into the layout in the first field, where dBASE III Plus places you when you create a new file. Press Return. This is a character field, so you can leave the next field unchanged by pressing Return. Type 18 into the Width column of the layout and press Return. You are now ready to define the second field.

STEP 11. Define the field FIRSTNAME as a character field with a length of 18

The procedure here is the same as in step 10.

STEP 12. Define the field GRADE as a numeric field with a length of 2 and 0 decimal places

---

The procedure here is the same as in steps 3 through 5 above except that the length of this field is two, rather than three, digits.

STEP 13. End your database file definition and save the database structure

---

This step is identical to step 8.

Designing the Data Entry Systems

We will now turn our attention to designing the data entry expert system interfaces for each of these database files. We will use VP-Expert to create this interface rather than going through dBASE III Plus directly primarily as an instructional exercise.

Clearly, a person could design an interface to these database files with appropriate error checking without using an expert system. The real strength of the expert system interface approach in this assignment lies in the ultimate "use" to which the data is to be put. Still, we can do some reasonably intelligent data validation in the EXPLIMIT.DBF file.

Data Validation in EXPLIMIT.DBF

As the user enters information into the EXPLIMIT.DBF file, the numeric data must meet two basic criteria to be valid:

- It must be smaller than $1000, the upper limit we have imposed on any single daily expense figure in the database file

- It must be consistent within each city and category — in other words, the maximum allowed for an administrator, for example, should not be larger than that allowed for a manager

Data Validation in EXECS.DBF

The only entry in the EXECS.DBF file that requires validation is the employee's grade, which must be between 1 and 15.

Building the EXPLIMIT.DBF Interface

We will take a modular approach to building the data entry interface for the EXPLIMIT.DBF file, beginning by constructing the portion of the interface that will accept and validate hotel expense maximums. Since all other processing is nearly identical, once we have built and debugged this module, the others will fall into place quite nicely. At the same time as we build the hotel module, we will add the code it will take to get the city entered into the system.

Listing 9-1 presents the ACTIONS block and the single rule it takes to manage the entry of the hotel expense maximums.

Listing 9-1

```
! (c) 1989, Dan Shafer

! This knowledge base first appeared in "Designing
! Intelligent Front Ends for Business Software,"
! published by John Wiley & Sons, Inc., 1989.

ENDOFF;
ACTIONS

FIND city
WHILETRUE hotels_ok<>Yes THEN
        RESET hotel_exec
        RESET hotel_mgr
        RESET hotel_adm
        RESET hotels_ok
        FIND hotels_ok
END
DISPLAY "Done!";

RULE  Hotel_Limits
IF    hotel_exec < 1000
AND   hotel_mgr < 1000
AND   hotel_adm < 1000
AND   hotel_exec >= (hotel_mgr)
AND   hotel_mgr >= (hotel_adm)
THEN  hotels_ok=Yes
ELSE DISPLAY"
Sorry, but there is an inconsistency here. You have
entered the following:
```

```
          Executive Hotel Limit = ${hotel_exec}
          Managerial Hotel Limit = ${hotel_mgr}
          Administrator Hotel Limit = ${hotel_adm}

No expense item maximum can be greater than $999.99.
Also, limits for executives must be equal to or greater
than those for managers, which in turn must be equal to
or greater than those for administrators.

Please re-enter the data.

          PRESS ANY KEY TO CONTINUE~"
          hotels_ok=No;

ASK city:"For which city do you wish to enter expense
maximums?";

ASK hotel_exec:"What is the maximum amount an executive
can spend per day for a hotel in {city}?";

ASK hotel_mgr:"What is the maximum amount a manager can
spend per day for a hotel in {city}?";

ASK hotel_adm:"What is the maximum amount an
administrator can spend per day for a hotel in
{city}?";
```

The kernel of this system is the single rule called Hotel_Limits. It has five premises and one of its conclusions is a relatively complex DISPLAY statement. The rule is driven by the familiar WHILETRUE loop in the ACTIONS block. If you run this module through some tests, you'll find that the message in the DISPLAY statement scrolls partly off the top of the consultation window.

To see what this looks like in the finished system, you can add the RUNTIME clause to the beginning of the knowledge base. If you do so, however, be sure to comment out that line or delete it before proceeding with development or you'll be unable to follow the inference engine if you need to trace its actions. Notice that we use the curly braces in the ASK statements to display the name of the city with which we are working. This approach is useful to the end user, particularly a large number of cities' information is being entered at one sitting and the possibility of losing track of one's location exists.

Figure 9-4 shows part of the interaction the user might have with this module of the interface.

```
For which city do you wish to enter expense maximums?
 Detroit

What is the maximum amount an executive can spend per day
for a hotel in Detroit?
 195

What is the maximum amount a manager can spend per day
for a hotel in Detroit?
 165

What is the maximum amount an administrator can spend per day
for a hotel in Detroit?
█




Enter to select       ? & Enter for Unknown      /Q to quit
 1Help 2How? 3Why? 4Slow 5Fast 6Quit
```

Figure 9-4. Sample Interaction with Hotel Expense Module

Adding the two remaining modules to enter and check for valid entries for meals and transportation costs is a simple matter of copy-paste-edit techniques. Using a good text editor, you should be able to copy the WHILETRUE loop for hotel expenses and then insert it twice. Change the labels from "hotel" to "meals" for the first new loop and to "trans" for the second. Similarly, copy, paste, and edit the ASK statements. Your program will now look like Listing 9-2.

Listing 9-2

```
! (c) 1989, Dan Shafer

! This knowledge base first appeared in "Designing,
! Intelligent Front Ends for Business Software,"
! published by John
! Wiley & Sons, Inc., 1989.

ENDOFF;
ACTIONS

FIND city
```

```
WHILETRUE hotels_ok<>Yes THEN
        RESET  hotel_exec
        RESET  hotel_mgr
        RESET  hotel_adm
        RESET  hotels_ok
        FIND   hotels_ok
END

WHILETRUE meals_ok<>Yes THEN
        RESET  meals_exec
        RESET  meals_mgr
        RESET  meals_adm
        RESET  meals_ok
        FIND   meals_ok
END

WHILETRUE trans_ok<>Yes THEN
        RESET  transport_exec
        RESET  transport_mgr
        RESET  transport_adm
        RESET  transport_ok
        FIND   trans_ok
END

DISPLAY "Done!";


RULE  Hotel_Limits
IF    hotel_exec < 1000
AND   hotel_mgr < 1000
AND   hotel_adm < 1000
AND   hotel_exec >= (hotel_mgr)
AND   hotel_mgr >= (hotel_adm)
THEN  hotels_ok=Yes
ELSE  DISPLAY"
Sorry, but there is an inconsistency here. You have
entered the following:

        Executive Hotel Limit = ${hotel_exec}
        Managerial Hotel Limit = ${hotel_mgr}
        Administrator Hotel Limit = ${hotel_adm}

No expense item maximum can be greater than $999.99.
Also, limits for executives must be equal to or greater
than those for managers, which in turn must be equal to
or greater than those for administrators.

Please re-enter the data.

        PRESS ANY KEY TO CONTINUE~"
        hotels_ok=No;

RULE  Meal_Limits
IF    meals_exec < 1000
```

```
AND   meals_mgr < 1000
AND   meals_adm < 1000
AND   meals_exec >= (meals_mgr)
AND   meals_mgr >= (meals_adm)
THEN  meals_ok=Yes
ELSE  DISPLAY"
```

Sorry, but there is an inconsistency here. You have
entered the following:

```
        Executive Meal Limit = ${meals_exec}
        Managerial Meal Limit = ${meals_mgr}
        Administrator Meal Limit = ${meals_adm}
```

No expense item maximum can be greater than $999.99.
Also, limits for executives must be equal to or greater
than those for managers, which in turn must be equal to
or greater than those for administrators.

Please re-enter the data.

```
        PRESS ANY KEY TO CONTINUE~"
        meals_ok=No;
```

```
RULE  Trans_Limits
IF    trans_exec < 1000
AND   trans_mgr < 1000
AND   trans_adm < 1000
AND   trans_exec >= (trans_mgr)
AND   trans_mgr >= (trans_adm)
THEN  trans_ok=Yes
ELSE  DISPLAY"
```

Sorry, but there is an inconsistency here. You have
entered the following:

```
        Executive Transportation Limit = ${trans_exec}
        Managerial Transportation Limit = ${trans_mgr}
        Administrator Transportation Limit = ${trans_adm}
```

No expense item maximum can be greater than $999.99.
Also, limits for executives must be equal to or greater
than those for managers, which in turn must be equal to
or greater than those for administrators.

Please re-enter the data.

```
        PRESS ANY KEY TO CONTINUE~"
        trans_ok=No;
```

```
ASK city:"For which city do you wish to enter expense
maximums?";
```

```
ASK hotel_exec:"What is the maximum amount an executive
can spend per day for a hotel in {city}?";
```

```
ASK hotel_mgr:"What is the maximum amount a manager can
spend per day for a hotel in {city}?";

ASK hotel_adm:"What is the maximum amount an
administrator can spend per day for a hotel in
{city}?";

ASK meals_exec:"What is the maximum amount an executive
can spend per day for meals in {city}?";

ASK meals_mgr:"What is the maximum amount a manager can
spend per day for meals in {city}?";

ASK meals_adm:"What is the maximum amount an
administrator can spend per day for meals in {city}?";

ASK trans_exec:"What is the maximum amount an executive
can spend per day for local transportation in {city}?";

ASK trans_mgr:"What is the maximum amount a manager can
spend per day for local transportation in {city}?";

ASK trans_adm:"What is the maximum amount an
administrator can spend per day for local
transportation in {city}?";
```

Building the EXECS.DBF Interface

The interface to the EXECS dBASE III Plus file is obviously much simpler and smaller than the one for the more complex EXPLIMIT.DBF file. It must check only one entered value: the employee's job grade to ensure a number higher than 15 is not entered.

Since this type of validation has by now become commonplace, we will simply produce the program in Listing 9-3 and leave its explanation to your reading of its contents.

Listing 9-3

```
ENDOFF;
ACTIONS

FIND  last_name
FIND  first_name
```

```
WHILETRUE  grade_ok <> Yes THEN
      RESET  grade
      RESET  grade_ok
      FIND   grade_ok
END
DISPLAY "Done!";

RULE  1
IF    grade <= 15
THEN  grade_ok=Yes
ELSE  DISPLAY"
Sorry, but there is no job grade higher than 15!

Please re-enter the data.

      PRESS ANY KEY TO CONTINUE~"
      grade_ok=No;

ASK last_name:"What is the new executive's last name?";

ASK first_name:"What is the new executive's first
name?";

ASK grade:"What is the new executive's job grade?";
```

Another approach to this problem is to supply the user with a menu of all choices (in this case, numbers 1 to 15) and obviate the necessity to check the entry since we can guarantee the entry is in a valid range. Listing 9-4 shows how that approach would look in this case.

Listing 9-4

```
ENDOFF;
ACTIONS

FIND last_name
FIND first_name
FIND grade
DISPLAY "Done!";

ASK last_name:"What is the new executive's last name?";

ASK first_name:"What is the new executive's first
    name?";

ASK grade:"What is the new executive's job grade?";
CHOICES  grade:1,2,3,4,5,6,7,8,9,10,11,12,13,14,15;
```

Notice that because we used a menu, we did not even need a rule to confirm the validity of the entry. We have created a single-purpose expert system without a rule.

Updating the dBASE Files

Depending on how the expert system tool you're using interacts with dBASE III Plus files, you will have to alter the instructions in this section. We will describe how to do this in VP-Expert. To update a dBASE III Plus file from a VP-Expert knowledge base, we need to ensure only two things:

1. That the names of variables in the knowledge base correspond precisely to the names of fields in the database file

2. That there is a value for each variable or column to which we want to assign a value

Now we can use the simple APPEND statement in VP-Expert to add a new record to the end of a database file. Note that we have always used the same names in VP-Expert for variables as in the .DBF file. This makes updating the database file much easier. While we are updating the database file, let's also make the "Done!" message we've been satisfied with during debugging a little more informative. The statement that will add a new record to the EXECS.DBF file, which should be placed after the point where you've obtained all of the necessary data from the user, is:

```
APPEND execs
```

Once the update is complete, the system will use this new DISPLAY statement to keep the user informed:

```
DISPLAY"{city} added to database!"
```

Similarly, we update the EXPLIMIT.DBF file with this command:

```
APPEND explimit
```

and notify the user of the file addition in this statement:

```
DISPLAY"{firstname} {lastname} added to data-
base!"
```

Listing 9-5 shows the new ADDEXECS knowledge base, including the last round of changes in which we converted from a rule to a menu approach to confirm data validity.

Listing 9-5

```
ENDOFF;
ACTIONS

FIND last_name
FIND first_name
FIND grade
APPEND execs
DISPLAY "{firstname} {lastname} has been added to the
   database!";

ASK last_name:"What is the new executive's last name?";

ASK first_name:"What is the new executive's first
name?";

ASK grade:"What is the new executive's job grade?";
CHOICES grade:1,2,3,4,5,6,7,8,9,10,11,12,13,14,15;
```

There are other methods for updating a dBASE file from within VP-Expert. The shell with which you are working may also offer such alternatives. For example, positioning a new record at a specific point in the database. Or you can modify an existing record's contents.

Entering the Sample Data

With the interfaces for data entry built and tested, you should now enter the sample data shown in Tables 9-3 and 9-4. Before doing so, you may want to enter the RUNTIME command at the beginning of each of the data entry interface systems. This will allow you to use the full screen for entering the sample information.

Building the Expense Approval Interface

Once the files are set up and initialized with the sample data, we are ready to build the main expert system interface. This program checks the contents of the database to confirm the validity of an expense item. The program requires a logic flow as shown in Figure 9-5.

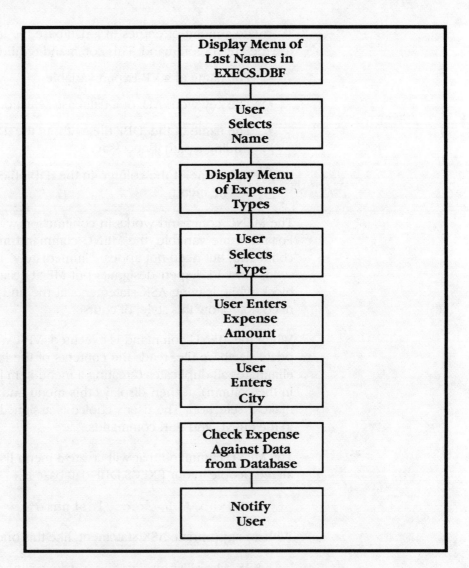

Figure 9-5. Logic Flow of Expense Validation System

Note our menu-driven approach to the interface. This saves the finance clerk typing and eliminates typographical errors. It also greatly speeds up the expense validation process. VP-Expert can easily generate the first menu, which presents a list of all the staff people known to the system; other shells may not be able to produce it at all, in which case you must resort to the typing method of data entry here and then add the ability to confirm the accuracy of the entry.

To create a menu of entries in a database file in VP-Expert, you will use the MENU command. This command requires four arguments:

- The name of a VP-Expert variable

- The key word ALL or a database selection rule

- The name of the .DBF file, without the .DBF extension and including a path if necessary

- The name of the column in the .DBF file to be used to generate the menu

The MENU command works in conjunction with an ASK command. For the same variable, the MENU command must precede the ASK command, but need not appear "immediately" before. As a matter of style, most VP-Expert designers put MENU clauses in the ACTIONS block while leaving ASK statements at the end of the program. You need not follow this style, of course.

When the MENU command is executed, VP-Expert opens the appropriate database file, reads the contents of the indicated column, and eliminates all duplicates (creating a menu item for each unique entry in the column). It then displays this menu and waits for the user to make a selection. The user's choice is assigned to the variable used in the MENU and ASK commands.

The MENU command that will create a menu listing the last names of all the people in our EXECS.DBF database is:

```
MENU who, ALL, execs, lastname
```

With an appropriate ASK statement, like this one:

```
ASK who:"What is the name of the traveler?";
```

this MENU command will generate from our sample database a question that looks like the one shown in Figure 9-6.

(You may already have noticed that this design approach has a drawback in our situation. If two employees have the same last name, the MENU clause will only display one choice for them. The first one will be the only one you will be able to access. This problem is caused in large part by VP-Expert's lack of string concatenation facilities in Ver-

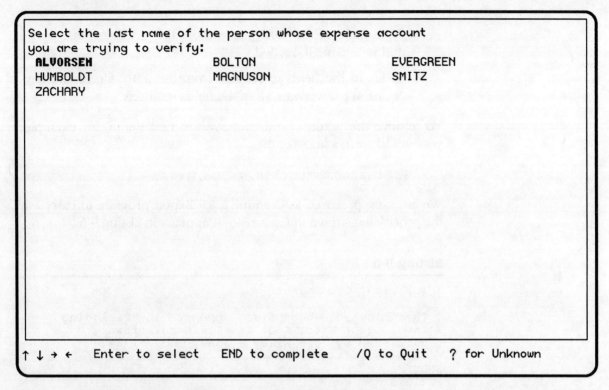

```
Select the last name of the person whose expense account
you are trying to verify:
ALVORSEN           BOLTON              EVERGREEN
HUMBOLDT           MAGNUSON            SMITZ
ZACHARY



















↑ ↓ → ←   Enter to select   END to complete   /Q to Quit   ? for Unknown
```

Figure 9-6. Sample MENU Question from Database File

sion 2.02 (the version used for this book). In a real-world situation, we would probably have a unique employee number assigned to each person and use that number for the menu, rather than using last names. However, the principle would be the same and since our emphasis is on expert system design rather than on database design for expert system use, we have elected to use a simplified approach despite its clear practical drawback in this scenario.)

Other than the use of the MENU command, the only other new element we must introduce before we examine the expert system module for expense validation is the GET command. This command retrieves information from a .DBF file and stores it in a VP-Expert variable or variables. This makes the data, in our case, available for comparison. The GET command has three arguments:

- A database rule instructing VP-Expert which record(s) to retrieve, or the keyword ALL meaning that it should retrieve all of the records in the file

- The name of the .DBF file without the extension but with a full pathname if needed

- A list of the fields to retrieve from the .DBF file or the keyword ALL if we want all of the fields returned

To retrieve the grade of the employee named Berlin, for example, you would write a line like this:

```
GET lastname=Berlin,execs,grade
```

We are now prepared to examine a VP-Expert program to carry out the processing shown in Figure 9-5. It appears in Listing 9-6.

Listing 9-6

```
! (c) 1989, Dan Shafer

! This knowledge base first appeared in "Designing
! Intelligent Front Ends for Business Software,"
! published by John Wiley & Sons, Inc., 1989.

ENDOFF;
ACTIONS

MENU    who,ALL,execs,lastname
FIND    who
GET     who=lastname,execs,grade traveler_grade=(grade)
MENU    where,ALL,explimit,city
FIND    where
GET     where=city,explimit,ALL

! Set up dimensioned variable DATA to retrieve expense
! limits later using an indexed approach.

DATA[1]=(HOTEL_EXEC)
DATA[2]=(HOTEL_MGR)
DATA[3]=(HOTEL_ADM)
DATA[4]=(MEALS_EXEC)
DATA[5]=(MEALS_MGR)
DATA[6]=(MEALS_ADM)
DATA[7]=(TRANS_EXEC)
DATA[8]=(TRANS_MGR)
DATA[9]=(TRANS_ADM)

FIND    expense_type
FIND    expense_amount
FIND    expense_ok

DISPLAY
        "That expense is {expense_ok}.";
```

```
RULE    Confirm_Expense
IF      job_class<>UNKNOWN
AND     exp_limit<>UNKNOWN
AND     expense_amount<=(exp_limit)
THEN    expense_ok=accepted
ELSE    expense_ok=rejected;

RULE    Assign_Class1
IF      traveler_grade <=5
THEN    job_class=3; ! We use this and expense type to
        index data

RULE    Assign_Class2
IF      traveler_grade >5
AND     traveler_grade <=10
THEN    job_class=2;

RULE    Assign_Class3
IF      traveler_grade > 10
THEN    job_class=1;

RULE    Get_Hotel_Limit
IF      job_class<>UNKNOWN
AND     expense_type=hotel
THEN    exp_limit=(data[job_class]);

RULE    Get_Meals_Limit
IF      job_class<>UNKNOWN
AND     expense_type=meals
THEN    indx=((job_class)+3)
        exp_limit=(data[indx]);

RULE    Get_Trans_Limit
IF      job_class<>UNKNOWN
AND     expense_type=trans
THEN    indx=((job_class)+6)
        exp_limit=(data[indx]);

ASK who:"Select the last name of the person whose
expense account you are trying to verify:";

ASK expense_type:"What type of expense is it?";
CHOICES expense_type:hotel,meals,transportation;

ASK expense_amount:"How much is this {expense_type}
expense?";

ASK where:"In what city were the expenses incurred?";
```

Note in Listing 9-6 that after we read the expense account limits from the EXPLIMIT.DBF file, we rearrange their order by placing the individual fields' values into a dimensioned variable called DATA. This will facilitate our use of a calculated index to retrieve them. We set them up so that the hotels occupy elements 1 through 3 of the variable DATA, meals occupy elements 4 through 6, and local transportation elements 7 through 9. Then we translate the traveler's grade into a number: 1 for executives, 2 for managers, 3 for administrators.

This arrangement means that to examine the expense limit for a hotel for a manager, we look at the second element in the variable DATA, which corresponds to the number for managers (2) plus zero (because the hotels are first and do not need to be increased). Similarly, administrators' food limits will always be in element 6 of DATA, which can be found by adding the job classification number (3) for an administrator to the number by which we have to increase the index to get to where the food limits are stored (items 4 through 7). Examine the code and you can see how we take advantage of this.

We should comment, too, on the fact that we cannot directly index this variable by the simple expedient of:

```
data[((job_class)+3]
```

because doing so violates VP-Expert's rules about math operations. Thus we create a new variable called `indx` (leaving out the "e" because the word "index" is a reserved word in VP-Expert and would create a syntax error if used in this way), calculate it, and then use the result to retrieve the appropriate element of the DATA variable.

The rest of Listing 9-6 should be familiar to you by now.

A Driving Control Center

The only serious drawback to the expert system approach we've taken to construct here is that each module is isolated from the other. If you want to update the file of people, for example, you have to call on the expert system called ADDEXECS.KBS. Updating the expense limits file requires the system EXPLIM.KBS, while validating the expenses uses VALIDEXP.KBS.

VP-Expert allows us to connect two knowledge bases, even retaining the values of facts as we move between them. Using the CHAIN command, we can create a small but functional driver interface that will allow the user to run any of these programs from a central control point. This program appears in Listing 9-7.

Listing 9-7

```
RUNTIME;
ENDOFF;
ACTIONS

FIND action_complete;

RULE 1
IF    action=Add_Cities
THEN  CHAIN explim
      action_complete=Yes;

RULE 2
IF    action=Add_People
THEN  CHAIN addexecs
      action_complete=Yes;

RULE 3
IF    action=Validate_Expenses
THEN  CHAIN validexp
      action_complete=Yes;

RULE 4
IF    action=Quit
THEN  action_complete=Yes;
ASK   action:"Select the action you want to take:";
CHOICES action:Add_Cities,Add_People,Validate_Expenses,
        Quit;
```

This driver routine is relatively self-explanatory. To make the entire system of four expert systems work well together, however, you will have to make some changes to the other expert systems. Specifically, you will have to:

- Add a CHAIN EXPDRIVER command at the end of each of the ACTIONS blocks of those other systems so that when the user finishes using them, he will be brought back to this menu

- Add an EXECUTE command to the beginning of each system, so that the user won't have to press Return to resume the consultation after a CHAIN command has executed

The RECORD_NUM System Variable

Our discussion of using VP-Expert to interact with dBASE III compatible files would not be complete without a brief discussion of a system variable we have not had occasion to use. You might well need it in your specific application, however.

To keep track of which record in a database is the "current record," VP-Expert keeps a special system variable called RECORD_NUM. This variable always contains the record number of the last dBASE file record accessed with a VP-Expert GET clause. You can check the contents of this variable any time to find out which record is currently being accessed by VP-Expert. Because it is a system variable, you need neither declare nor initialize it before using it in your expert systems.

RECORD_NUM is a passive variable. You cannot use it to access a record in a dBASE file with a GET clause. Nor can you change its value by assignment (e.g., RECORD_NUM = 49). VP-Expert will permit you to make the assignment (i.e., it will not complain about a syntax or other error) but the location of the pointer remains unchanged. Therefore treat RECORD_NUM as a read-only variable.

Summary

In this chapter, we have learned a great deal about how to write an intelligent interface for a dBASE file. We have developed both data entry/validation routines and analytical routines. We have also seen how to use the VP-Expert CHAIN command to create a "driver" system that acts as a control center for the user to direct the actions of a series of related expert systems.

In Chapter 10, we look at a slightly more complex application involving a spreadsheet and a database.

CHAPTER 10
Case Study: Time and Billing

This chapter presents a case study in the use of a spreadsheet, database, and several small expert systems to manage time and billing operations. It presents a practical example of data entry and validation, supplying an interactive interface. It also shows how to use expert systems to combine what might otherwise be incompatible spreadsheet and database applications. Spreadsheets and databases are good at doing different things. Some spreadsheets are multifunction programs that include the ability to create database capabilities within a worksheet. However, companies often have related information stored separately in a database file or files created using one publisher's program, and in worksheets built using a different publisher's spreadsheet application. Integrating those disparate sets of information can be a difficult or impossible task. In this chapter, we'll see how expert systems technology can be brought to bear to make the underlying data appear seamlessly integrated to the end user.

The Application

Figure 10-1 provides a diagram of the application we build in this chapter. As you can see, there are four expert system modules involved:

- One similar to the one we built in Chapter 9 whose function is to provide an interactive way to control what the user sees as one total application

- One for adding clients to the database file whose purpose is to ensure the uniqueness of the client ID and the reasonableness of the hourly billing rates entered

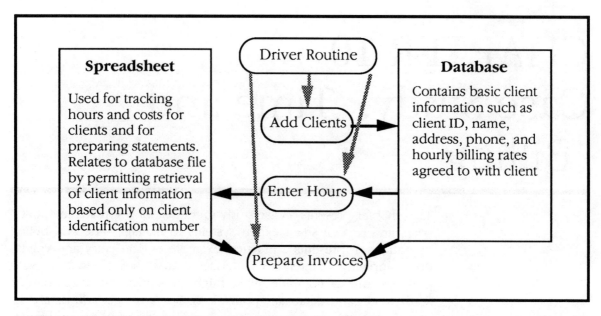

Figure 10-1. Application Overview

- One for entering hours into the worksheet whose function includes validating the client number entered by the user and checking for anomalous hours entries

- One for preparing invoices by combining information from both the worksheet and the database files to create and/or print a separate file

The graphic design consultant who uses this system built it himself with a little help from a friend who is a power computer user. He has always entered his own time into the system and prepared his own reports. He feels the system serves his needs well for the moment and is reluctant to change unless there is a good reason to do so. Now the business has grown too large for him to continue to spend his time on this administrative work. A local high school student has been hired to come in after class and keep up this part of the designer's records. This student is reasonably knowledgeable about using computers but is totally unfamiliar with the business operations of the consulting firm. The student is also occasionally unable to make it to work because of extracurricular activities or family travel, so a fellow student has been trained to do the job when he can't be there. Obviously, an easy-to-use system with as much error-trapping and correction as possible is in order.

This system is designed with 12 ranges in the worksheet file, one for each month of the year. Time is entered into the appropriate month's range by the user entering three values: client identification, a code for the type of work performed, and the number of hours billed. To prepare a month's invoices, the consultant generates a separate worksheet file for each client for the month — using a macro he and his friend built, but the process is not terribly automatic. Invoices are then printed using these worksheets. Because the consultant has a small number of clients, this system works quite well for him. For hundreds of clients, the approach would clearly need reworking.

The consultant has hired us to make his system more smoothly integrated so that a relatively untrained person can use it. We've decided to use VP-Expert to develop the interface and management routines.

The Worksheet

The structure of the worksheet where billing information is stored is relatively simplistic. It is shown in Table 10-1 and discussed below.

As you can see, the worksheet has five columns. The first contains the client code. The consultant uses a simple code in which the first two characters are alphabetic and are the first and last initials of the person or firm. The last character is a number that is used to differentiate between two clients who happen to have the same initials. Thus, if he has a client named Robert Smith and another named Reed-Smithers Corporation, he could give them codes RS1 and RS2. Columns 2 through 4 are used to enter hours for the client each month for the kind of activity involved: consultation, layout, and design. Each holds a numeric value with two decimal places. Finally, the materials column holds a dollar amount for out-of-pocket expenses incurred. It is formatted as a currency value.

Table 10-1. Worksheet Structure

Client	Consultation	Layout	Design	Materials
Alpha Code	Hours-2.2	Hours-2.2	Hours-2.2	Costs-Currency

You might wonder why we don't include this information on hours worked and costs incurred in the database file where the client data is. There are several reasons for this, including the wasted space in the database file that would result from having to create a separate record for each transaction, leaving in most cases all but one of the four financial columns blank. However, the most important rationale for this design is that the consultant wants to be able to perform some analysis on the information in the worksheet. He wants, for example, to be able to find out what percentage of his time he's spending on consultation. Or what the total number of hours billed to a specific client for design work has been. A spreadsheet application is particularly adept at such calculations, while most databases perform such operations less efficiently if at all.

We want this worksheet to be able to accommodate customer charges for each of the 12 months in a year, and in each of the categories shown in Table 10-1. There are a number of ways we could accomplish this, including simply copying the worksheet 12 times and naming each one after a month. But we'll use the range-naming capability of the spreadsheet application to define regions of the worksheet and give them names that correspond to the month to which they pertain. The primary reason for choosing this approach is because VP-Expert (and other expert system shells as well) provide commands and statements for dealing with ranges in a spreadsheet. They are less adept at referencing a worksheet file by name using a variable, which is what we want to be able to do here.

As we'll see later in this chapter, choosing this approach makes it possible for us to reference, retrieve, and update each month's values independently of the others while using a VP-Expert variable to define the range of cells with which we want to work.

The Database

We'll walk through the construction of the worksheet shortly, but first let's look at the database file that makes up the second leg of this application. Table 10-2 summarizes its contents.

Table 10-2. Database Structure

Field Name	Contents	Type/Format	Comments
ID	Unique customer ID	Character-3	2 alpha, 1 numeric
Lastname	Last or co. name	Character-18	
Firstname	First name	Character-18	
Address	Street	Character-40	
City	City	Character-30	
State	State	Character-2	
Zip	Zip code	Character-5	
Phone	Customer phone	Character-10	Unformatted
Consult	Chg for consulting	Numeric-2 dbs	Hourly rate, up to
Layout	Chg for layout	Numeric-2 dbs	$99.99 for each
Design	Chg for design	Numeric-2 dbs	service indicated

There is nothing surprising or particularly difficult about this database layout. Note that it includes a per-hour charge for each type of activity for which the graphics consultant bills his clients. This is the only information that requires data validation in the expert system we will build to add clients to the system.

Constructing the Worksheet

The worksheet itself has the format shown in Table 10-1. It also has one additional row and one additional column, each containing formulas for the calculation of totals. We will follow the same step-by-step procedure we used in earlier chapters to construct this worksheet. Again, we use the commands and approaches common to Lotus 1-2-3, VP-Planner Plus Version 2, Quattro, and other Lotus workalikes. If you are an accomplished spreadsheet user, you should not need to read most of the explanatory text that follows the boxed description of each step.

STEP 1. Create a new worksheet

Load the spreadsheet program so a blank worksheet is displayed.

STEP 2. Enter the column headings: Client, Consultation, Layout, Design, Materials, Total beginning in cell A1 and continuing to cell F1

To enter these labels, since all begin with a letter, all you have to do is position the cursor in row 1 of each column and simply enter the label name as shown. When you finish, your screen should look something like Figure 10-2.

STEP 3. Set all of the columns' widths to 10, then change column B's width to 13 to accommodate the full title of "Consultation"

In Lotus 1-2-3 and workalikes, the key sequence to set all of the cells' widths to 10 is:

```
/WGCS10
```

followed by the Return key

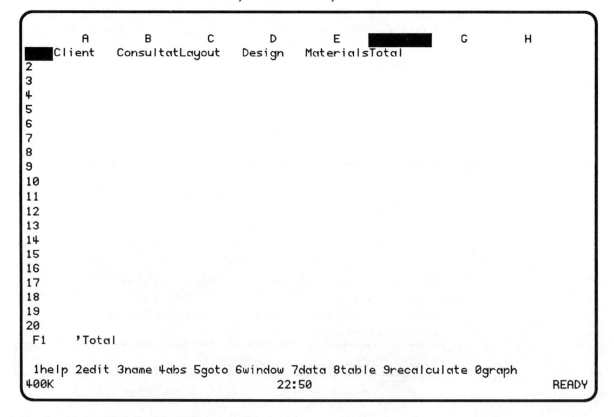

Figure 10-2. Worksheet Labels Entered

(for Worksheet Global Col-width Set 10). Once the entire worksheet has been set to a column width of 10, position the cursor in cell B1, under "Consultation." Then set the width of this column to 14:

```
/WCS <Return> 13 <Return>
```

(for Worksheet Col-Width Set 13). Because you are positioned in cell B1, the your command will set only that column's width to 13. Notice, though, that in VP-Planner Plus (but not in 1-2-3 or Quattro) you can set the width of multiple columns by using the Range Col-width Set command and defining the range.

STEP 4. Set the format of columns B through D and F to be floating-point format with two decimal places and column E to be currency format with two decimal places

---

There are a number of sequences you could use to accomplish these formatting changes. The most efficient is to first reformat columns B through F to be floating-point numbers with two decimal places, then move to column E and reset its format. To do this, start with your cursor in cell B1 and then type this command sequence:

```
/RFF
```

(for Range Format Fixed) followed by the Return key (because you're accepting the default of 2 decimal places). Then press the right arrow key four times so that the range is defined as B1..F1 and press Return.

Now position the cursor in cell E1 and reset its format with this command sequence:

```
/RFC
```

(for Range Format) followed by two carriage returns (because you're accepting both the default range of E1..E1 and the default decimal places of 2).

STEP 5. Save your work

This is your first save of this worksheet, so you will have to supply a file name. The key sequence is:

```
/FS
```

(for File Save) followed by the file name (we suggest CONSULT) and a Return.

STEP 6. Enter the formula in column F to add the contents of columns B through D to determine total hours for a given client

---

Position the cursor in cell F2. Type this formula:

    @SUM(B2..D2)

and press the Return key. (You can, of course, accomplish this differently by using the cursor to select the range of cells whose values are to be added, but we are using the direct programming method here in the interest of space and clarity.)

Now we need to copy this formula through the rest of the cells in column F to the end of the area in which we are working. We will assume for the sake of this example that the consultant never works with more than 17 clients in a given month. This means that, allowing a blank line for readability, we will put the totals on row 20. It also means that the total range of the worksheet is A1..F20.

To copy the formula in F2 into cells F3 through F18, follow these steps:

1. Be sure the cursor is still positioned in cell F2

2. Type /C (for Copy) and then accept the suggested range of source cells as F2..F2 by pressing the Return key

3. Press the down arrow to start the copy destination range at cell F3

4. Now you can either type two periods followed by the final cell in the range (F18), or type a period and then press the down arrow 16 times. In either case, the final result should be a defined destination of F3..F18

5. Press Return

In a few moments, the worksheet will recalculate and zeros will appear in cells F3 through F18, exactly as you'd expect given worksheet cells with no data.

STEP 7. Enter the label "Totals" in cell A20

STEP 8. Enter the formula in cell B20 to total cells B2 through B18 into cell B20

This formula is:

```
@SUM(B2..B18)
```

As usual, you can simply type the formula or you can use pointing techniques to tell the spreadsheet application the range of cells to be totaled.

STEP 9. Copy the formula in cell B20 into cells C20 through F20

The procedure is essentially the same as that used in step 6. Rather than pressing the down arrow once you've defined the source range as cell B20, however, you'll press the right arrow. Then you can type a period and "F20" or you can type a period and press the right arrow three times. In either case, the range defined will be C20 through F20. Press Return and the recalculation places zeros in all of these cells.

STEP 10. Save the worksheet

Since you've already saved this worksheet earlier, just confirm the replacement of the existing file. The command sequence is:

```
/FS <Return> R
```

(meaning File Save using the current file name and Replace the existing copy of the file).

Now your worksheet should look like Figure 10-3. It is ready for information to be entered into it.

STEP 11. Copy the range of cells from A1 through F20 to a starting location of A22. Repeat the copy process 10 more times, each time leaving a blank row between the Totals line of one copy and the start of the next

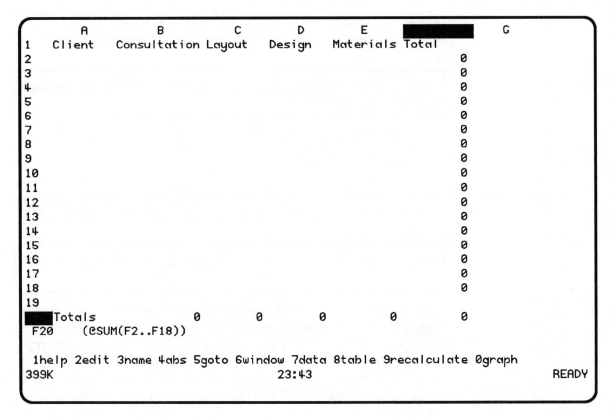

Figure 10-3. Consulting Worksheet in Final Form

Recall that we said the consultant uses a separate range in the work-sheet for each month of the year. We will name those ranges JAN, FEB, MAR, APR, MAY, JUN, JUL, AUG, SEP, OCT, NOV, and DEC.

To copy the first range of cells, follow these steps:

1. Position the cursor at cell A1.

2. Type /C (for Copy). Notice that the spreadsheet application is now asking you to identify the range of cells to be copied.

3. You can identify the range either by pointing (moving the cursor with the arrow keys down and to the right until the entire range is highlighted), but in this case it is probably much more efficient simply to "type" the range. Type A1..F20 and press the Return key. (You can type just one period between the two cell locations if you wish, but most experienced spreadsheet users get into the habit of typing two simply because that's the way the system displays range addresses.)

4. You will now be asked for the destination location for the copy. Here, you need only supply a single cell's address, since the spreadsheet will start the copy at that location and continue for as many cells in both directions (down and to the right) as necessary to copy all of the cells in the identified range. Type A22 and press Return.

5. After a few moments, the system will finish recalculating and moving and it will be ready for the next Copy command.

6. Repeat steps 2 and 3 above for each range copy we need. Table 10-3 summarizes the 13 ranges, their starting and ending cell locations, and the names we will give them at the next step in our processing.

STEP 12. Save the worksheet

Remember, the Lotus 1-2-3 and VP-Planner Plus command to save the worksheet at this point is /FS<Return>R. Whenever you've made changes as extensive as we just have to a worksheet, it's a good idea to save it.

STEP 13. Name the 11 ranges you just created, using the three-letter month abbreviation for each month
---

In VP-Planner Plus and Lotus 1-2-3, the command to name a range is

   /RNC

(for Range Name Create), followed by the name of the range and then the definition of the starting and ending cells of the range. As usual, you can use pointing or direct definition by typing to identify the range of cells.

To name the first range, from cell A1 to cell F20, JAN, follow these instructions:

1. Type /RNC

2. Give the range name, JAN, and press Return

3. Type A1..F20 and press Return (if you prefer, you can type only one period between the two cell addresses)

Naming the remaining ranges follows the same procedure, using the names and cell information in Table 10-3 for each range.

Table 10-3. Range Names for 12 Months

Start Cell	End Cell	Range Name
A1	F20	JAN
A22	F41	FEB
A43	F62	MAR
A64	F83	APR
A85	F104	MAY
A106	F125	JUN
A127	F146	JUL
A148	F167	AUG
A169	F188	SEP
A190	F209	OCT
A211	F230	NOV
A232	F251	DEC

Constructing the Database

Using dBASE III Plus, constructing the database used in this case study requires only six basic steps after starting dBASE III Plus, though one of them involves the entry of all 11 fields in the database. Here are step-by-step instructions for building the database. (In keeping with our established principle, you need only read the material that follows the step if you need further explanation of that step.)

STEP 1. In dBASE III Plus, set up a new database file called CLIENTS

At the dot prompt in dBASE III Plus, type

```
CREATE CLIENTS
```

and press Return. You will be taken immediately to the field-definition screen.

STEP 2. Define the 11 fields shown in Table 10-2

The process is the same for the first eight fields, all of which are character fields of various lengths. Simply enter the name of the field (upper- or lowercase is not material; dBASE III will convert all of your entries to uppercase letters), then press Return twice and enter the length of the field as shown in Table 10-2. Then press Return again and you will be ready to enter the next field definition.

Once you've defined the PHONE field this way, you'll be entering definitions for three numeric fields. These require two additional steps each. Enter the name of the field, then press Return and then the Space Bar to change the field type from the default of Character to Numeric. Press Return and enter the total field length (in this case, 5), then Return again. Finally, enter a 2 for the number of decimal places. Press Return once more and you're ready to enter the next numeric field.

When you're done, your dBASE III Plus screen should look like Figure 10-4.

STEP 3. Press Control-End to terminate field definition

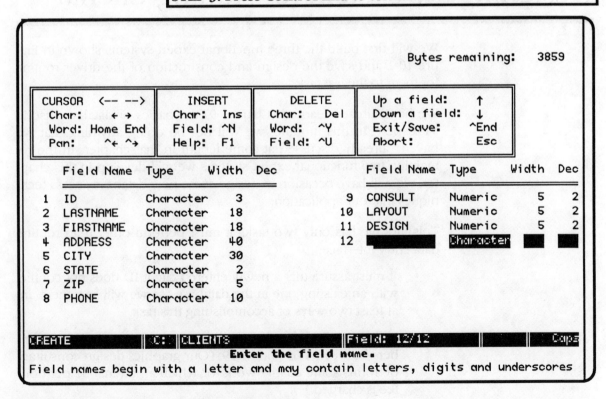

Figure 10-4. dBASE File Definition Complete

> **STEP 4. Press the Enter key to confirm you really want to end this phase of database definition**

> **STEP 5. Answer "N" when asked if you want to enter records now**

Since we are designing a VP-Expert module to enter clients, we do not wish to enter any records through dBASE III Plus itself (though there's no technical reason not to do so).

> **STEP 6. Quit dBASE III Plus**

Just type QUIT and press the Return key at the dot prompt and you will return to the Operating System level.

Designing the System for Adding Clients

We will first build the three functional expert systems shown in Figure 10-1 and save the design and construction of the driver routine for them to the last task.

We have already learned (Chapter 9) the basics of database use in VP-Expert. In this module, we will not be doing anything that we haven't already discussed at some length in that chapter. In the remaining two functional expert systems we will develop in this chapter, we will have occasion to design some new database access techniques into our application.

This module has only two tasks it must perform other than routine data entry interface:

- It must assure that a newly entered client ID does not conflict with an existing one in the database. As we will see, there are at least two ways of accomplishing this task.

- It must confirm that the hourly rates entered are positive numbers between 1.00 and 99.99. (Our graphics design consultant performs some charity work for which a nominal $1 per hour fee is charged.)

Other than these two data-validation tasks, this expert system is simply a more user-friendly front end to the database than would be possible to design completely within the confines of dBASE III Plus or any of its work-alikes.

This expert system will therefore be designed to follow the logic path shown in Figure 10-5. Notice that we retain the logical order of entry dictated by the database structure even though we could, if there were a reason to do so, alter it to be more "logical" from the expert systems perspective (e.g., entering all information requiring validation before allowing the user to enter the address and phone).

Designing the System for Entering Hours

When the consultant wants to enter billing time into the system, he currently follows these basic steps:

1. Open the worksheet for the month in question.

2. Check visually to see if the client for whom he wants to enter billable time is already in the worksheet

3. If the client is already in the worksheet, he adds the hours to the appropriate columns; if not, he creates a new spreadsheet row for this client

An expert systems approach requires that we automate the second and third steps, that is, determine whether a new row needs to be added to the spreadsheet or whether we simply need to update the existing hourly totals for a client who already has billable time during the month. We also need a way to determine which worksheet file to open at step 1.

The logic flow for this expert system is shown in Figure 10-6.

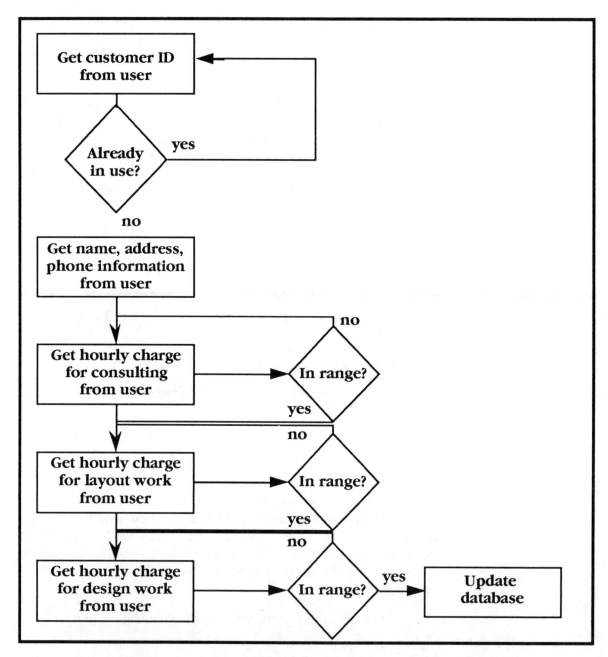

Figure 10-5. Logic Flow of System for Adding Clients

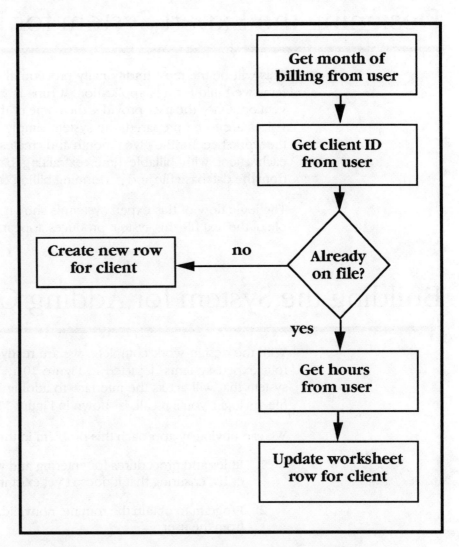

Figure 10-6. Logic Flow of System for Entering Hours

Designing the Expert System for Invoicing

This will be the most traditionally procedural of the four expert systems we build for this application. It runs largely without user intervention. Once the user provides the name of the month for which invoices are to be prepared, the system simply runs. It loops through the worksheet for the given month and creates a separate text file for each client with billable time, extracting basic client information from the database file and performing billing calculations as it runs.

The logic flow of this expert system is shown in Figure 10-7. A sample of the text file this system produces appears in Figure 10-8.

Building the System for Adding Clients

With the design work complete, we are ready to begin building the four expert systems depicted in Figure 10-1. We will start with the system that will act as the interface to adding clients to the database file. Its logic, you'll recall, is shown in Figure 10-5.

We can obviously approach this problem in three major modules:

1. Rules and procedures for entering and validating the customer ID, ensuring that it doesn't yet exist in the database file

2. Program to obtain the routine, nonvalidatable information from the user

3. Three nearly identical routines to enter and validate the hourly rate to be charged for consulting, layout, and design

If we approach the problem in this stepwise fashion, we will be more likely to succeed in creating an efficient system.

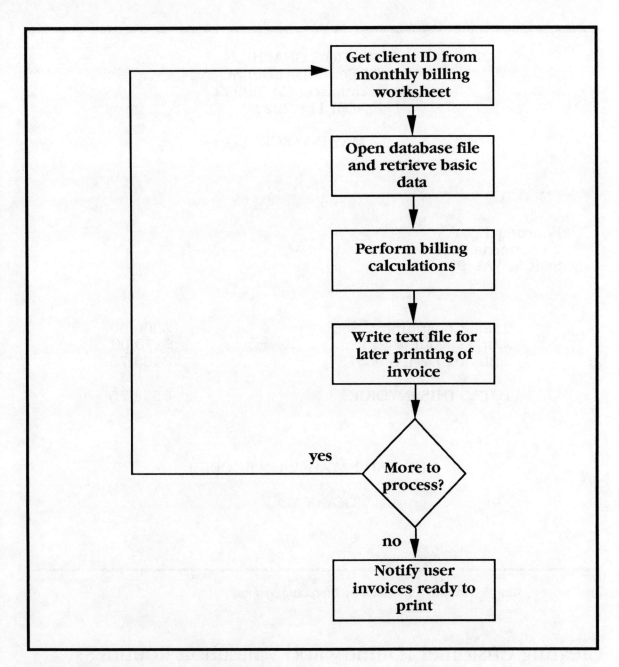

Figure 10-7. Logic Flow of System for Invoicing

HOWARD'S GRAPHICS
1234 South Division St.
San Francisco, CA 99999
(405) 111-2222

MAY INVOICE

SOLD TO:

Fourtney Brooks
23 Alameda Dr. #9
Seattle, WA 99444

6 hrs. Consulting @ $50 $300.00
2 hrs. Layout @ $35 $ 70.00
2.25 hrs. Design @ $75 $168.75

TOTAL THIS INVOICE $538.75

DUE AND PAYABLE ON RECEIPT

THANK YOU

Figure 10-8. Sample Text File Produced by Invoicing System

Creating Customer ID Entry and Validation Routines

There is only one new thing to be done in the process of entering and validating the customer ID. The routine for handling this phase of the design appears as Listing 10-1.

Listing 10-1

```
ENDOFF;
ACTIONS

FIND cust_id
GET cust_id=id,clients,id
FIND dupe_id
DISPLAY"Client successfully added to database.~";

RULE confirm_cust_id
IF      cust_id<>UNKNOWN
AND     id=(cust_id)
THEN    dupe_id=Yes
        DISPLAY"Sorry, but that ID is already being used
        in the file."
        WHILETRUE dupe_id=Yes THEN
            FIND cust_id
            RESET cust_id
            RESET dupe_id
        END
ELSE    dupe_id=No
        cust_id_ok=Yes;

ASK cust_id: "What customer ID do you want to assign to
    this customer?";
```

As you can tell from looking at Listing 10-1, the new element in the routine is the GET statement in the second line of the ACTIONS block. Notice that it follows the FIND statement that asks the user for the customer ID to be used. The GET statement requires three arguments:

- A "database rule" which can either be a set of matching criteria or the keyword ALL

- The name of a dBASE or compatible file, omitting the .DBF extension

- The name(s) of the field(s) to be retrieved from the dBASE file, or the keyword ALL if you want to retrieve all of the fields

Notice, too, that the database rule used in the GET statement in Listing 10-1 places the VP-Expert variable first and the dBASE file field name to be matched second. This order is important; reversing these two arguments is a fairly common cause of problems in VP-Expert database interface routines.

The GET statement, translated into English, tells VP-Expert: "Open the file CLIENTS.DBF and look in the field called ID for an entry that matches the current value of the VP-Expert variable `cust_id`. If you find such a matching record, return with the contents of the field called ID." Notice that the field names are not case sensitive, so we can use the lowercase `id` rather than the more traditional uppercase field name `ID`. Once the GET statement has retrieved a database record if it can find one, then the rule called `confirm_cust_id` can be used by the next FIND command to confirm that the ID the user has entered is not already in use. That rule uses the WHILETRUE loop approach we became familiar with in earlier chapters.

Testing Customer ID Routines

Because of the critical nature of this phase of the design and because the GET statement is new, we will pause here to suggest that you test this routine. Doing so takes relatively little effort and can save a great deal of time later when we have a more complete and complex system to test. Do the following steps to set up a test of this routine.

STEP 1. Make a copy of your CLIENTS.DBF file

Use DOS (disk operating system) or database program techniques to create the copy. If you don't know how to do this, consult the user manual for your database program or for your version of DOS. In general (without considering pathnames where you might have your file stored), the DOS COPY command will work:

```
COPY CLIENTS.DBF CLIENT1.DBF
```

STEP 2. Enter a value into the ID field of the file CLIENTS.DBF

This step requires that you open the database file and instruct the program to add a record. In dBASE III Plus, the sequence of commands is:

```
USE CLIENTS
APPEND
```

This brings up a screen like that shown in Figure 10-9. Just enter an arbitrary value into the ID field and terminate the entry by pressing the Control-End key combination. Then type QUIT at the next dBASE prompt and you will be back at the DOS level.

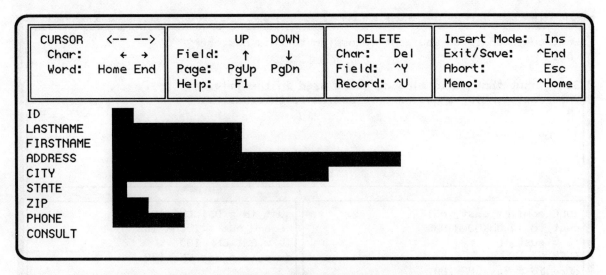

Figure 10-9. Data Entry Screen for CLIENTS.DBF in dBASE III Plus

STEP 3. Run the expert system and enter the same value for the customer ID when asked

You are by now familiar with how to run VP-Expert or whatever tool you are using to follow along in this discussion. When you are asked for the customer ID to be entered, respond with the same ID as the one you placed into the database file at step 2. The result should look like Figure 10-10 if you are using VP-Expert, somewhat different if you are using some other shell.

STEP 4. Enter a nonduplicated value for the customer ID in response to the system's request for a new ID

In VP-Expert, simply enter the new ID in response to the second request for a customer ID for this new client. You can enter any value other than the one you stored in the database at step 2.

STEP 5. Abort this run and then restart the expert system; enter a valid, nonduplicated customer ID this time

In VP-Expert, type /Q when you are being asked a question, then press the F4 function key to restart the consultation. This time, when you are asked for the customer ID, enter one you know isn't in the file. You should simply be asked for the customer's last name. If you are, then the system is working correctly. You may now quit VP-Expert. If problems arise, check your program against Listing 10-1.

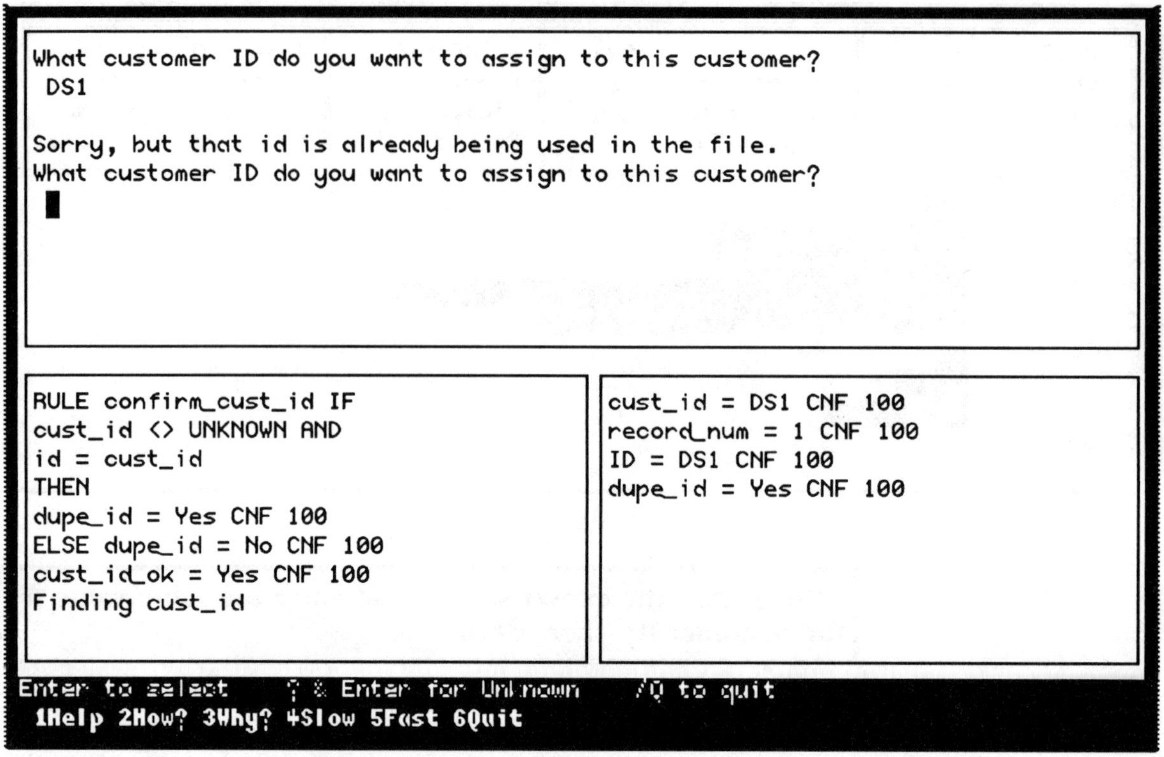

```
What customer ID do you want to assign to this customer?
 DS1

Sorry, but that id is already being used in the file.
What customer ID do you want to assign to this customer?
█
```

```
RULE confirm_cust_id IF          cust_id = DS1 CNF 100
cust_id <> UNKNOWN AND           record_num = 1 CNF 100
id = cust_id                     ID = DS1 CNF 100
THEN                             dupe_id = Yes CNF 100
dupe_id = Yes CNF 100
ELSE dupe_id = No CNF 100
cust_id_ok = Yes CNF 100
Finding cust_id
```

```
Enter to select      ? & Enter for Unknown      /Q to quit
 1Help 2How? 3Why? 4Slow 5Fast 6Quit
```

Figure 10-10. Entering Duplicate ID in Expert System

STEP 6. Rename the copied database file to CLIENTS.DBF

Again, you can do this from the DOS prompt:

```
COPY CLIENT1.DBF CLIENTS.DBF
```

Depending on how your DOS system is set up and on whether you are using any kind of DOS shell, this will either simply accomplish the task or it may ask you to confirm that you wish to overwrite an existing file with the COPY routine.

It is important that you get rid of CLIENTS.DBF after the testing and replace it with CLIENT1.DBF. Otherwise, problems will arise later when you use this expert system.

Building Routine Data Entry Module

The next several pieces of information our expert system needs to help the user enter are all routine data that are not subject to any validation, so we will simply build them all in one step. As you may recall, each of these items will be the subject of a FIND command and of an ASK statement. Listing 10-2 presents these statements as we defined them. They should be added to the appropriate points in your program as it appeared after testing the first module.

Listing 10-2

```
FIND lastname
FIND firstname
FIND address
FIND city
FIND state
FIND zip
FIND phone

ASK lastname: "What is the customer's last (or company)
name?";

ASK firstname: "What is the customer's first name?
(Skip for companies.)";

ASK address: "Enter the customer's street address.";

ASK city: "In what city is this customer located?";

ASK state: "Enter the two-letter state abbreviation.";

ASK zip: "Enter the Zip Code.";

ASK phone: "Enter the telephone number as 10 digits
with no punctuation.";
```

This new set of routines is so straightforward that no additonal testing is appropriate at this level. You should probably save your work, but we'll just continue constructing the last three modules.

Building the Rate Entry and Validation Routines

In creating the rules and related statements to obtain from the user the three hourly rate charges and validate them, we will use a two-tier approach. We will first ask the user if a predetermined default value for the rate is to be used. If the answer is yes, no validation is necessary. If some other value is to be entered, then we must validate that it falls between $1 and $99.99. For the purposes of our demonstration, we will assume that the graphics consultant normally charges $75 per hour for consultation, $50 per hour for design, and $35 per hour for layout work. The statements that will ask the user to choose either the normal rate or indicate a desire to enter a different rate will all look the same (see Listing 10-3).

Listing 10-3

```
ASK consult:"What is your agreed upon hourly rate for
consulting?";
CHOICES consult: 75,other;

ASK layout:"What is your agreed upon hourly rate for
layout work?";
CHOICES consult: 35,other;

ASK design:"What is your agreed upon hourly rate for
design work?";
CHOICES consult: 50,other;
```

These statements, of course, require accompanying FIND commands. Those commands will follow our usual pattern of naming, so that the value to be located to confirm that the user's entered rate for consulting is valid will be called *consulting_ok*, and the others will be similarly named.

This leaves us with only the rules to be defined. Each entry validation will require two nearly identical rules. The rule set for confirming the consultation rate is shown in Listing 10-4.

Listing 10-4

```
RULE standard_consulting
IF       consult<>other
THEN     consult_ok=Yes;
```

```
RULE      special_consulting
IF        consult=other
THEN      FIND amount
          consult=(amount)
          WHILETRUE consult<1 OR consult >= 100 THEN
              DISPLAY"Sorry, but the fee must be between
              $1 and $99.99."
              RESET consult
              FIND consult
          END
          consult_ok=Yes;
```

```
ASK amount:"Please enter a fee between $1 and $99.99.";
```

Notice that we define a new VP-Expert variable called amount in-side the rule special_consulting. This enables us to ask a fol-low-up question when the user indicates that a rate other than the default value provided should be used. If we tried to use the variable *consult* here, we would end up with an impossible situation of trying to assign a variable its present value and then test it against some range. The variable amount obviously requires its own ASK state-ment with no accompanying CHOICES clause.

Because we defined the question for the variable amount generical-ly, we can make it do triple duty, serving as the question we ask in the event that any of the fees entered by the user is nonstandard.

The rules for entering and validating the fees to be charged the new client for design and layout work make up Listing 10-5.

Listing 10-5

```
RULE      standard_layout
IF        layout<>other
THEN      layout_ok=Yes;

RULE      special_layout
IF        layout=other
THEN      FIND amount
          layout=(amount)
          WHILETRUE layout<1 OR layout >= 100 THEN
              DISPLAY"Sorry, but the fee must be between
              $1 and $99.99."
              RESET layout
              FIND layout
          END
          layout_ok=Yes;
```

```
RULE       standard_design
IF         design<>other
THEN       design_ok=Yes;

RULE       special_design
IF         design=other
THEN       FIND amount
           design=(amount)
           WHILETRUE design<1 OR design >= 100 THEN
               DISPLAY"Sorry, but the fee must be between
               $1 and $99.99."
               RESET design
               FIND design
           END
           design_ok=Yes;
```

Updating the Database

As you may recall from Chapter 9, updating the dBASE file in which
clients are being stored requires the use of the APPEND command in
VP-Expert. Immediately before the DISPLAY statement in the AC-
TIONS block, enter the line:

```
APPEND clients
```

and the database file will be updated after you finish entering all of
the needed information for each client.

Testing the ADCLIENTS.KBS Knowledge Base

We have now completed the construction of the knowledge base
that adds new clients to the database file and validates all critical information. We have tested independently the portions of this knowledge base that enter and validate the customer ID (to be sure it's
unique) and the consulting fees charged for the three major tasks (to
be sure they are in a valid range). We can now test the entire system
simply by entering a few sample clients. As you do so, you should
exercise the validation routines of the system by entering:

- Duplicate customer IDs in response to the first query about
  the customer ID

- Duplicate customer IDs in response to the follow-up query

- Invalid fee amounts in response to the first request

- Invalid fee amounts in response to the repeated requests that will continue so long as you enter invalid amounts

Having completed this testing, you should open the database file in dBASE III Plus (or whatever database you are using) and examine its contents to be sure they are as you expect them to be.

Building the System for Entering Hours

The first of the four expert system modules we are constructing in our case study is now complete, tested and ready to use. Now let's turn our attention to the routine that will enter the number of hours and charges into the worksheet. Because this system works with both the database and the worksheet and because of the relative complexity of the validation involved, it is the most complicated of the expert systems we will build in this book.

As you can see from Figure 10-6, the basic logic flow of this system does not appear to be as complex as we are suggesting it is. That is because the box labeled "Get hours from user" was purposely made simplistic. In reality, the flow involved in that box alone will look like that in Figure 10-11. Further complicating the process is the fact that the entire processing flow embodied in Figures 10-6 and 10-11 must take place within a major outside loop which continues to execute until the user has entered all of the charges for a given month. This is highly procedural programming, something to which, as we have seen, expert systems do not lend themselves particularly well. Still, it is possible to construct this knowledge base. Let's take our usual modular approach.

First, we'll build the part of the system that obtains from the user the month of billing and the client ID to whom the hours and costs are to be charged. It then examines the appropriate worksheet file to see if this client already has a charge record for the month. If not, it creates a new row for this client.

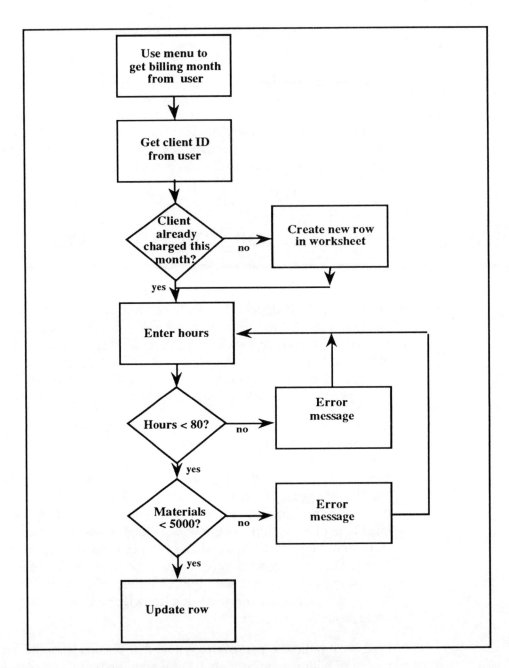

Figure 10-11. Detailed Processing of Hours Entry

Second, we'll build the hours-entry and validation portion of the system. This segment of the knowledge base asks for the type of activity for which hours are to be entered and validates the range of the subsequent hours entered.

Finally, we'll construct the worksheet update routine and enclose the entire processing system in a loop so that the user can continue to enter time for a given month until all the data to be entered in a single session has been processed.

Building the Basic Entry Routines

Entering the month of billing, retrieving the appropriate range of the spreadsheet, and obtaining the client ID from the user are trivial assignments. What makes this phase of the project interesting and challenging is the need to rearrange data from the way the VP-Expert WKS command reads it from the worksheet to the way we can use it to validate a client's ID. This requires that we do some procedural programming. Fortunately we'll find VP-Expert up to the task.

The first phase of this module is to ask the user for the billing month that is to be worked with, and then retrieve that month's range from the worksheet file we've called CHARGES.WKS. Listing 10-6 shows this step in the process.

Listing 10-6

```
ENDOFF;
ACTIONS

FIND month
WKS result,NAMED=(month),charges
DISPLAY"Please wait while I organize the billing
information."
x=1
y=1
WHILETRUE x<21 THEN
        client[x] = result[y]
        x=(x+1)
        y=(y+5)
END;

ASK month:"For what month do you want to enter time and
charges?";
CHOICES month:Jan,Feb,Mar,Apr,May,Jun,Jul,Aug,Sep,Oct
Nov,Dec;
```

This program segment shows some of VP-Expert's procedural power and a main reason the ACTIONS block is an important part of a typical VP-Expert knowledge base. The user is asked to provide a month, using the ASK and CHOICES statements shown. The result is then used as a variable to tell VP-Expert which range in the worksheet to retrieve. The results of the WKS retrieval are placed into the dimensioned variable called `result`. When VP-Expert reads a worksheet range, it reads the data into the indicated variable row-wise. Thus the first cell in row 1 of the range is in element 1, the second element of row 1 in element 2, and so forth. This arrangement means that when we're done reading a range, we have a variable called `result` with, potentially, 100 elements (20 rows of 5 columns each).

Unfortunately, in our case this means that the client IDs in the worksheet are separated from one another by five elements. The first client ID in the worksheet is in element 1, the second in element 6, and so on. This makes the job of comparing a customer ID provided by the user against those already on the file quite time-consuming. So we simply rearrange their order so that the first client ID is the first element of a variable, the second one the second element, and so forth. To do this, we create a new variable, `client`, and use a WHILETRUE loop to assign values to each of its elements, each element consisting of a customer ID from the worksheet.

When this task is complete, we have a small array of 20 or fewer elements containing only the client IDs of clients who have a billing entry in the month in which we are working.

Now we need to get the client ID from the user and find out if this client is already in the worksheet. This requires an ASK statement and some rules, as shown in Listing 10-7.

Listing 10-7

```
FIND      client_id
FIND      client_exists

RULE      find_client
IF        client_id<>UNKNOWN
THEN      count=1
          WHILETRUEclient_id<>(client[count])
              count=(count+1)
          END
          file_searched=Yes;
```

```
RULE      client_on_file
IF        file_searched=Yes
AND       count<20
THEN      client_exists=Yes
ELSE      count=1
          WHILEKNOWN client[count]
              count=(count+1)
          END
          client[(count)]=(client_id)
          client_exists=Yes;

ASK client_id:"Enter the ID of the client whose account
you are charging.";
```

The only element of the rules in Listing 10-7 that might seem unfamiliar is the WHILETRUE loop in the rule called find_client. It does not perform a FIND/RESET combination like other similar loops we've used in data validation. That's because we are working with a dimensioned variable, client, and since we keep changing the value of its index (count in the example), we need not reset its value. The value changes each time we go through the loop and the value of count is incremented.

This loop will essentially exit when it finds in the dimensioned variable client a value corresponding to the client ID entered by the user. We will then know which row of the worksheet the client is in.

The rule called client_on_file uses the value of count to determine if the client ID was found. If it was, the value of count will be less than 21, since there are only 20 possible entries in the worksheet range for each period. In that case, we need to assign the next available slot in the variable called client to the newly entered client ID. To do this, however, we cannot use the value of count obtained from the rule find_client because it is obviously 20 (meaning the client ID wasn't found in the range), and we don't want to assign a new client to a nonexistent row of the range. So we execute another loop, this one using the VP-Expert command WHILEKNOWN, which functions similarly to WHILETRUE as if the WHILETRUE command had an argument of <> UNKNOWN associated with it. In other words, it executes until it encounters a value of UNKNOWN for the variable it is using. Then it exits.

Two examples will help to illustrate how these rules work.

First, assume that the client ID code DS3 has been entered into the worksheet for March and some time has been charged to the account. Now we want to enter some new March time for this account. We will assume client DS3 is the fourth entry of 11 in the March worksheet at this point.

When the first rule executes, it will go through its WHILETRUE loop until `count` is 4. Then its condition, `client_id<>(client [count])`, will become false because a match will occur. With count at 4, the value of the VP-Expert variable `file_searched` will become Yes.

Now the second rule is executed (since the inference engine is looking for a value for the variable `client_exists` due to the FIND command in the ACTIONS block). It finds that the variable `file_searched` is Yes and that the value of count is less than 20, so it sets the value of `client_exists` to Yes and exits the rule.

Let's take another client ID entered by the user, this time RJ1. Let's assume this client has not yet had any time billed in March, so there is no matching entry among the 11 entries in the worksheet. The first rule executes its WHILETRUE loop 20 times, until it finally runs out of elements in the variable `client` and has to exit. At that point, `count` will have a value of 20 .

The second rule executes and a test indicates that although the value of `file_searched` is Yes, the value of `count` is not less than 20. It is in fact exactly 20. So the ELSE clause is executed. This time, the WHILEKNOWN loop will go through the variable `client` item by item until it encounters the first unknown element, which will be at item 12 (since there are 11 values in the worksheet). It then assigns the twelfth element the value of the client ID entered by the user, and then sets the value of the goal variable `client_exists` to Yes. The inference engine is satisfied, and we have entered a new client into the dimensioned variable `client`. (Note: We have "not" added this client to the worksheet variable `result` yet. This must be done before we update the worksheet, but we will do all the updating in one step after all the data has been entered.)

You should note, too, that it is important that we do not now reuse the variable `count` because we need it later to tell us where in the main data array `result` to put the hours the user is about to enter.

This is a good time to save your knowledge base. You might also test it by making a copy of the worksheet, entering a few values into the original file via the spreadsheet application, then testing to see if VP-Expert correctly identifies present and absent IDs in the range. If it works in one range, it will obviously work in all ranges, assuming you have properly identified and named all the ranges.

Building the Hours Entry Routine

The routine that allows the user to enter hours into the system should probably first confirm that the user has named the correct client to be charged. To do that, we have to use the client ID furnished by the user to access the dBASE file where we store the names of clients. Then we can display the client's name and ask the user if this is the client that is to be charged with the time and costs about to be entered. If the answer is yes, we have the right client and proceed to enter the time. Otherwise, we want the system to ask for a new client ID.

To create this process in VP-Expert, we must create a small loop surrounding the FIND clauses in the ACTIONS block so that they will execute repeatedly until the user confirms that we have found the right client. This construct looks like Listing 10-8.

Listing 10-8

```
restart=Yes
WHILETRUE restart=Yes THEN
        FIND client_id
        FIND client_exists
        FIND client_rec_ok
END
```

We can then use this new VP-Expert variable *restart* to determine later when to reinitiate the process because the user has found an error in the entry of the client ID. That part of the processing requires the rules shown in Listing 10-9.

Listing 10-9

```
RULE      locate_client_in_db
IF        client_exists=Yes
THEN      GET client_id=(id), CLIENTS, ALL
```

```
                     data_found=Yes
                     FIND right_client;

RULE       confirm_client
IF         right_client<>Yes
THEN       RESET client_id
           restart=Yes
ELSE       restart=No
           client_rec_ok=Yes;

ASK right_client:"Enter time and charges for
{FIRSTNAME} {LASTNAME}?";
CHOICES right_client:Yes,No;
```

These rules are relatively straightforward. The first finds the client's record in the CLIENTS.DBF file. (Note: We have not built in protection against the possibility that the user might delete a valid client from the database file and then try to enter hours for that deleted client. In a real-world application, you probably want to build in some form of protection against that eventuality, but that would properly be the function of managing the client file.)

Once we've retrieved the client data, we display the client's name and ask the user to confirm its accuracy. If "No" is the answer, then the rule resets the value of `client_id` to UNKNOWN and ensures that the variable `restart` has a value of Yes. This causes the loop in the ACTIONS block to re-execute. If, however, the user answers "Yes" when asked to confirm that this is the right client to be working with, *restart* is given the value "No" and the goal variable `client_rec_ok` is given a value so that the ACTIONS block loop completes its execution and the inference process can continue.

Now that we know we're working with the right client, we are ready to enter the hours. This requires two steps: naming the category of hours to be entered, and then entering and validating the number of hours. These routines are quite straightforward. The consultant has decided based on experience that it is highly unusual for any entry of hours to exceed 80 or for any single cost entry to exceed $5,000. This leads to the rules, ACTIONS block additions and ASK statements with CHOICES options shown in Listing 10-10.

Listing 10-10

```
! Additions to ACTIONS block
FIND entry_type
FIND entry_ok
```

```
! New rules
RULE      validate_hours
IF        entry_type<>Materials
AND       amount<=80
THEN      entry_ok=Yes
ELSE      WHILETRUE amount >80
              RESET amount
              DISPLAY"Sorry, but no single entry can
              exceed 80 hours!"
              FIND amount
END;

RULE      validate_costs
IF        entry_type=Materials
AND       amount<5000
THEN      entry_ok=Yes
ELSE      WHILETRUE amount > 5000
              RESET amount
              DISPLAY"Sorry, but no single entry can
              exceed $5,000!"
              FIND amount
END;

! New user interface commands
ASK entry_type:"What type of charge do you want to
enter?";
CHOICES entry_type:Consulting,Design,Layout,Materials;

ASK amount:"Please enter the charge (hours or cost of
materials.)";
```

The techniques depicted in Listing 10-10 are identical to those we used in earlier chapters. Therefore, no elaboration will be given.

Building the Worksheet Row Update Routine

When we have received and validated all the data for a particular entry, we are ready to update the information we brought in from the worksheet to reflect the new values. This necessitates that we:

- Examine the type of entry (stored in the VP-Expert variable `entry_type`)

- Determine the beginning position in the dimensioned variable `result` in which to store the updated information

- Add the newly entered amount to the existing amount in that element of the worksheet

Recall that earlier we stored in a VP-Expert variable count the element of the dimensioned variable client where the current client is stored. You may also recall that the variable client was generated by taking every fifth element of the dimensioned variable result, into which the worksheet was originally read. Now we need to translate this location back to the original position in the variable result. The formula to do this conversion requires us to multiply the location in client by 5 and then subtract 4 from the result. You will see this formula in the ACTIONS block of Listing 10-11, where we assign the result of the calculation to the variable location.

Once we know where in the dimensioned variable result performs updating, the process of calculating and updating the value stored there is straightforward. We simply add to the value of the variable location a value corresponding to the type of entry relative to the beginning of a worksheet row. Thus, consulting hours are found at element location+1, layout work at location+2, and so forth.

We will not write the updated worksheet data to the disk file until we have completed all of the updates for this session. That will be our final task of this module construction.

Listing 10-11

```
!ACTIONS block additions
!Add after all previous ACTIONS block clauses
location=((5*count)-4)
FIND update1

!New rules
RULE      update_consulting
IF        entry_type=Consulting
THEN      result[(location+1)]=((result[(location+1)]+
          amount)
          update1=Yes;

RULE      update_layout
IF        entry_type=Layout
THEN      result[(location+2)]=((result[(location+2)]+
          amount)
          update1=Yes;

RULE      update_design
IF        entry_type=Design
THEN      result[(location+3)]=((result[(location+3)]+
          amount)
          update1=Yes;
```

```
RULE      update_materials
IF        entry_type=Materials
THEN      result[(location+4)]=((result[(location+4)]+
          amount)
          update1=Yes;
```

Building the Worksheet Update Routine

The final step in this module of the expert system used in this case study involves updating the worksheet file. This in turn requires us to take the following steps:

1. Confirm that the user is finished with entries

2. Update the client ID entries in the VP-Expert dimensioned variable `result` in case any new clients have been added in this session

3. Write the dimensioned variable `result` to the worksheet

Confirming that the user is ready to end this data entry session requires that we enclose the appropriate ACTIONS block statements in a WHILETRUE loop. Listing 10-12 shows the complete ACTIONS block revised to include this new loop, as well as the ASK and CHOICES statements that control its execution.

Listing 10-12

```
! Revised ACTIONS block to include action loop to
! control completion
ENDOFF;
ACTIONS
FIND action
WHILETRUE action<>Quit THEN
        FIND month
        WKS result,NAMED=(month),charges
        DISPLAY"Please wait while I organize the
        billing information."
        x=1
        y=1
        WHILETRUE x<21 THEN
            client[x] = result[y]
            x=(x+1)
            y=(y+5)
        END
END
```

```
WHILETRUE action=Enter_data THEN
        restart=Yes
        WHILETRUE restart=Yes THEN
            FIND client_id
            FIND client_exists
            FIND client_rec_ok
        END
        FIND entry_type
        FIND entry_ok
        location=((5*count)-4)
        FIND update1
        RESET action
END;

! Additions to user interface portion of program
ASK action:"What do you want to do now?";
CHOICES action:Enter_data, Print_invoices, Quit;
```

As you can see by examining Listing 10-12, we have added a large WHILEKNOWN loop which continually asks the user after each step in the processing what is to be done next. As long as he keeps indicating he has more data to enter, the system will keep asking for a new client ID, and update the client's data as appropriate. (Note: Because we have read in the entire range of a month's data, we do not allow the user to change his mind about the month to be worked on without quitting the run. This enables us to keep better track of the monthly billing data in the worksheet without risking errors caused by system crashes and failures with a great deal of unrecorded changes in the system's memory.)

Now let's add the routine to the ACTIONS block that will ensure that the dimensioned variable `result` has the latest client IDs stored in it. This will ensure that if we have had to add any clients during this entry session, they will be added to the worksheet. Listing 10-13 shows the ACTIONS block addition needed to accomplish this task.

Listing 10-13

```
! ACTIONS block additions
WHILETRUE counter<21 THEN
        result[((5*counter)-4)] = client[(counter)]
        counter=(counter+1)
END
```

Notice that we use the same formula as earlier for determining what position in the variable `result` to update based on the contents of the other dimensioned variable `client`.

Writing the revised data to the worksheet file is a one-line command, but we'll add a second line to DISPLAY the fact that we have completed the task. These additions appear in Listing 10-14.

Listing 10-14

```
! ACTIONS block additions
PWKS result,NAMED=(month),charges
DISPLAY"Billing information has been successfully
updated!";
```

Building the Invoice-Creating Routine

The last step in building our case study application is to create the routines that will generate invoices for our hypothetical graphics consultant. We will use VP-Expert's FDISPLAY command for this purpose. This command takes two arguments:

- The name of a file to be used (with or without a path name)

- The string (enclosed in quotation marks) to be placed at the end of that file

We will know that the user wants to print invoices because he will have indicated that as the desired activity in response to the question associated with the variable `activity_type`. Rather than embedding the test for the response, `Print_invoices` in the ACTIONS block, we'll use a rule. This serves two purposes. First, it removes some otherwise potentially confusing clutter from the ACTIONS block. Second, it removes the necessity of asking the user after each file is created what is to be done next, as would be the case if we placed the test in a WHILETRUE loop as we do the other activities.

A single rule and two additions to the ACTIONS block will produce the invoices we want. (See Figure 10-8 for an illustration of what the file contents will be for each invoice.) We are going to produce a separate file, named for the client, for each invoice to be produced. The rule is long because the amount of text to be placed in the file with the FDISPLAY command is extensive. Don't let that fool you; the rule itself is simple. Listing 10-15 provides the additions we will make to our expert system to cause it to print invoices on demand.

Listing 10-15

```
! ACTIONS block additions
CHR 13,CR
CHR 10,LF

! New Rule
RULE      print_invoices
IF        action=Print_invoices
THEN      counter=1
          WHILEKNOWN client[(counter)]
               GET client[(counter)]=ID,CLIENTS,ALL
               location=((5*counter)-4)
               consult_amt=result[(location+1)] *
               consulting
               layout_amt=result[(location+2)] * layout
               design_amt=result[(location+3)] * design
               total=(consult_amt + layout_amt +
               design_amt + materials)
               FDISPLAY {client_id},"{CR}{LF}
                  HOWARD'S GRAPHICS{CR}{LF}
               1234 South Division St.{CR}{LF}
               San Francisco, CA 99999{CR}{LF}
                     (415) 111-2222{CR}{LF}
{CR}{LF}
                  {month} INVOICE{CR}{LF}
{CR}{LF}
SOLD TO:{CR}{LF}
{CR}{LF}
{firstname}{lastname}{CR}{LF}
{address}{CR}{LF}
{city}, {state}  {zip}{CR}{LF}
{CR}{LF}
               {result[(location+1)]} hrs. Consulting
@${consulting}     ${consult_amt}{CR}{LF}
               {result[(location+2)]} hrs. Layout
@${layout}        ${layout_amt}{CR}{LF}
               {result[(location+3)]} hrs. Design
@${design}     ${design_amt}{CR}{LF}
               Materials and Expenses
 ${result[(location+4)]}}{CR}{LF}
{CR}{LF}
               TOTAL THIS INVOICE
                                            ${total}
{CR}{LF}
{CR}{LF}
{CR}{LF}
                  DUE AND PAYABLE ON RECEIPT{CR}{LF}
{CR}{LF}
                     THANK YOU{CR}{LF}
"
          counter=(counter+1)
          END;
```

The strange-looking {CR} and {LF} characters insert a carriage return and line-feed combination into the text stream being stored in the file. They ensure proper formatting of the file. Other elements of the rule should be familiar to you. We define the values of the VP-Expert variables CR and LF in the ACTIONS block with the command CHR. This command can be used to generate any ASCII character in a DISPLAY, FDISPLAY, or other output statement in VP-Expert.

How About a Macro?

Since the knowledge base we have created is quite large and somewhat complex, you may wonder if a worksheet macro could be used just as easily as an expert system for this application. Such an approach, however, would not be very straightforward.

First, most spreadsheet programs do not allow for the selective access of database records through spreadsheet commands. VP-Planner Plus does allow such an approach but neither Lotus 1-2-3 nor Quattro does. (Add-on programs to these spreadsheet programs can be used to provide such access but that only further complicates the question.) Lotus 1-2-3 and Quattro can both read an entire dBASE file into a worksheet but the process can't be controlled conditionally from inside a macro.

Second, the resulting macro would be extremely large, difficult to write, complicated to understand, and probably impossible to maintain. The best solution is clearly to use an expert system to tie together the spreadsheet and database files in a user-friendly, seamless manner. This results in a system that is easy to implement, test, use, and expand.

Summary

We have now completed our expert system interface to a time and billing package. You now know how to make a spreadsheet program and a database system work together to solve a problem by means of an expert system acting as the "glue." Even where the underlying applications are created using conceptually incompatible tools, an expert system can help tie them together and give the user a seamless, integrated interface.

You have now reached the end of your formal study of spreadsheets, databases, and expert systems. You should now be ready to look at the spreadsheet and database demands of your business or that of your clients with a new, intelligent eye, and to create highly usable interfaces that not only make data entry easier but more accurate as well.

Chapter 11 discusses the use of hypertext techniques to make expert systems more useful and usable.

CHAPTER 11
Extending Intelligent Interfaces: Hypertext

One of the key features of intelligent front ends with which we have dealt in this book has been the use of context-sensitive help. It is possible to extend the intelligence of an interface beyond the help level and to provide a "layered" approach to the knowledge contained in an expert system.

In this chapter, we will look at how the concept of hypertext — a method of linking related pieces of information in such a way that the user can traverse a collection of such data as desired — can be used to enhance intelligent front ends. We begin by exploring the idea of hypertext and how it relates to the broader concept of hypermedia. Then, we look at how VP-Expert and KnowledgePro implement hypertext as part of their approach to expert system design.

What Is Hypertext?

The idea of hypertext is not new, though it is enjoying a major resurgence of interest in the computing community. Hypertext as an idea traces back to the early 1950s when a forward-thinking philosopher named Vannevar Bush came up with the idea of linking vast numbers of related pieces of information in a machine that would act as an extension of human memory.

Computer industry visionary Ted Nelson built on that concept and began the process of popularization of the concept of hypertext that is now reaching a crescendo. Nelson pioneered the idea of a global network of deeply interconnected knowledge that he calls Project Xanadu.

While experts and aficionados differ on the details, what all hypertext designers and thinkers can probably agree with is that hypertext is a method of linking together otherwise isolated or unrelated pieces of knowledge. The key idea is that of the link. At Hypertext '87, the first international gathering of people interested in the application of hypertext technology, Professor Dieter Meiser of the University of Saarlands, Saarbrücken, West Germany described two types of links as he explained the structure of hypertext documents: "Hypertext entities of type text are called DOCUMENTS; documents are partitioned into logical units (pages). The links between pages of one document are called INTERNAL REFERENCES, links to other documents are called EXTERNAL REFERENCES."

Some people would prefer to call the logical units into which documents are partitioned chunks rather than using the more traditional (and thus more easily misconstrued) term "pages," but the fundamental idea of internal and external links would ring true. The link points themselves are often referred to as hypertext nodes.

Hypertext documents can be related to one another in interesting and unexpected ways. Links can be circular, interminable, or one directional. There is some debate over whether true hypertext requires the support of bidirectional links (i.e., the ability to traverse a path among numerous hypertext documents and then reverse it at will) or whether simple one-directional links (where one idea builds on another to which you cannot return over the same path) is sufficient. For our purposes, that discussion is of only academic interest, but the idea of bidirectional linking is one we will deal with later in this chapter, so you need to be aware of its role.

Hypertext and Knowledge

The importance of hypertext in the creation, use, and maintenance of knowledge bases derives from two important observations about knowledge.

First, knowledge is layered — beginning with a given topic, you can delve more and more deeply into its background, related subjects, and even tangents almost limitlessly. For example, start a discussion on a topic like the last Super Bowl, for example, and see how quickly the knowledge begins to reveal itself in layers. One person never heard of a Super Bowl and thinks it's a great way to eat soup. Another knows the Super Bowl is a football game, but doesn't know when it is played, why, or who won the last one. The next person in the conversation sat on the 50-yard line at Super Bowl XXIII and watched the San Francisco 49ers make short work of the Cincinnati Bengals. Still another hasn't seen a Super Bowl since Super Bowl IX but can recite the play-by-play of that game as if still on the sidelines. Finally, there's the inveterate sports nut who can tell you the total statistics of every quarterback who ever threw a Super Bowl pass.

Second, all knowledge is ultimately connected to all other knowledge. This deep philosophical thought was put into proper perspective by Nelson, who said it more succinctly: "Everything is deeply intertwingled." (Inventing new words is one of Nelson's hobbies.)

The connectedness of knowledge results in the fact that we can provide users of knowledge-based systems such as our expert systems with richer and more useful information by using hypertext.

Hypertext and Expert Systems

As we have seen in our study of expert systems and their applications to everyday business problems, a user's interaction with an expert system usually takes the form of a dialogue. The system asks the user a question, the user provides some information, the system infers some new knowledge from that information, and goes on to the next question. This process continues until the expert system reaches a conclusion, whether intermediate or final. When it reaches a conclusion, it often presents its findings to the user.

At the dialogue and presentation points of an expert system consultation, hypertext can come into play in one of two ways: to provide context-sensitive help, or to allow the user to explore tangents and byways of knowledge of interest. Each of these uses of hypertext enhances the expert system's ability to provide useful information to the user.

Context-Sensitive Help

Context-sensitive help is most often useful at the point when the user is being asked a question. It may also find a use when conclusions are being presented, but that is not its usual application in an expert system.

Assume that you are building an expert system to allow a user to enter insurance information into a database application. The consultation has reached the place where the system asks the user this question: "Has a complete Form 143B-1 been filed for this applicant?" Most users of the system know what a Form 143B-1 is; they work with them all the time. However, a new person or a temporary worker faced with this question might not be certain about the form.

By making the text "Form 143B-1" a hypertext link, you can provide such a user with additional information. By selecting this text — with a mouse or pointing device or via the keyboard, depending on the implementation — the user can be shown a new piece of information. "The Form 143B-1 is a special physical examination form required of certain classes of applicants. It is light blue in color and is prepared by the agent, then completed by the applicant's physician.

If you answer "No" to this question, you will be asked to have a Form 143B-1 sent to the agent. The forms are kept in the third drawer of Filing Cabinet 18 in the Forms Supply Office."

You can immediately see two advantages to this hypertext approach to context-sensitive help. First, the extended information is not cluttering up the screen for the knowledgeable user who doesn't need it. Second, you can create further hypertext links within the context-sensitive help text. For example, in the above link we could create a hypertext link for the phrase "Forms Supply Office" so that the user who didn't know where that office was located could be given directions, a phone extension, the name of the office manager, or even a map to help clarify the issue.

Knowledge Exploration

When an expert system presents the user with a conclusion it has reached, it may be supplying new information to the user. This new information may trigger a desire to explore other avenues of knowledge. Hypertext links can provide a vehicle by which the user can access those avenues. This use of hypertext is less common in intelligent front ends than it is in other kinds of expert systems applications (see Chapter 13).

Most expert systems, including VP-Expert, incorporate an explanation facility through which the user can ask why or how (i.e., by what inference process) a particular conclusion was reached. This notion of hypertext knowledge exploration goes beyond such one-time queries. It permits the user to indicate a desire to explore some tangential information that may be only obliquely related to the topic at hand.

Assume you are designing an expert system designed to evaluate spreadsheet data to help a finance clerk recommend changes in short-term cash management strategies. When the system makes a recommendation to change from one kind of checking account to another, for example, the user might want to learn more about the decision. Selecting a hypertext node labeled "checking" could lead to some additional information about how checking accounts work. Another node in that knowledge bank could then lead to a discussion of the various types of deposits accepted by banks, and hence to an understanding of how banks work. Figure 11-1 shows the kind of ultimate goal to which such a knowledge trek could lead if Nelson's Xanadu project were functioning so that massive amounts of information was available.

Hypertext in VP-Expert

VP-Expert Version 2 was enhanced to include hypertext concepts. Hypertext in VP-Expert is relatively easy to implement but it is designed so that it lends itself better to knowledge exploration than to context-sensitive help.

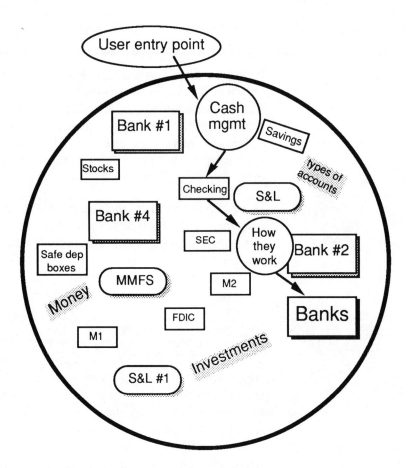

Figure 11-1. Knowledge Exploration in Hypertext

Hypertext in VP-Expert uses external text-only files that follow some basic format rules. These files are read into the computer's memory when the value of a variable changes, and the selected portion of the hypertext file marked by a "hyperword" is displayed. You can define the location and size of the window in which hypertext appears, and the foreground and background colors to be used in that window.

VP-Expert Hypertext File Format

A file to be used by VP-Expert as a hypertext file must follow certain conventions. These are illustrated in Figure 11-2.

```
* HYPERWORD

  up to 23 lines of up to 78 characters

* HYPERWORD

  up to 23 lines of up to 78 characters
```

Figure 11-2. VP-Expert Hypertext File Format

If you want to use a hyperword in a chunk of hypertext but do not want that occurrence of the hyperword to act as a link, you simply precede the word in the text file with a vertical bar (I) and VP-Expert will treat it as ordinary text.

Note that although VP-Expert permits up to 23 lines of text, each of which can be up to 78 characters long, you are responsible for formatting the text in such a way that it fits within the window you define with the call to the hypertext function. VP-Expert does not automatically word-wrap and reformat text to match the window.

A VP-Expert hypertext file can be any size and can include up to 2,000 different hyperwords.

The HYPERTEXT Statement

Figure 11-3 shows the syntax of the HYPERTEXT statement in VP-Expert. Such a statement will only execute when the variable that appears as its first parameter is assigned a value matching a hyperword in the text file.

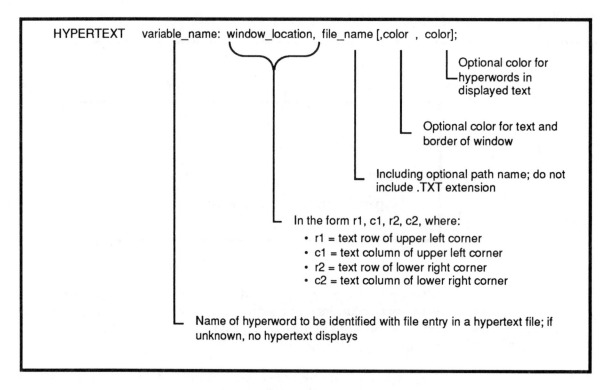

Figure 11-3. Format of VP-Expert HYPERTEXT Statement

The HYPERTEXT statement must be executed while VP-Expert is in a graphics mode. Only one hypertext window can be displayed at a time. If the user selects a hyperword in an open hypertext window, that window is removed and the newly selected one is opened and its contents displayed. For example, you could place the following statement in the ACTIONS block of your knowledge base:

```
HYPERTEXT Checking: 5,5,20,65,Banking,5,8;
```

When it encounters this command, VP-Expert will set up its internal routines so that when the value of the variable Checking changes to correspond to a hyperword contained in the file BANKING.TXT, the hypertext function will execute. When the value of the variable Checking does change to that of a hyperword in the file, a window with magenta text and border (color 5) and gray (color 8) hyperwords will appear on the screen. This window will be 15 rows deep (from row 5 to row 20) and 60 columns wide (from column 5 to column 65).

The LBUTTON Statement

Your program must provide a way to dismiss the hypertext from the screen when the user is done reading it. There are a number of strategies for doing so; we will concentrate on the easiest and most likely approach in our discussion.

Since hypertext only works in a graphic mode, you can use a graphic "button" to give the user a way of dismissing the hypertext when he is through reading it. The easiest command to create such a button is the LBUTTON (the "L" stands for "label") statement whose syntax is shown in Figure 11-4.

The value of the boolean variable that is the first argument to LBUTTON toggles between Yes and No as the user presses the mouse with the pointer positioned over the button.

As the value changes, the background color of the button toggles between the two values describing the colors. The LBUTTON statement usually appears in the ACTIONS block in close proximity to the HYPERTEXT (or other) statement whose actions it is designed to affect. Such an LBUTTON statement might look like this:

```
LBUTTON Exit: 40,2,4,14,CANCEL;
```

When VP-Expert encounters this statement and enters a graphics mode, it will display a rectangular button beginning at column 40 of row 2 of the display. The button will be red if the value of the variable Exit is No, light yellow if it is Yes.

The button will consist of the word CANCEL surrounded by a rectangular border sized to fit the label.

Generally, the variable used in an LBUTTON statement is used in a WHENEVER rule so that when its value changes, the WHENEVER rule fires and causes the value of the variable associated with the HYPERTEXT statement to be set to UNKNOWN. When that happens, VP-Expert takes the hypertext window off the screen. For example, you could include the following WHENEVER rule in your knowledge base to handle dismissal of the hypertext window:

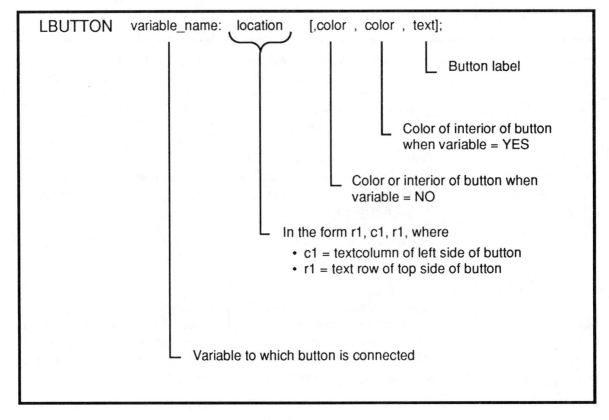

LBUTTON   variable_name: location   [,color , color , text];

- Button label
- Color of interior of button when variable = YES
- Color or interior of button when variable = NO
- In the form r1, c1, r1, where
  - c1 = textcolumn of left side of button
  - r1 = text row of top side of button
- Variable to which button is connected

Figure 11-4. Syntax of VP-Expert LBUTTON Statement

```
WHENEVER 1
IF Exit=Yes
THEN RESET Checking;
```

This, combined with the previous LBUTTON and HYPERTEXT rules and other related logic leads to a skeletal HYPERTEXT routine that looks like that shown in Listing 11-1.

Listing 11-1

```
ACTIONS
        ***
        GMODE 14
        Exit = No
        Checking = OK
        WHILETRUE Exit = No THEN END
        TMODE;
        ***
```

```
HYPERTEXT Checking: 5,5,20,65,Banking,5,8;
LBUTTON Exit: 40,2,4,14,CANCEL;
***
WHENEVER 1
If Exit=Yes
THEN RESET Checking;
```

The rules portion of the knowledge base would then include one or more rules that would give the variable Checking a value corresponding to a hyperword in the file BANKING.TXT. At the point when that variable assignment occurred, a hypertext window would appear and the appropriate text would be shown. At the top of the screen, nearly in the center, a button labeled CANCEL would be shown. When the user presses this button with the mouse pointer, the value of Checking will be set to UNKNOWN by the RESET command. That causes VP-Expert to remove the hypertext window from the screen and return to text mode.

(There would be some condition that would cause the system to go into graphics mode 14 in the first place, of course. This could be a special circumstance that triggered the hypertext need or it could be the mode in which the system is designed to run, using "hot graphics" as described in Chapter 12.)

Hypertext in KnowledgePro

KnowledgePro from Knowledge Garden, Inc. (see Appendix B for a full description of this product) is inherently hypertext oriented. As a result, its integration of hypertext is far more seamless than that of VP-Expert. Hypertext can easily be used both for context-sensitive help and for knowledge exploration from conclusion screens.

In KnowledgePro, hypertext can be embedded directly into the program code, including both questions posed to the user via the ASK command and screen outputs using any of several commands. It can also be stored in an external file and read into the knowledge base dynamically.

We examined the basic structure, flow and approach to a KnowledgePro knowledge base in Chapter 8. If you did not work through that chapter, it might be a good idea to read it before you attempt to understand the following discussion.

Marking Hypertext in KnowledgePro

Any text appearing between two hypertext-marking characters in a KnowledgePro knowledge base will act as hypertext without any further programming effort on your part. The special hypertext marking characters are "#m". When you mark hypertext in a KnowledgePro knowledge base, it will appear highlighted on the user's display. The user can then select the hypertext either with a mouse or by using the F3 and F4 keys to select and view the appropriate topic.

When the user does select a hypertext node in KnowledgePro, the system executes a topic with the same name as the text. If no topic with a corresponding name can be found, KnowledgePro looks for a topic named "mark" and passes the hypertext node name to that topic as a parameter. This allows you to create very general-purpose hypertext management topics and to deal with the dynamic definition and use of hypertext in KnowledgePro knowledge bases.

Here is a sample of how hypertext can be marked in a question being posed as part of a KnowledgePro expert system:

```
ask('Has a complete #mForm 143B-1#m been filed
for this applicant?',response,[Yes,No]).
```

When KnowledgePro executes this ASK command, it poses the question, highlighting the text phrase "Form 143B-1" and displays a pop-up menu with the two choices, Yes and No. If the user clicks on or selects the hypertext phrase, KnowledgePro looks for a topic called "Form 143B-1" and, if it finds one, executes it. Listing 11-2 shows how such a topic might be programmed.

Listing 11-2

```
topic 'Form 143B-1'.
window().
say('The Form 143B-1 is a special physical
examination form required of certain classes of
applicants.  It is light blue in color and is prepared
```

```
by the agent, then completed by the applicant's
physician.  If you answer No to this question, you will
be asked to have a Form 143B-1 sent to the agent.  The
forms are kept in the third drawer of Filing Cabinet 18
in the #mForms Supply Office#m.').
    close_window().
    end.
```

Notice that the SAY clause in Listing 11-2 contains another hypertext phrase, "Forms Supply Office." Assume that there's a text file called OFFICES.TXT where directions to various offices in the building are stored. Further assume that the knowledge base includes numerous references to hypertext nodes stored in that file. Rather than programming individual KnowledgePro topics for each office name, you could use the special MARK topic as shown in Listing 11-3.

Listing 11-3

```
topic mark (find_string).
text is READ ('OFFICES.TXT', ?find_string, '/end').
window().
say (?text).
close_window().
end.
```

The READ command opens the file OFFICES.TXT and searches until it locates the find_string parameter passed by the hypertext call, in this case, "Forms Supply Office." It then reads that text until it reaches the text "/end," which we have (arbitrarily) decided to use as the marker indicating the end of one office instruction and the beginning of the next. All of this text is placed into the variable text, which is then displayed in a special window.

Summary

In this chapter, we have looked at how hypertext can be used to extend the intelligence and usefulness of expert systems. We have seen that hypertext is a relatively old idea that is enjoying a resurgence today. We have learned that hypertext revolves around the idea of links connecting various kinds of information. And we have seen how two expert system tools — VP-Expert and KnowledgePro — implement and manage hypertext.

Chapter 12 focuses on using interactive graphics — which many people see as extending the hypertext concept — in expert systems.

CHAPTER 12
Extending Intelligent Interfaces: Hot Graphics

Modern computer systems are becoming increasingly more graphic in their interface design. Building on the success of Apple's Macintosh among users, other major hardware and software publishers and manufacturers, including IBM and Microsoft, have begun moving toward creating such interfaces for their systems.

Interfaces that do not incorporate graphics, or at least the ability to include graphics if desired, will undoubtedly be viewed with decreasing favor in the months and years ahead.

Expert systems have been slow to move into this arena. However, at least three of the tools with which we are working in this book provide the ability to create interactive, or "hot," graphics as part of their interface design.

As their name implies, these graphics are images through which the user can interact with the system, that is, enter data and provide information. VP-Expert Version 2, KnowledgePro, and Personal Consultant Plus all provide this ability, although KnowledgePro and Personal Consultant require the purchase of add-on packages.

What Are Hot Graphics?

In some ways, hot graphics are extensions of the ideas of hypertext discussed in Chapter 11. If we can link textual information with strategies that result in hypertext, the thought goes, why can't we also link text to graphic images and vice versa, creating the kernel of an extended idea called hypermedia?

A hot graphic image is contrasted with a static image, which is designed only for aesthetic purposes or to focus the user's attention or assist the user in identifying a response. Hot images accept input from the user if they are active input images, and convey changing information graphically if they are output images.

This difference is depicted in Figures 12-1 and 12-2. In Figure 12-1, the user is presented with several shapes and asked to select the one that corresponds to the object being looked at by typing the number of the shape. In Figure 12-2, however, the user is asked to click directly on the shape that corresponds to the object.

An interactive graphic usually includes more than one area which will respond to the user's input. These areas are called "hot regions" because they are dynamically linked to objects in the system. Most hot regions change the value of a fact or variable, though in some systems it is possible to define a hot region so that it has a more tangible effect. One such effect is the display of another graphic.

Comparing Interactive Graphics

Expert system shells that include interactive graphics or offer add-on toolkits that enable you to use them differ from one another in at least four important respects:

- The source or type of images that the system can import

- The process of defining the hot regions

- The availability of predefined graphic images or shapes

- The kinds of actions that can be triggered by the user

Source or Type of Image

VP-Expert does not allow you to import pictures from other graphics or drawing packages for use in the expert system. Graphic images

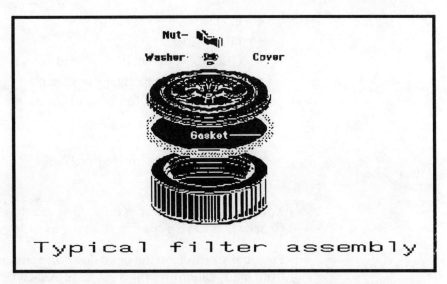

Figure 12-1. Static Graphic Image for User Information

used in a VP-Expert system must be one of two types: a predefined active image (see the following discussion) or an image drawn using one of VP-Expert's built-in drawing commands. These commands include:

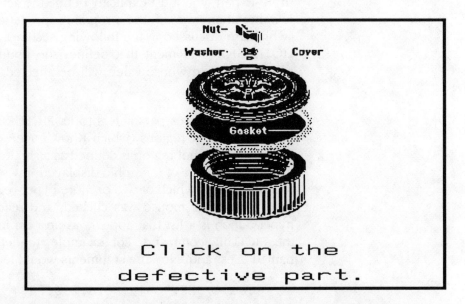

Figure 12-2. Dynamic Graphic Image for User Interaction

- ELLLIPSE
- FILL
- GBCOLOR (to set background color)
- GCLS (to clear the graphic screen)
- GCOLOR (to set foreground color)
- LINETO
- MOVETO
- PSET (to draw a single pixel)
- RECTANGLE

KnowledgePro supports only files created using PC Paintbrush (whose files have a specific format and a file extension of .PCX).

Personal Consultant Images allows the importation of graphic files from many other programs via its SNAPSHOT utility. However, these images can not be made active. Instead, they provide a graphic backdrop for active images created within PC Images.

Defining Hot Regions

In VP-Expert, you must explicitly define the active region of a graphic other than one of the program's predefined dynamic images (which are discussed in the following section). You do this with the HOTREGION statement that defines the boundaries of the region and the variable whose value will be affected by the user selecting that region.

KnowledgePro uses parameters to its PICTURE command to define one or more hot regions (which KnowledgePro refers to as "hyper-regions"). Each hot region is defined as a single point. When the user clicks on any part of a graphic displayed in KnowledgePro, the system determines which of two or more hyper-regions is nearest to the point where the mouse was clicked, and reacts accordingly. Each hyper-region is a list that appears as an item in the argument list to the PICTURE command. For example, to define two hot regions named "Yes" and "No," the arguments would look like this:

```
[Yes,T,528,105],[No,G,296,238]
```

The first argument in each list names the region. The second is a "T" if activation of the hyper-region should result in a text screen being displayed, "G" if it should bring up another graphic screen. The last two arguments are the x-y (column-row) address of the point.

PC Images does not allow you to define hot regions. Instead, it supplies a range of built-in dynamic images (see following section) which can be overlayed on a more traditional graphic design. Because PC Images and Personal Consultant Plus do not provide built-in mouse support, manipulation of graphic images is via arrow keys on the keyboard.

Built-In Images

KnowledgePro does not supply any prebuilt graphic images with predefined hot regions with which you can work with single-command approaches. All graphics must be built externally to KnowledgePro and then used with hot regions as described in the preceding section.

Both VP-Expert and PC Images have several kinds of built-in active graphic images. These features make these systems quite powerful where the ability for the user to enter data using one of these direct-manipulation approaches is important.

VP-Expert defines the following types of dynamic images:

- BUTTON (two types, labeled and unlabeled)

- HGAUGE (horizontal slide gauge)

- METER (semicircular dial)

- VGAUGE (vertical slide gauge)

- TRACK (read-only time-series graph to monitor a variable)

Defining any of these types of dynamic images is straightforward. For example, to display a vertical gauge designed to ask the user for the temperature of an object, you could write a command like this:

```
VGAUGE Temperature: 30,30,-20,120;
```

Once such an image is defined, the user can manipulate the gauge directly with the mouse, dragging its active portion to change the value of the underlying variable.

PC Images predefines the following wide range of dynamic images:

- DIAL (circular gauge)

- DIGITAL DISPLAY PANEL (similar to a digital clock)

- DISPLAY PANEL (shows text or numbers)

- HORIZONTAL BAR GRAPH

- HORIZONTAL SELECTION BOX (two or more mutually exclusive values in a single unit)

- SEMICIRCULAR DIAL

- THERMOMETER

- VERTICAL BAR GRAPH

- VERTICAL SELECTION BOX

These images can be displayed in color with or without borders, labeled in various ways, and otherwise modified.

Actions to Be Taken

The user's interaction with dynamic graphic images in PC Images and VP-Expert can only modify the value of a variable. In fact, each image is defined so that it is related specifically to a variable. Of course, the changing of a variable's value is often the trigger event for a rule to fire, and rules can be designed so that their entire purpose is to take such actions as display another graphic or open a database.

In KnowledgePro, each hot region is tied directly to a topic. Since, as we have seen (Chapter 8) a topic in KnowledgePro can be any of several kinds of object, there is practically no limit to the kinds of actions that can be directly triggered by a user's interaction with a hot graphic in KnowledgePro.

Uses of Interactive Graphics

Hot graphics have a wide range of possible uses in expert systems. Some of the more interesting are:

- To enter numeric values without typing. Temperatures, pressures, values of stocks, and other numberic values can be created as dynamic images (particularly in VP-Expert and PC Images). To indicate the value of such a variable in response to a question, the user simply moves the image's indicator (needle, horizontal or vertical bar, etc.).

- To create graphic menus. A menu from which the user can select an option for the consultation can be created as a graphic image with hot regions. The activation of a region is then translated into the user's instruction to perform a specific action.

- To provide a point-and-click method of pinpointing problems in diagnostic systems. Display a picture of the copier and ask the user to click on the part that's causing the problem. The system can then explode the view to get more specific or provide the user with information or advice on how to repair the part, how to remove it for replacement, and so forth.

- To create "intelligent forms" for data entry. As we have seen in this book, most expert systems interact with the user through a dialogic process: the system asks a question, the user responds. However, it may be more convenient in some cases to ask the user to supply some basic information before the consultation begins. Using some of the graphic images in PC Images and VP-Expert, you can easily construct full-screen forms that the user simply completes. This form of interaction with expert systems has been gaining favor in recent months.

Summary

This brief chapter has introduced you to the idea of using hot, or interactive, graphics to convey and accept information between the system and the user. You have seen that this concept is to some degree an extension of the use of hypertext discussed in Chapter 11. You have seen how the approaches taken by three different expert system tools — VP-Expert Version 2, KnowledgePro, and PC Images for Personal Consultant Plus — vary from one another.

This concludes our discussion of intelligent front ends for business applications. Chapter 13 turns its attention briefly to other possible uses of expert systems in everyday business settings to point out that intelligent front ends are but one part of a potentially huge impact AI technology can have on the way we use business computers.

CHAPTER 13
Intelligent Back Ends

This concluding chapter takes a brief look at another possible use for combinations of expert systems with spreadsheets and databases. While the focus of this book has been on using expert systems to create intelligent front ends for such applications, there are dozens of other possible uses for the technology. Most of these other uses can be grouped under the heading of intelligent "back" ends.

What's a "Back End"?

As we have seen in this book, an intelligent front end is an expert system used to assist the user in getting information into a worksheet or a database file. It is thus concerned with the data entry process.

By contrast, an intelligent back end is concerned with using the data that has already been entered into a worksheet or database file.

Any process, whether it is a spreadsheet application or a manufacturing line, has three major components. These are:

- Front end or interface portion, where interaction with the user or other parts of the system take place

- Processing module, where the "black box" actions — largely transparent to the user and to the other components of the system — take place

- Back end, where delivery of the finished product takes place

In the case of a business application created using a spreadsheet or a database, this back end is typically one or more reports that present the information in the file in some useful or interesting way. Such reports are capable of performing calculations, even very complex ones, and of formatting their contents in such a way that they are easy to read and understand. However, such back-end reports are not generally capable of providing new insights into the information on which they are based.

What's an Intelligent Back End?

This is where intelligence can be added to back ends of such systems to the benefit of the business. An expert system can be designed so that it looks at the information in the system, draws some conclusions, and makes some recommendations based on the information.

Such recommendations need not be particularly startling or insightful to be useful. Quite often, these recommendations are mere applications of company policies to information stored in spreadsheet and database files.

Intelligent back ends can be used to assist a business in such worksheet and database-oriented tasks as data analysis and pattern recognition. These uses in turn can lead to expert systems playing a major role in the support of management decision-making, long-term planning, and other tasks for which spreadsheets and databases alone are inadequate.

Some specific examples of how such systems might be used will be presented later in the chapter. First, let's look briefly at each of these types of systems and how they relate to the availability and implementation of expert systems technology.

Analyzing Data

Reports generated by spreadsheet programs and database applications typically produce formatted listings of raw data, possibly including some calculations.

A manager looking at such data performs analysis. "What is the real meaning of the numbers?" is the question he is asking as he reviews the reports. If accounts receivable are up over last quarter by some substantial percentage and at the same time current orders are lagging behind, he may probe further to determine if customers have stockpiled the product. Spotting such a trend or problem in data analysis can be an important part of the role of data in managing a business.

An expert system can be designed to retrieve information stored in a worksheet or a database file, perform calculations on it and then compare the results against a set of rules that are designed to spot trends and potential problems.

Pattern Recognition

Buried in the mounds of data that are stored in any company's worksheets and database files are hidden patterns. Some of these patterns are incidental and insignificant. However, others can provide early warnings of a need to change business strategies or policies, identify major problems before they impact the company's financial health, and otherwise assist in decision making.

These patterns are difficult to see, no matter how many different ways you look at the data. This is because the individual pieces of data — which are probably myriad — are not stored consecutively or grouped logically by the kinds of criteria that lead to important patterns.

Analyzing the data with a set of rules designed to ferret out patterns of data combinations that always or frequently have certain results can make business planning easier. Pattern-recognition systems can help businesses answer such questions as:

- "What kinds of customers always go through the final step of the selling process and then decide not to buy?"

- "Are there any relationships between major insurance claims we experience and any other aspect of the claimants' applications, locations, occupations, or other factors?"

Applying Intelligent Back Ends

There are as many ways of putting intelligent back ends to work as there are decisions that have to be made every day where data is a major factor. A few examples will suffice to show the breadth of potential application of this expert system approach to business data management and utilization.

Example One: Debt Collection Practices

Your company keeps its accounts receivable information in a database file. This file contains information about each customer's current and historical sales, order, and payment activity as well as current order and invoice status. Each month, the accounting department runs a report from the database showing the aged accounts receivable. This report is sent to the president, who alone knows the accounts well enough to decide what kind of collection action should be applied to the accounts.

As the company grows, the president is spending more and more time on what is essentially a fairly routine task. The president is able to articulate to some degree at least the basis for his decisions made each month. A good customer who has been dealing with the firm a long time is not a good candidate for a nasty collection letter when their account is 90 days past due. Instead, a routine invoice with a hand-written note from the president will usually result in payment. However, a customer who has been dealing with the company for several years but whose payment record is poor may be best shifted into collection-letter status.

By working with the president to refine some rules, it should be possible to write an expert system that would go through the database each month, examine the status of accounts, and apply its heuristic rules to the decision making. The system could recommend to a clerk that certain actions be taken. The president might then only spot-check findings, or deal with certain flagged accounts.

Over time and with more experience with the system, it could be refined so that the president could develop enough confidence in its ability to deal with such problems that he could largely remove himself from the task.

Example Two: Checkbook Management

Your company operates with a reasonably large amount of cash flow. It maintains several bank accounts, some checking and some savings, in Metro City Bank. There is no particular pattern to how it decides what funds to place in each kind of account at the moment.

The bank has set up several categories of checking and savings accounts. Each has its own requirements: minimum balances, service charge limits and levels, minimum and maximum monthly transaction levels, and so forth. And each pays different interest if you abide by its rules. You'd like to maximize your company's return on cash in the bank but to do so would require you to spend a huge amount of time analyzing each account and its transactions each month.

In its policies, the bank has given you the basic rules for account management. The task of converting those rules into a rule base that will work with your account information stored in a spreadsheet (probably) would be a fairly straightforward assignment.

Set up an expert system that the accounting clerk can run each month. If the information is all stored in files, it need not even ask the clerk a single question. It just looks at the data, analyzes it, and proposes changes in your current cash management strategy that will return maximum interest on your money without crippling your liquidity. The value of such a system is easy to see.

Risk Analysis

Your company, an insurance provider, depends on the accuracy of its assessment of the degree of risk it assumes in underwriting a policy. Actuarial tables and other standard industry tools can provide a basis for such decisions, but the difference between a highly profitable company and a less than attractive one often lies in the use to which such data is put.

Three of your firm's top underwriters spend more than half of their time reviewing the records of claims filed against the company to see if they can spot patterns of fraud, abuse, unexpected risk or other problems that could potentially affect the company's ability to stay in business. If their time could be spent on real underwriting work, the company could write 10 percent more coverage every year.

These three underwriters can describe at least to some degree how they determine what kinds of claims to investigate deeply and which apparent anomalies have valid explanations. They are typically examining information stored in the company's database.

By designing an expert system to examine the database and compare findings against the rules developed in conjunction with these expert underwriters, your firm can increase its business and profitability. It may also be able to do an even better job of this assessment than the human experts alone could do. The computer can analyze far more data in a short time than can a human being. As a result, the program can look through more data for more kinds of patterns and spot problems sooner.

Vendor Monitoring

Your company manufactures complex systems. A major part of these systems consists of components supplied by other manufacturers. Your company integrates their parts with several that it manufactures to create the final product.

When these systems fail, troubleshooting and repair costs are extremely high. Reliability is critical, so your customers rely on you supplying them with systems that will work well under a variety of circumstances. Your company, in turn, depends heavily on its vendors for quality parts. Several of the components you use come from different vendors.

The company maintains a database that records for each system built some basic information about the component parts of which it was assembled.

When a customer returns a defective part, your company would like to be able to see if the problem is with a particular company's product, a specific batch or run of a particular product, or some other isolatable element. If such a determination can be made, other customers whose systems have potential flaws can be field-upgraded to prevent a problem from arising.

It would be straightforward to design an expert system that could look at a collection of failed systems, identify common parts and vendors, use some rules to determine if these faults were important and potentially serious enough to warrant action, and then analyze other past and current manufacturing plans to warn the company.

Designing Intelligent Back Ends

This book does not discuss designing intelligent back ends primarily because they are, as you can see from the above examples, more context-dependent than front ends.

In many ways, intelligent back ends can be seen as traditional expert systems that derive much of their data from databases and worksheets. The same design principles that apply to diagnostic and other major categories of expert systems (see Chapters 2 and 3 for some discussion of these topics) can be brought to bear on the design of intelligent back ends.

Summary

This chapter concludes our discussion of expert systems. We have looked briefly at other methods spreadsheets, databases, and expert systems that might be able to work together. In particular, we looked at back ends — expert systems that analyze information stored in databases and spreadsheets and give user advice about policy and other decisions to make — and provided two examples of its use.

APPENDIX A
Induction of Rules from Spreadsheets and Databases

While the primary focus of this book has been on designing intelligent interfaces between users and their spreadsheet and database applications, there is another way these widely used business applications and expert systems can work together. Many expert system tools, including VP-Expert and Knowledge Maker (a KnowledgePro-based system from Knowledge Garden, Inc.), permit *induction* of rules from the contents of spreadsheet and database files.

This appendix deals briefly with such induction approaches to rule set construction. You should note that the discussion is neither exhaustive nor tutorial. It is, rather, a treatment of the subject so that if it is a technique you might find useful in your work with spreadsheets and databases via expert systems technology, you will know that it exists and be able to assess its possible importance.

What Is Induction?

Beginning with a worksheet file, database, or properly formatted text file, VP-Expert can create a set of rules that describe that worksheet, provided that the worksheet meets certain criteria. Those rules are then available for you to edit, add to, combine, and otherwise manipulate in the VP-Expert editor or in your favorite word processor.

Induction is reasoning from example. In human terms, you can think of it as an apprentice approach to learning, where rules are more of a tutorial approach. If you were living a few centuries ago, you might have become an apprentice to a craftsman of some sort. You would learn his trade by watching what he did and perhaps listening to him explain. "Now, when I get into a situation where I need one of these kinds of cuts," he might say as he worked, "I use this tool over here and I angle it just so and...." In your mind, you would be storing this and hundreds or thousands of other pieces of information in an expanding network of knowledge about the skill.

In expert systems terms, induction is the process of examining a table of factors, values, and outcomes, and moving from that information to a rule or set of rules that describe the data. Each individual collection of factors, values, and outcome can be thought of as an example. The accumulation of several related examples into a table produces information from which an inductive process can derive a rule set that defines the behavior described in the examples.

Some expert system shells — notably Fusion (see Appendix B) — specialize in induction. It is their primary means of building and maintaining rule sets. Others, like VP-Expert and KnowledgePro (also Appendix B), have an induction capability built in (e.g., VP Expert) or available as an add-on function (e.g., KnowledgePro).

Induction has some interesting advantages over the normal process of building rules by typing and editing. In some situations, it is a better approach to the initial design, at least, of an expert system. Induction is most useful in situations where the knowledge to be reduced to a set of rules is not now in rule form, even in someone's mind, but is instead in the form of a collection of historical data. For example, an insurance company might have a large number of files containing information about policyholders that would be able to tell them the relationships among certain policyholder traits such as age, region of residence, type of occupation, and other factors, and the claims experience on their policies. The company might not even know or be able to easily determine what rules ought to be involved in an expert system that builds on that experience base. However, an inductive system could well be designed to give them at least a start in the direction of codifying that experience into usable rules.

This example-based approach leads to another advantage of induction: it sometimes provides insight into the knowledge and patterns contained in the knowledge that would escape even an expert. In this sense, an inductive expert system tool can act as an analyst, examining the data and essentially proposing ways the various pieces relate to one another.

The process of induction uses some kind of algorithm to massage the data into rules. There are several in popular use, but the most important and widely used is the so-called ID3 algorithm. It is the one used, for example, by Fusion.

Induction in VP-Expert

To understand how induction works in VP-Expert, we'll look at a small example. This example uses an induction table, a text file that follows some basic format guidelines:

- Its top line must be a list of factors involved in the decision

- The rightmost column in the table is the goal variable, or outcome, of the example described in the row

- Each row must end with a carriage return

- There must be no blank lines in the table

Table A-1 shows the induction table.

Table A-1. The Induction Table

Job_Type	Rating	Bonus_Last_Year	Bonus
Sales	Excellent	No	Yes
Sales	Excellent	Yes	Yes
Sales	Good	No	No
Sales	Good	Yes	Yes
Sales	Fair	Yes	No
Sales	Fair	No	No
Manager	Excellent	Yes	Yes
Manager	Excellent	No	Yes
Manager	Good	No	No
Manager	Good	Yes	No
Manager	Fair	Yes	No
Manager	Fair	No	No

Obviously, from looking at the table, we are working with some knowledge regarding bonus decision making. These are some examples of people who have a job type, a current performance rating, and about whom we know whether they earned a bonus last year or not. The final column tells us the decision that was made in each case regarding a bonus for this year.

When we run this table through VP-Expert's induction capability, we get a knowledge base shown in Listing A-1.

Listing A-1

```
ACTIONS
        FIND Bonus;


RULE 0
IF      Job_Type=Sales AND
        Rating=Excellent AND
        Bonus_Last_Year=No
THEN    Bonus=Yes;

RULE 1
IF      Job_Type=Sales AND
        Rating=Excellent AND
        Bonus_Last_Year=Yes
THEN    Bonus=Yes;

RULE 2
IF      Job_Type=Sales AND
        Rating=Good AND
        Bonus_Last_Year=No
THEN    Bonus=No;

RULE 3
IF      Job_Type=Sales AND
        Rating=Good AND
        Bonus_Last_Year=Yes
THEN    Bonus=Yes;

RULE 4
IF      Job_Type=Sales AND
        Rating=Fair AND
        Bonus_Last_Year=Yes
THEN    Bonus=No;

RULE 5
IF      Job_Type=Sales AND
        Rating=Fair AND
        Bonus_Last_Year=No
THEN    Bonus=No;
```

```
RULE 6
IF      Job_Type=Manager AND
        Rating=Excellent AND
        Bonus_Last_Year=Yes
THEN    Bonus=Yes;

RULE 7
IF      Job_Type=Manager AND
        Rating=Excellent AND
        Bonus_Last_Year=No
THEN    Bonus=Yes;

RULE 8
IF      Job_Type=Manager AND
        Rating=Good AND
        Bonus_Last_Year=No
THEN    Bonus=No;

RULE 9
IF      Job_Type=Manager AND
        Rating=Good AND
        Bonus_Last_Year=Yes
THEN    Bonus=No;

RULE 10
IF      Job_Type=Manager AND
        Rating=Fair AND
        Bonus_Last_Year=Yes
THEN    Bonus=No;

RULE 11
IF      Job_Type=Manager AND
        Rating=Fair AND
        Bonus_Last_Year=No
THEN    Bonus=No;

ASK Job_Type: "What is the value of Job_Type?";
CHOICES  Job_Type: Sales,Manager;

ASK Rating: "What is the value of Rating?";
CHOICES Rating: Excellent,Good,Fair;

ASK Bonus_Last_Year: "What is the value of
Bonus_Last_Year?";
CHOICES Bonus_Last_Year: No,Yes;
```

As you can see, VP-Expert has given us a very good start on a rule base, even creating the appropriate FIND statement in the ACTIONS block and all of the questions and choice lists for the variables it needs to know to reach a conclusion. We could now go into the editor and make the questions more meaningful, add a DISPLAY command to the ACTIONS block to show the user the outcome of the consultation, and other things to make the knowledge base more aesthetically pleasing. But it will run exactly as it is provided to us by VP-Expert.

(You may have noted, however, that the rules the knowledge base created for us aren't particularly "smart." For example, it creates separate no-bonus rules for a salesperson with a Fair rating, whether or not a bonus had been awarded last year. It would obviously be more efficient for the system rule to be more like Listing A-2. As we'll see shortly, a tool like Fusion that is "designed" for inductive reasoning does a far better job of optimizing rules than VP-Expert, which really uses induction as a way to get us started on a knowledge base where we have a collection of examples and no idea where to begin constructing a rule base.)

Listing A-2

```
RULE   fair_salesperson
IF     Job_Type=Sales
AND    Rating=Fair
THEN   Bonus=No;
```

In fact, VP-Expert has one other induction table capability worth mentioning that can greatly streamline the inductive process. It requires you to know something about the patterns in your data. However, if you know, for example, that any employee, regardless of job classification, with a Fair performance rating, is not going to earn a bonus whether earned last year or not, you can create an example with "don't care" elements in appropriate places. An asterisk is used in a VP-Expert induction table to mean that we don't care what value is in that column for this example set.

Using that approach, our earlier decision table would become more compact, as Table A-2 indicates.

When this table is used to induce a new rule set by VP-Expert, the rule set shown in Listing A-3 results.

Table A-2. Compact Induction Table

Job_Type	Rating	Bonus_Last_Year	Bonus
*	Excellent	*	Yes
Sales	Good	Yes	Yes
Sales	Good	No	No
*	Fair	*	No
Manager	Good	*	No

Listing A-3

```
ACTIONS
      FIND Bonus;

RULE 0
IF     Rating=Excellent
THEN   Bonus=Yes;

RULE 1
IF     Job_Type=Sales AND
       Rating=Good AND
       Bonus_Last_Year=Yes
THEN   Bonus=Yes;

RULE 2
IF     Job_Type=Sales AND
       Rating=Good AND
       Bonus_Last_Year=No
THEN   Bonus=No;

RULE 3
IF     Rating=Fair
THEN   Bonus=No;

RULE 4
IF     Job_Type=Manager AND
       Rating=Good
THEN   Bonus=No;

ASK Job_Type: "What is the value of Job_Type?";
CHOICES Job_Type: Sales,Manager;

ASK Rating: "What is the value of Rating?";
CHOICES Rating: Excellent,Good,Fair;

ASK Bonus_Last_Year: "What is the value of
Bonus_Last_Year?";
CHOICES Bonus_Last_Year: Yes,No;
```

Obviously, by the time you got to the point where you could define the induction table well enough to create this more efficient rule base, you would have been able to discern the rules without the aid of an expert system. Still, it would save you the time to edit the rules.

In a larger application setting, with far more examples, you would probably not have seen the rule pattern even if you could do some consolidation of factors like that shown above.

Thus far, this may seem to have little to do with the subject of this book, however, VP-Expert extends induction a step farther than we have described by allowing you to use a worksheet or database file as an induction table.

Therefore, your business applications can not only benefit from the application of expert system technology, they can participate in the process of creating such a system.

To be used as an induction table by VP-Expert, worksheet and database files must meet certain format requirements. A database file is typically usable in the form in which it is stored by dBASE III Plus or VP-Info, though you will usually have to modify its content somewhat to remove irrelevant factors and add a decision or conclusion field unless one already exists.

A worksheet file must have:

- A blank row under the column headings

- No blank columns

- No blank rows above or to the left of the table to be used for induction

You can see now how the induction table we used in our example knowledge base above could have been extracted from a worksheet file. The worksheet file might have contained a good deal of other data about the employee (e.g., name, ID, date of hire, address, department) that was irrelevant to the decision-making process here. Using VP-Planner or Lotus 1-2-3, the user could simply choose the relevant columns of the larger worksheet and put them into their own worksheet in the proper format for a VP-Expert induction table.

Optimized Induction in Fusion

As we said earlier, VP-Expert does not claim to have a terribly powerful or usable induction capability. Rather, it provides you with a convenient way to start building a knowledge base under the right circumstances.

Fusion, an expert system tool from 1st-Class Expert Systems, Inc. (see Appendix B for contact information), is centered on the inductive process, and includes a rule editor only for situations where induction is not an appropriate solution. Fusion does not rely on external induction tables for its processing, however. Instead, you build your expert system as a decision table completely within the Fusion environment. You define the factors involved, the values those factors can have, and the outcomes of each combination. Fusion then creates a decision tree and a rule base that you can then edit.

Just so you can see how much more effective a tool dedicated to such an approach could be, Listing A-4 shows the rule set induced by Fusion from the first listing of factors above. (Fusion, too, lets you put "don't care" values into columns of factors. It also uses the asterisk to mean "don't care." However, we wanted to show you the worst-case scenario here, so we chose the more normal situation, that is, that in which the user doesn't have a clue what pattern might emerge or what factors might be subject to combination or elimination. With Fusion, you can even include irrelevant factors in the table and the program will eliminate those factors from consideration when the user consults with the knowledge base. You can force Fusion to leave those factors in, but left to its own devices, it will eliminate them from consideration.)

Listing A-4

```
1:    Rating??
2:          Excellent:---------------------- Yes
3:          Good:BonusLastYr??
4:               Yes:JobType??
5:                    Sales:--------------- Yes
6:                    Manager:------------- No
7:               No:--------------------- No
8:          Fair:----------------------- No
```

This listing is, of course, in different format than we're used to seeing with VP-Expert. Fusion approaches the rule-construction process radically differently from the way VP-Expert does. Still, Listing A-4 is quite readable. If you look closely, you can see that it does an interesting thing that we haven't seen VP-Expert do (because it can't): it prioritizes the factors in the knowledge base in decreasing order of focus. As it analyzed our examples, it concluded that the most important filtering factor is the employee's current rating. If that rating is Excellent, the employee gets a bonus regardless of job type or whether one was received last year. If it's fair, no bonus is given again without regard to the other factors. Only if the rating is Good does the system need to undertake further exploration.

When you run a consultation (which Fusion calls the Advisor) with this rule, the system actually asks the rating question first. If you give the employee a rating of Excellent, the system does not ask the other questions, instead moving right to the conclusion.

There are pros and cons to this optimized approach. Fusion, in fact, permits you to choose other methods of rule induction which do not perform this optimization in the event you want the user to be asked all of the questions regardless of the answer. (You might, for example, want to store those answers for use elsewhere, or you may just want to be sure the user can fall into a pattern of use that minimizes the chance of mistakes.)

APPENDIX B
Using Other Expert System Shells

Although we have concentrated on the use of VP-Expert to create intelligent front ends to business applications, there are obviously other expert system tools capable of providing the same kind of result. In this appendix, we'll take a brief look at six other PC-based tools that could be used to create the interfaces in this book and others modeled on those interfaces.

We'll discuss the following tools in this appendix:

- Crystal
- Fusion
- KnowledgePro
- Level 5
- Nexpert-Object
- Personal Consultant Plus

Not all of these tools have facilities for both database and spreadsheet access, but all support one or the other. There is considerable variety among these tools with regards to their price, style of development, multiple-platform support, and other criteria.

There may be other expert system tools that are also capable of providing intelligent interfaces to worksheets and database files. This selection is not necessarily intended to be exhaustive, though I have looked at more than a dozen PC-based tools before creating this list. Like all other software, expert systems tools are constantly changing. For example, a tool I looked at during the development of this book and concluded was unable to do enough to make it interesting to you may have subsequently been enhanced to afford the support it once lacked. I have also focused exclusively on tools that work on

IBM PCs and compatibles. Those that run on other desktop computers, notably the Apple Macintosh, have been omitted from consideration primarily because their interaction and use are so different that explaining them would require a separate book.

As we discuss each of these tools, we will use the same approach. First, we'll provide publication information. Second, we'll look at the general tone and flavor of the tool, keeping in mind the principles we discussed in Chapter 2. Third, we'll summarize the means by which the tool interacts with spreadsheet and/or database applications, pointing out the methods and the limitations. Finally, we'll make some observations about how the differences between the tool and VP-Expert would impact the design and construction of intelligent interfaces. Our aim is not to provide an exhaustive treatment of each shell's capabilities, strengths, and weaknesses. It is, rather, to give you some idea as you make tool-selection decisions how these other tools differ from and relate to the base-line criteria established by VP-Expert. In each case, if you think one of these tools might be more useful or usable for your situation than VP-Expert, you should contact the publisher (contact information is given at the start of each discussion) for more current and complete information.

Crystal

Crystal is available from Intelligent Environments, PO Box 388, One Village Square, Chelmsford, MA 01824, (508-256-6412).

Crystal is a powerful, yet easy-to-use expert system design tool that uses a structured approach to system construction. It makes extensive use of the function keys, pop-up menus, windows, and other modern interface techniques to make the creation of an expert system as straightforward as possible.

Crystal features separate interface modules for designing interactions between its expert systems and spreadsheets and databases. Clearly it has the widest range of functions and therefore offers the most power of any of the expert system shells discussed in this book for interacting with traditional business applications.

The Lotus interface — which will work equally well with VP-Planner Plus Version 2, Symphony, and Quattro files — features 21 separate functions. These functions include the capability of creating and using spreadsheet files, managing ranges, loading cells, generating Lotus column headings, and finding a named range in the worksheet. All functions begin with the key letters "LT" to flag them as Lotus worksheet calls.

To open a spreadsheet file, you would use the `LTflopen` function. Creating a new one requires the use of the `LTflcreate` function while `LTflclose` will close an open spreadsheet file. Both the open and create functions require a worksheet name, but the close command does not. Only one worksheet can be open at one time, so the close command is always nonambiguous.

Most worksheet access in Crystal will be through ranges, which are essentially buffered (though you can work around this approach if you want to do so). This approach would be a problem (since most worksheets do not define ranges for all cells), but Crystal allows you to create new ranges in the worksheet. On the positive side, this range-based approach provides a standard syntactical way of interacting with the worksheet. The command to create a range is `LTrng`. This range can then be loaded (with `LTrngload`) or saved (`LTrngsave`) from and to a file of any type. Reading and writing ranges from and to a worksheet require use of the `LTarrread` and `LTarrwrite` (the "arr" stands for "array") functions.

Once a range has been read or loaded into Crystal, it can be used with the following read and write commands, each of which takes as parameters the row and column of the cell involved:

```
LTrddate (reads date or time value)
LTrdnum (reads a numeric value)
LTrdtxt$ (reads labels and other text values)
LTwrdate (writes date or time value)
LTwrint (writes an integer value)
LTwrnum (writes a numeric value)
LTwrtxt (writes a text value)
```

You can read information directly from a worksheet file without going through the range operations with the "load" functions:

```
LTlddate (loads a date or time value)
LTldnum (loads a numeric value)
LTldtxt$ (loads a text value)
```

Crystal also allows you to translate a column number into its equivalent character heading with the LTcol$ command. This is handy in looping constructs where you can use the number to control the loop but translate it into the appropriate character string the worksheet recognizes as a column address. You can also translate a range name into an array of cell addresses with the LTnamerng command.

The dBASE interface in Crystal is equally powerful. It permits the use of up to 15 open files at one time, and it supports indexed files. As with its Lotus interface, Crystal's dBASE interface permits you to create new dBASE files as well as manipulate existing ones.

You can create a new dBASE file with the DBcreate function. The DBopen function opens an existing dBASE file, while DBclose can be used to close a single open dBASE file. If you use multiple dBASE files, however, you can use DBselect to choose the one to use for a particular set of instructions, and you can close all open files with the DBcloseall function.

From within Crystal, you can create a new index for a dBASE file (using DBicreate), open an existing index (DBiopen), reindex a file (DBreindex), choose an index to use for a particular file (DBorder) and close an index file (DBiclose).

Moving around inside a dBASE file can take two approaches: navigation or searching. Navigation commands let you go to the first (DBfirst) or last (DBlast) records in the file, or to move sequentially or by index to the next (DBnext) or previous (DBprior) record. You can also move to a specific record (using the DBgoto function). If you want to move to a record based on content, you can search for a matching field using the DBfsearch function. It has a reverse-search equivalent, DBbsearch. The function DBtfind will locate a record using an index and DBnfind will use a numeric index for the same purpose. You can always find out what record number you are currently accessing with the DBrecno function.

Reading a record from the dBASE file requires use of the DBreadrec function, which always reads the current record from the named file. You can also find out how many fields the file has (DBcountflds) and what they are called (DBgetflds).

Writing information into a dBASE file is supported by five commands. The DBwriterec function writes a record to the database in the current record position, while DBappend puts the new data at the end of the file. DBdelete marks a record for deletion. The deletion can then be finalized with the DBpack command or reversed before packing with the DBrecall function.

All of the examples in this book could be created using Crystal, though the process of expert system design and definition would be far more interactive and menu-driven and far less programmerlike.

Fusion

Fusion is a product of 1st-CLASS Expert Systems Inc., 286 Boston Post Road, Wayland, MA 01778, (617-358-7722).

Fusion is a relatively new product on the expert system scene but is an outgrowth of one of the most established tools on the PC market: 1st-CLASS. (In fact, the company actually lists Fusion as "1st CLASS-Fusion" but most practitioners drop the historical first part of the name, and we've adopted that approach here) For this appendix, we used Version 1.04.

At heart, Fusion is an induction shell. It is normally used to induce rules from examples provided to it. (Appendix A provides a more in-depth discussion of the inductive process as it applies to expert system shells.) However, it does allow for the editing of rules induced by the system and even the custom entry of rules.

Fusion supports only dBASE III file interface; it has no spreadsheet support. However, you can build expert systems in Fusion that call programs written in Pascal, BASIC, or C, or even interact through DOS batch files. This combined with Fusion's ability to exchange data with any other program using intermediate files means you *could* theoretically develop an interface to a worksheet using Fusion. The process would not be as seamless and straightforward as it is with other tools, but it is certainly possible.

Accessing dBASE files from Fusion requires the use of command statements, specially marked text that appears in the text area associated with factors, values, or results. The basic Fusion commands that access dBASE III files are GET, PUT, and APPEND.

The GET command retrieves a single field from a record in a dBASE file. The syntax of the GET command is:

```
{GET filename, specification, fieldname}
```

The `specification` term can be either a record-selection criterion or the key word THIS which tells Fusion not to move to the next record (which is the normal behavior associated with the GET command) but to retrieve another field from the current record. Specifications can be complex, using the logical connectors AND and OR to link criteria together. To retrieve the price of an axle from a dBASE III file called SUPPLY.DBF, you would use the following command:

```
{GET SUPPLY, PRODUCT = AXLE, PRICE}
```

If you then wanted to retrieve the stock number for the same item, you could write a command line like this:

```
{GET SUPPLY, THIS, STOCKNUM}
```

Like GET, the PUT command deals with dBASE records one field at a time. Its syntax is:

```
{PUT filename, fieldname}
```

where `filename` is the name of one of up to four currently open dBASE files. If you had used the GET command in the above examples to retrieve the price of an axle and now wanted to change the price in the database, you would calculate a new value for PRICE and then use a command line like this:

```
{PUT SUPPLY, PRICE}
```

Unlike the GET command, PUT does not automatically advance one record in the database after executing. So you can update the values of several fields with a succession of PUT commands.

To add a new record to a dBASE III file in Fusion, you use the AP-PEND command, which takes only one argument: the name of the dBASE file to which the record should be appended. Fusion then supplies a new value in the file for every field corresponding for which a Fusion variable exists. Any dBASE fields without corresponding values in Fusion are filled with blanks.

The other dBASE-related commands available in Fusion are:

- SEEK is used to position a pointer to a desired record in the file, either by means of a specification similar to the GET command or by specific record number.

- CLOSE is not required but is useful for accessing more than four dBASE files in one consultation session.

- SCAN presents a summary of the field names, types, and sizes, as well as sample records if you wish, so you can determine the structure of a dBASE file.

If the problem for which you are designing an interface has a number of examples available in some tabular or other usable form (e.g., a procedures manual or a decision tree), then Fusion may be a good tool to choose for your project. If, however, you will be building production rules from scratch rather than inducing them, you may find the rule editing capability of Fusion less intuitive than a more programming-oriented approach. However, it is true that Fusion's rule editor is designed for nonprogramming users. If it is adequate to the rules you need to build, Fusion may merit your investigation.

Assuming you want to construct the examples in this book using Fusion, you will find the translation of the production rules themselves fairly straightforward. But you will have to place the validation criteria — places where VP-Expert uses the WHILETRUE approach, for example — into the matrix that makes up the central structure of Fusion. A significant reworking of the examples in this book would be required to produce identical results in Fusion.

KnowledgePro

KnowledgePro is available from Knowledge Garden, Inc., 473A Malden Bridge Road, Nassau, NY 12123, (518-766-3000). Its use is discussed in some limited contexts in Chapters 8, 11, and 12.

As delivered by its publisher, KnowledgePro cannot engage in direct database or spreadsheet file access. It does, however, offer a flexible and usable interface to external programs, with which you could design interfaces to such files. However, Knowledge Garden makes available a separate and inexpensive Database Toolkit which permits access to both dBASE III and Lotus 1-2-3 spreadsheet files. Unfortunately, the tool does not permit you to write any information to a database or worksheet file. Your interaction with business applications, then, is confined to read-only access. This makes KnowledgePro unsuited to many of the applications discussed in this book.

Still, the ability to access database and worksheet files for retrieval and analysis can be useful in business applications. KnowledgePro's raw processing power, due to its implementation of the data structure known as lists and its own special concept called topics, is sufficient to warrant investigation if your need for database and spreadsheet access is limited to reading files and performing analysis.

KnowledgePro comes from the term "Knowledge Processor." Its developers hope to establish the principle that their product is more than an expert system shell, that it should be considered more like a word processor for knowledge. The program features a very powerful, flexible language which is both simple and complex. It is simple in that you can learn to do some very basic tasks in KnowledgePro with an understanding of a relatively small handful of commands. Because KnowledgePro implements hypertext (the idea of linking one piece of textual information to another somewhat dynamically, allowing the user to explore a knowledge base in more or less freeform fashion), some very powerful applications can be built without a great deal of programming experience or understanding.

There are many unique aspects to KnowledgePro, making it difficult to summarize its operations in a treatment as brief as this must of necessity be. The key idea to understand, though, is that of the topic. In KnowledgePro, a topic can:

- Contain commands, much like a procedure in a conventional programming language

- Store values, much as variables do in conventional programming languages and other expert system tools

- Return values, like functions in conventional programming languages

- Be assigned properties, like frames in a frame-based system (see Chapter 2)

- Inherit values from other topics (creating an object-oriented framework for programming)

- Behave like system commands, or extensions to the KnowledgePro language

- Be connected (or threaded) to hypertext so that they display information or carry out actions based on the user's selection of hypertext information in other topics

- Be arranged hierarchically, so that forward and backward chaining can be structured and organized intelligently

As you can tell, topics are a highly flexible concept in expert systems tools. (See my article, "The Ultimately Flexible Knowledge Representation Scheme" in the July/August 1988 issue of *PC/AI* magazine for more details.)

Database access in KnowledgePro requires the use of two commands: `open_dbf` and `read_dbf`. A third database-related command, `close_dbf`, is seldom needed but is available if the number of open files becomes too large for your system to handle.

To open a dBASE III file for KnowledgePro access, then, you must assign the results of the execution of the `open_dbf` command to a topic, as in this example:

```
db_desc = open_dbg('supply').
```

After this command executes, the topic `db_desc` will contain a collection of lists and other data describing the contents of the database file SUPPLY.DBF. Among other things, this description tells KnowledgePro the record structure, how many records are in the file, and the length of each record.

This topic is important because the `read_dbf` file uses it to reference the file. To read a record from the file SUPPLY.DBF after it has been opened with the above statement requires the command:

```
db_data = db_desc(?db_desc).
```

(Use whatever names for the topics `db_desc` and `db_data` that you like.) The question mark before the name of the topic `db_desc` means that KnowledgePro is to use the value of that topic — which is a collection of descriptive information — to access the file.

When a record has been read from the database file, its field values are accessible to KnowledgePro, which can then use its built-in production-rule or other techniques to analyze, process, display or otherwise manipulate the contents. The values are actually stored in a list, which KnowledgePro can then use to perform whatever processing is appropriate.

Database files are closed when the knowledge base finishes its execution, but if you must explicitly close a database file, KnowledgePro has provisions for doing so.

Spreadsheet data can be retrieved in KnowledgePro either for a specific cell, a group of separate, noncontiguous cells, or a block of cells. To retrieve one or more cells that do not fall into a definable range or block, you use the `read_spreadsheet` command. As with all such commands in KnowledgePro, you must assign the results of the operation to a topic, as in this example:

```
test_data = read_spreadsheet ('scores',[A6,
C8, G8]).
```

This command would read the contents of cells A6, C8, and G8 of a worksheet called SCORES.WK1 into a topic called `test_data`. (KnowledgePro uses the .WK1 file extension by default, but you can supply any other extension and override the default assumption.)

If you wish to retrieve a range of cells — whether that range has been named or not — you can do so by adding the KnowledgePro command `spreadsheet_range` to a `read_spreadsheet` command. Here's an example:

```
test_data = spreadsheet_range ('scores',

    spreadsheet_range(A1,F20)).
```

This command would read the contents of cells A1 through F20 into a topic called `test_data`.

It would, as we said at the outset, be impossible to recreate the examples in this book without resorting to programming in Pascal or some other conventional programming language. Facilities for such external program interfaces exist in KnowledgePro, but their use is not transparent or seamless as the use of VP-Expert for these tasks.

Level 5

Level 5 is available from Information Builders, Inc., 1250 Broadway, New York, NY 10001, (212-736-4433).

Level 5 started life as Insight (later changed to Insight I), and became Insight II+ before Information Builders, Inc., one of the largest mainframe software publishers in the country, acquired the original publisher and changed the name to Level 5. (Level 5 Research was the name of the company that originally developed the tool.) For this discussion, we used PC Version 1.0.

Level 5 has always featured strong interaction with database programs and includes the ability to exchange information between its Production Rule Language (PRL) and dBASE II and III files directly using a vocabulary we'll discuss shortly. It does not, however, provide any built-in means of dealing with worksheets. Level 5 does include one of the most extensive and flexible means of dealing with external programs and files of any expert system tool, however, so writing a routine to access a worksheet file would at least be possible. It just wouldn't be as seamless as it is with VP-Expert. (I should also point out that Level 5 for the Macintosh does interface to a spreadsheet, namely Microsoft Excel, however, on that platform it does not yet have any means of accessing database files.)

The heart of Level 5 is its PRL language, an extended production-rule syntax that includes nearly 100 key words. This rich, Pascal-like language is accompanied by a strict structural design format for a knowledge base. Certain elements must precede others. Variables not of the default type must be predeclared. The inference engine's equivalent of VP-Expert's ACTIONS block takes the form of an outline listing goals and subgoals and directing the flow of the inference process in much the same way as VP-Expert's FIND commands.

You can build PRL knowledge bases using Level 5's built-in editor or your favorite word processor. You then compile these knowledge bases and run them under Level 5.

Before a dBASE II or III file can be accessed in a Level 5 PRL statement or rule, it must be opened and declared. The basic syntax for the OPEN command responsible for this task is:

```
OPEN filename AS database_type FOR access_type
CALLED pseudo_name
```

The database_type argument tells Level 5 whether the file is a dBASE II file (using the key word DB2) or a dBASE III file (using the key word DB3). You can open a database file for two types of access: READ or WRITE. If you use the key word CALLED, then you must use the pseudo_name you provide to reference the dBASE file. This permits you to use a short name for a file that might have a very long path name to access. It is not required.

Once you have opened a dBASE file for access in Level 5, you can use any of several PRL commands to access and update its contents. The primary commands are: ADVANCE, LOCATE, APPEND, and DE-LETE.

The ADVANCE command is an interesting Level 5 device that combines three functions in one command: advancing to the next record, writing any changes to the preceding record, and reading the values of the new record into what Level 5 refers to as the "context." (Simply put, the context is the working memory of information available to the expert system during a consultation.) Assuming the database file is opened for WRITE access (see the discussion of the OPEN command, above), the ADVANCE command works as follows:

1. The first time it is encountered, the command moves to the next (possibly first) record in the file and reads the values of all of its variables into the consultation context where the production rules can access them.

2. Each subsequent time it is encountered, the command determines whether any changes have been made to any of the values representing the database file contents. If so, it updates the record in the database accordingly. In either case, it advances to the next record and retrieves all the values of its fields into the consultation context.

To locate a record in the database file that meets some specific criteria in Level 5, you use the LOCATE command. Its syntax is:

```
LOCATE specification IN filename
```

For example, to find the next record in the file that has an axle in it, you would write a command like this:

```
LOCATE supply.part=axle IN supply
```

(The first part of the criteria shows how a database variable is accessed in Level 5. It consists of two parts: the name of the database and the name of the field, separated by a period. This permits you to use nearly identical variable names for database contents and uses inside the expert system and to differentiate them from one another.) If you issue another `LOCATE` command after this one (or under a number of other circumstances), Level 5 first performs an `ADVANCE` and then locates the next matching record.

The specification can be arbitrarily complex, using the logical connectors to create detailed retrieval criteria.

Adding a record to the end of a database file requires the use of the `APPEND TO` command. This command takes only one argument: the name (or pseudonym) of the file to which the record is to be appended.

Level 5 also allows you to remove a record from a database file, using the `DELETE FROM` command. Like the `APPEND TO` command, it takes only one argument: the name of the database file from which the currently chosen record should be deleted.

There are two additional database-oriented commands in Level 5:

- `POSITION`, which moves the current record pointer to a specifically numbered one in the file. Like `ADVANCE`, it updates the record it is leaving before moving to the indicated place in the file.

- `SIZE`, which is a numeric function that you can use to discover how many records are in a given database.

Level 5 is a highly structured, highly procedural environment in which people with some Pascal and C programming experience feel at home. Yet its syntax is straightforward enough that nonprogrammers can often understand and deal with it. It is notoriously fast when it is executing and database retrieval follows that pattern.

Recreating the knowledge bases in this book with Level 5 will take a little redesign. For example, criteria can be tested using IF-THEN-ELSE rules in conjunction with the Level 5 key word `LOOP`. Here is how such a rule might look in Level 5:

```
RULE to confirm cost in range
IF ASK cost
AND cost < 50
AND cost > 90
THEN we are done
ELSE LOOP
```

It may also be worth noting that Information Builders intends to provide Level 5 support for other types of database files on DEC VAX and other hardware platforms, so that the product may eventually become positioned as a premiere expert system tool for designing and building intelligent front ends to such systems.

Nexpert-Object

Nexpert-Object is available from Neuron Data, Inc., 444 High Street, Palo Alto, CA 94301, (415-321-4488).

Nexpert-Object is considered by many people to be the Cadillac of the expert systems arena. It features a rich array of knowledge representation schema, a highly windowed, graphically rich developer environment, and a degree of transportability across hardware platforms that is better than any competitive product available at this writing. It is a complex tool, one that requires some study and thought to master. Many consultants recommend that before you attempt to build a serious product using Nexpert-Object, you should attend formal training classes.

We should also point out that Nexpert-Object provides interfaces to many kinds of databases and to standard worksheet files as well. In addition, it has its own built-in database and spreadsheet routines to maintain internal business application files.

Entering rules and other knowledge into Nexpert-Object involves filling out a series of forms on the display screen that allow you to describe the functions of the rules while furnishing a template within which the rules are syntactically correctly defined. Thus we cannot really speak of "writing" rules in Nexpert-Object; instead, we build or create them in templates. Nonetheless, we will proceed as if we were simply writing them in a text editor. If you become interested in using Nexpert-Object for your projects, you will have no difficulty translating our text format into the templates furnished by the program. One of the consequences of this template approach is that arguments are in prefix notation, which is often harder to read. Thus, for example, if we want to express the relationship price >= 32000, we would code that in Nexpert-Object as:

```
>=  price  32000
```

Both database files and worksheets are accessed using two Nexpert-Object commands: Retrieve and Write.

The Retrieve command takes two sets of arguments. The first is the name of a database file. The second is a collection of relationships between database file names and Nexpert object properties (perhaps mixed with other elements that are not of interest to us at the moment). Here is a sample rule (adapted from the Nexpert-Object user manual) that shows how a database file called SUPPLY.DBF would be accessed:

```
If
        Yes  start_read_next_record
        >=   record_number  0
Then    read_next_record
And
        Retrieve "SUPPLY.DBF"
        FIELDS -->       PROPS
        part             part.id
        desc             part.desc
        price            part.price
```

This rule begins the process of retrieving the three named fields from the dBASE III file SUPPLY.DBF.

Database file update takes place via the Write command. Like the Retrieve command, this command also takes two arguments. The first is the name of the file. The second is a list of the database fields being updated and their corresponding Nexpert-Object properties names. (Again, there is other optional material in the rule, which we need not be aware of for the purposes of this discussion.) The following rule is adapted from the Nexpert-Object manual:

```
If
        Yes  start_read_next_record
        >    record_number  0
        <,   price          1
Then    UpdatePartsPrice
```

And

```
do    part.price * 1.25    part.price
Write              "SUPPLY.DBF"
                   FIELDS <--    PROPS
                   price         part.price
```

This rule would increase the price of any part whose current price is lower than $1.00 by 25%. The `Write` command would put the value of `part.price` into the database field called `price`.

Worksheet file access is identical to that for databases except that in naming the file, you use an appropriate file extension such as .WKS. Nexpert-Object figures out from the extension how to manage the file and manipulate its contents. You provide explicit mapping between cells or ranges and Nexpert-Object objects and properties.

Nexpert-Object is an object-oriented, highly flexible product. It is sufficiently high-priced that you probably are not going to acquire it if your only need is for a front end for a spreadsheet or database application. However, if you have other expert system needs and can use Nexpert-Object for the interface, you will find it to be a highly intelligent approach. Virtually all of the examples in this book would require a total revision to work with Nexpert-Object because of the different data structures the program uses when compared to VP-Expert and other expert system tools.

Personal Consultant Series

The Personal Consultant series, consisting of Personal Consultant Easy and Personal Consultant Plus, is available from Texas Instruments, ATTN: Data Systems Group, M/S 2151, PO Box 2909, Austin, TX 78769-2909, (512-250-4018). Its support of interactive graphics is described in Chapter 12.

Personal Consultant Easy and Personal Consultant Plus (PC-Easy and PC-Plus) are among the most widely used expert system tools in the world. They have the most comprehensive set of commands for dealing with dBASE III files. On the worksheet side, PC-Plus and PC-Easy allow read-only access to Lotus 1-2-3 compatible files.

Both of the entries in the Personal Consultant series feature highly structured, prompted design methodologies and are intended for use by people with little or no programming background. PC-Easy is a low-priced introductory product which is nonetheless capable of producing powerful and complex expert systems. PC-Plus adds to PC-Easy in a number of key ways, including the ability to extend the entire product by programming in the AI language known as Scheme, a dialect of the dominant AI language, LISP. PC-Plus differs in a number of other ways from PC-Easy, but knowledge bases built using PC-Easy can be used transparently in PC-Plus. As a result, many knowledge engineers and designers begin with PC-Easy, finish a prototype, and then graduate to PC-Plus when they need greater power and flexibility. It is not unlikely, though, that PC-Easy will suffice for your expert system needs if you are interested only in building intelligent front ends for databases. If your need for worksheet access can be limited to read-only, PC-Easy can be a good solution for all of your intelligent interface design needs.

There is no functional difference for the purposes of this discussion between PC-Easy and PC-Plus. We'll refer to PC-Easy in our comments, but you should know that if you have PC-Plus, all of the same procedures, commands, and techniques will apply equally to you.

PC-Easy is frame-based (see Chapter 2). In using dBASE files with PC-Easy, you will typically set the value of a parameter in the knowledge base with information in the database file or you will update information in the database using the contents of a PC-Easy parameter.

If you are using the PC-Easy parameter to retrieve information from a dBASE file, you have a choice of two approaches. First, you can set up the parameter's EXPECT list so that it looks into the database file for values. Second, you can attach a METHOD property to the parameter. This latter approach is most often used to initialize a parameter's value from a database record.

All parameters in PC-Easy can have an EXPECT list. This list specifies all of the possible values for a parameter. There are a number of options for this list, including SINGLE-LINE INPUT, MULTI-LINE INPUT, INTEGER, NUMBER, POSITIVE-NUMBER, and the database-related functions in which we are interested. The METHOD property, however, is only applicable to a dBASE retrieval approach for setting a parameter's value.

Whether you place the dBASE access in the EXPECT list or in a METHOD property, you have two ways to set the parameter's value in dBASE: you can simply retrieve some information from the database or you can execute a dBASE program (a set of dBASE instructions with a .PRG extension) from directly within PC-Easy.

The retrieval approach calls for the use of the PC-Easy command DBASE-RETRIEVE. If you want to run a program in dBASE, you will use the DBASE-EXECUTE-FILE command instead.

To use the DBASE-RETRIEVE command effectively, you will generally include the special key word QUAL, which stands for *qualifier*. This is the signal to PC-Easy that you are providing some criteria by which it should retrieve information from the database file. Here's an example, again following our parts inventory example:

```
DBASE-RETRIEVE "SUPPLY" (QUAL PART = "Axle")
PRICE
```

(Note: Because PC-Easy works with parameters one at a time, you can only read one field from the database at a time. If there are other parameters in your PC-Easy knowledge base that need information from this same file, you simply supply DBASE-RETRIEVE commands in the EXPECT list of each of them.)

This command could be placed in either the EXPECT list of the parameter or in the METHOD property. The syntax would be identical in either case. It would locate the record in the file SUPPLY.DBF where the field PART contains the value "Axle" and return the value of that record's PRICE field into the parameter to which the command is attached.

If the information you want to retrieve from a dBASE file for use in a PC-Easy parameter can best be obtained using a dBASE program file, you can use the DBASE-EXECUTE-FILE command. This function can be used in a METHOD property, in an EXPECT list or as part of the THEN statement of a traditional production rule. This approach is particularly useful if the dBASE program carries out some specific calculations to obtain a value for the parameter.

The dBASE program simply carries out its calculations and puts the result into a text file it names. PC-Easy then retrieves the value from that text file and assigns it to the parameter.

Updating a dBASE file can only be done from the THEN portion of a rule, of course. To do so in PC-Easy, use the DBASE-REPLACE function. Its syntax is as follows:

```
DBASE-REPLACE "filename" (QUAL qualifiers)
fieldname = parameter_name
```

For example, if we had increased the price of our axle and wanted to update the dBASE file accordingly, we would simply write the following statement in the THEN portion of a rule:

```
DBASE-REPLACE "SUPPLY" (QUAL part="Axle")
PRICE = NEWPRICE
```

The other means of updating the dBASE file is the DBASE-APPEND function, which requires a minimum of two arguments: the name of the dBASE file and one or more field names and associated values. To add a battery to our SUPPLY.DBF file:

```
DBASE-APPEND "SUPPLY" PART = "Battery" PRICE =
"39.07"
```

In addition to these basic dBASE commands and functions, PC-Easy includes the following commands for use with dBASE files:

- DBASE-DELETE, which marks for deletion information in the database file

- DBASE-RECALL, which unmarks information that has been previously marked for deletion

- DBASE-PACK, which removes from the database information marked for deletion with DBASE-DELETE

- DBASE-REPORT, which invokes a print routine inside dBASE III

- DBASE-BUFFER, which accumulates dBASE commands and requests for later execution in a group

- DBASE-BUFFER-APPEND, which adds more dBASE commands to an existing dBASE buffer

- DBASE-EXECUTE, which executes the instructions built up in the buffer by one of the two preceding commands

You can only read data from a Lotus 1-2-3 compatible worksheet in PC-Easy. The command to read information from such a file is LO-TUS-WKS. It takes one required argument and has an optional one. The required argument is the name of the worksheet file. If you are retrieving values for more than one parameter in a rule, you must also supply a list of all the parameters in PC-Easy for which values are to be retrieved. There must be a named one-for-one correspondence between the parameter name and the cell or range name in the worksheet. This means you must name individual cells in the worksheet that you expect to need in PC-Easy (or you must name the PC-Easy parameters the same as the cell address).

Appendix C
Sample Spreadsheet

Following is a listing of the spreadsheet macro that would implement the menu-driven interface to the worksheet described in Chapter 5. It is presented linearly, row-wise, so that its entries are keyed to the Range Name Table appearing at the end of the listing. Each grouped entry in the listing itself is marked with a comment delimited by the Pascal-style "(*" and "*)" symbol pairs. The comment defines the starting cell for the entries that follow it.

```
(*O14*)
\0 {let printdone,"N"}
   {menubranch menu}

(*O17*)
menu Sales
              enter sales slips
              {goto}salestable~
              /rvqoh~salesqoh~
              /rvytdunits~salesunit~
              /rvytddollars~salesdollar~
              {menubranch sales}

(*Q14*)
              Receiving
              enter shipmnents received
              {goto}receiptstable~
              /rvqoh~rqoh~
              /rvorders~roders~
              {menubranch receive}

(*R14*)
              Orders
              issue new purchase orders
              {goto}orderstable~
              {menubranch orders}

(*S14*)
              Print
              print the worksheet
              {branch print}

(*T14*)
              Quit
```

```
                         save the worksheet and quit to DOS
                         {branch quit}

(*O25*)
Sales A3SS
                           Disk Supply SD
                           {goto}
                           A3SS
                           ~
                           {branch sales entry}

(*Q25*)
                           A3SD
                           Disk Supply
                           {goto}
                           A3SD
                           ~
                           {branch salesentry}

(*R25*)
                           B35S
                           Granville SD
                           {goto}
                           B35S
                           ~
                           {branch salesentry}

(*S25*)
                           B35D
                           Granville DD
                           {goto}
                           B35D
                           ~
                           {branch salesentry}

(*T25*)
                           C35S
                           Woomera SD
                           {goto}
                           C35S
                           ~
                           {branch salesentry}

(*U25*)
                           C35D
                           Woomera DD
                           {goto}
                           C35D
                           ~
                           {branch salesentry}

(*V25*)
                           D35S
                           FSI SD
```

```
                        {goto}
                        D35S
                        ~
                        {branch salesentry}

        (*W25*)

                        D35D
                        FSI DD
                        {goto}
                        D35D
                        ~
                        {branch salesentry}

        (*X25*)

                        Main Menu
                        Return to the main menu
                        {home}
                        {menubranch menu}

        (*O32*)
        testcell
        testvalue
        dummy
        printdone N

        (*O37*)
        salesentry   /xnEnter unit sales from sales slip for
                        this product code (0

                                to exit):~~
                                /rv"testcell"
                                {if
                                testcell=0}/re~{goto}salestable~{menubr
                                anch sales}
                                {r 3}
                                /rv"testccell"
                                {if testcell<0{branch toomanyerr}
                                {l 2}
                                /xnEnter sales $ from sales slip for
                                this productg code:~~
                                {goto}salestable~
                                /rvnsalesqoh~salesqoh~
                                /rvnsalesunit~salesunit~
                        /rvnsalesdollar~salesdollar~
                        /resalesinput~
                        {menubranch sales}

        (*O53*)
        stoomanyerr {beep 5,5}
                        {getlabel "Sales can't cause QOH to become
                          less than 0.
                        Press ENTER to con tinue)",dummy}
                        {l 3}
```

```
                           /re~
                           {branch salesentry}

        (*O59*)
        receive            A35S
                           DiskSupply SD
                           {goto}
                           A35SR
                           ~
                           {branch receipts}

        (*P59*)
                           A35D
                           Disk Supply DD
                           {goto}
                           A35DR
                           ~
                           {branch receipts}

        (*Q59*)
                           B35S
                           Granville SD
                           {goto}
                           B35SR
                           ~
                           {branch receipts}

        (*R59*)
                           B35D
                           Granville DD
                           {goto}
                           B35DR
                           ~
                           {branch receipts}

        (*S59*)
                           C35S
                           Woomera SD
                           {goto}
                           C35SR
                           ~
                           {branch receipts}

        (*T59*)
                           C35DWoomera DD
                           {goto}
                           C35DR
                           ~
                           {branch receipts}

        (*U59*)
                           D35S
                           FSI SD
                           {goto}
```

```
                              D35SR
                              ~
                              {branch receipts}

            (*V59*)
                              D35D
                              FSI DD
                              {goto}
                              D35DR
                              ~
                              {branch receipts}

            (*W59*)
                              Main Menu
                              Return to the Main Menu
                              {home}
                              {menubranch menu}

            (*O69*)
            receipts          /xnEnter quantity of product code received
                                 (0 to exit):~
                              /rv"testcell"
                              {if
                                testcell=0}/re~{goto}receiptstable~{menub
                                ranch receive}
                              {r 2}
                              /rv"testcell"
                              {if testcell<0}{branch rtoomanyerr}
                              {goto}receiptstable~
                              /rvneworders~roders~
                              /rvnewqoh~rqoh~
                              /rvrqoh~salesqoh~
                              /rvrorders~oorders~
                              /rerinput~
                              {menubranch receive}

            (*O83*)
            rtoomanyerr {beep 5,5}
                              {getlabel "Receipts can't cause QOH to
                                become less than 0.
                                  Press ENTER to continue)",dummy}
                              {l 2}
                              /re~
                              {branch receive}

            (*O89*)
            Orders A3SS
                              Disk Supply SD
                              {goto}
                              A35SO
                              ~
                              {branch orderentry}

            (*Q89*)
```

```
                               A3SD
                               Disk Supply
                               {goto}
                               A3SDO
                               ~
                               {branch orderentry}

            (*R89*)
                               B35S
                               Granville SD
                               {goto}
                               B35SO
                               ~
                               {branch orderentry}

            (*S89*)
                               B35D
                               Granville DD
                               {goto}
                               B35DO
                               ~
                               {branch orderentry}

            (*T89*)
                               C35S
                               Woomera SD
                               {goto}
                               C35SO
                               ~
                               {branch orderentry}

            (*U89*)
                               C35D
                               Woomera DD
                               {goto}
                               C35DO
                               ~
                               {branch orderentry}

            (*V89*)
                               D35S
                               FSI SD
                               {goto}
                               D35SO
                               ~
                               {branch orderentry}

            (*W89*)
                               D35D
                               FSI DD
                               {goto}
                               D35DO
                               ~
                               {branch orderentry}
```

```
(*X89*)
                    Main Menu
                    Return to the main menu
                    {home}
                    {menubranch menu}


(*O96*)
orderentry    /xnEnter quantity you want to order (0 to
                  exit):~~
              /rv"testcell"
              {iftestcell=0}/re~{goto}orderstable~
                {menubranch orders}
              {r}
              /rv"testcell"
              {r}
              /rv"testvalue"
              {if testcell>testvalue}{branch otoomanyerr}


(*O104*)
ocontinue     {goto}orderstable~
              /rvoneworders~oorders~
              /reoinput~
              {menubranch orders}


(*O110*)
otoomanyerr {beep 9,5}
              {menubranch oyesno}


(*O113*)
oyesno        Yes
              The current quantity on hand exceeds the
                ROP; do you want to order anyway?
              {1 2}
              {branch ocontinue}


(*Q113*)
                    No
                    The current quantity on hand exceeds the
                      ROP; do you want to order anyway?
                        {1 2}
                    /re~
                    {menubranch orders}


(*O120*)
print         /ppgpq
              {let printdone,"Y"}
              {home}
              {menubranch menu}


(*O125*)
quit          {if printdone<>"Y"}{branch notprterr}
              {menubranch quityesno}


(*O128*)
```

```
quityesno   Yes
                    Do you really want to save the
                    worksheet and quit to DOS?
                    /fs~b
                    /qy

(*Q128*)
                    No
                    Do you really want to save the
                    worksheet and quit to DOS?
                    {home}
                    {menubranch menu}

(*O133*)
notprterr   {beep 5,5}
                    {getlabel "You must print the worksheet
                    before quitting

                    (press ENTER to continue)",dummy}

(*Range Name Table*)

A35D              AC6
A35DO             AX6
A35DR             AO6
A35S              AC5
A35SO             AX5
A35SR             AO5
B35D              AC8
B35DO             AX8
B35DR             AO8
B35S              AC7
B35SO             AX7
B35SR             AO7
C35D              AC10
C35DO             AX10
C35DR             AO10
C35S              AC9
C35SO             AX9
C35SR             AO9
CEILING           G5..G12
D35D              AC12
D35DO             AX12
D35DR             AO12
D35S              AC11
D35SO             AX11
D35SR             AO11
DUMMY             AO34
MACROS            M14
MENU              O17
NOTPRTERR         O133
NSALESDOLLAR      AJ5..AJ12
NSALESQOH         AF5..AF12
NSALESUNIT        AH5..AH12
```

```
OCONTINUE          O104
OINPUT             AX5..AX12
ONEWORDERS         BC5..BC12
OORDERS            BB5..BB12
ORDERENTRY         O96
ORDERS             O89
ORDERSTABLE        AW3
OTOOMANYERR        O110
OYESNO             O113
PRINT              O120
PRINTDONE          O35
QOH                E5..E12
QUIT               O125
QUITYESNO          O128
RECEIPTS           O69
RECEIPTSTABLE      AN3
RECEIVE            O59
RINPUT             AO5..AO12
RNEWORDERS         AQ5..AQ12
RNEWQOH            AS5..AS12
ROP                F5..F12
RORDERS            AP5..AP12
RQOH               AR5..AR12
RTOOMANYERR        O83
SALES              O25
SALESDOLLAR        AI5..AI12
SALESENTRY         O37
SALESINPUT         AC5..AD12
SALESQOH           AE5..AE12
SALESTABLE         AB3
SALESUNIT          AG5..AG12
STOOMANYERR        O53
TESTCELL           O32
TESTVALUE          O33
YTDDOLLARS         I5..I12
YTDUNITS           H5..H12
\0                 O14
\A                 O14
```

GLOSSARY

In VP-Expert, the exclamation point is used to indicate a comment, which is ignored by the program and serves to document the functions of the expert system or provide incidental or legal information such as author's name, copyright, date of last modification, and the like.

algorithm
A method or procedure for solving a problem.

argument
When a command is carried out in a computer program, it often has one or more parameters associated with it. These parameters are also called arguments. Generally, arguments and parameters supply the command with information about how to carry out its instructions or provide the data on which the command operates. Also sometimes termed operands.

backward chaining
An *inference engine* strategy involving a process of attempting to prove a preset goal by successively evaluating more precisely defined subgoals until the main goal is proven, disproven, or is shown to be not susceptible to proof with the rules and facts known. Contrast with forward chaining.

blackboarding
A design strategy using a master control program and an intermediate computer file or area of memory as a place for two or more programs to exchange data. The term was originally restricted to the sharing of such data by two or more expert systems working on problems in semi-parallel ways, but has expanded to include sharing data between expert systems and other programs such as databases and spreadsheets.

certainty factor	A numeric value that reflects the degree of confidence an expert has in the validity of a rule's conclusion or of a fact. Also called confidence factors, certainty factors are typically reported in the range of 0 (no confidence) to 100 (total confidence) but should not therefore be confused with a probability of correctness.
concatenate	Joining two or more objects, typically but not necessarily strings of characters, together to form one new object.
conclusion	In a production rule, the THEN portion of the rule that results in fact values being changed and/or actions being taken.
consultation	The interaction of a user with an expert system during which the expert system program asks the user questions and provides answers to problems.
counter	A *variable* used in a program to keep track of how many times a process is carried out, what row or column of a table is now being examined, and other similar iterative processes.
debugging	The process of identifying, isolating, and repairing or removing errors in computer programs.
declarative	An approach to computer programming and a description of programming languages that emphasizes describing the problem to be solved and letting the computer solve it without explicit step-by-step directions. Contrasted with *procedural* programming. Declarative languages include *Prolog* and Smalltalk, among others.
descendant	In frame-based knowledge representation schemes, a *frame* can have child frames which inherit properties of the parent but may also add other properties and functions. Such children are referred to as descendants or descendant frames.
domain	The specific problem area addressed by an expert system's knowledge base.

forward chaining	An *inference engine* strategy involving a process of working from a given collection of one or more facts and reasoning to a conclusion that is now known in advance. Contrast this with backward chaining.
4th-generation language	A special-purpose programming language, usually embedded in a program such as a spreadsheet or database management system and designed to be usable by people with less programming experience than more traditional languages such as Pascal or C. Both dBASE III and Lotus 1-2-3 include such languages aimed at making the design of applications using the tools easier to build and more powerful than would otherwise be the case.
frame	An architecture for *knowledge representation* that ties together facts, rules, defaults, and sometimes procedures for dealing with this knowledge into one object. Frames usually contain slots that can further describe the object.
heuristic	A rule of thumb garnered from experience.
hypertext	Term coined by computer visionary Ted Nelson to describe nonlinear writing and communication of written materials. Some expert system tools make it possible to use hypertext to enrich the amount of information they can convey to users.
induction	The process of reaching a conclusion by inference from particular facts. (See Appendix A for a discussion of induction as a method of generating expert system rules from tables of data.)
inference engine	A computer program that is part of most expert system tools and which is designed to infer, or draw conclusions, from data furnished to it. It can be thought of as the "brains" in an expert system.

knowledge acquisition	The process of obtaining knowledge from experts and other sources for inclusion in an expert system. Often perceived as the major bottleneck which is keeping expert systems from wider application because the knowledge acquisition process has traditionally been manual and time intensive.
knowledge base	The collection of rules and facts that make up the specific knowledge about the *domain* of an expert system and on which the *inference engine* operates to draw its conclusions.
knowledge engineer	A professional trained in the skills of *knowledge acquisition* and knowledge-based programming. Wide disagreement exists as to where to draw the line in defining the limits of a knowledge engineer and many would include programming and/or expert system shell usage among the requisite skills for such a person.
knowledge representation	The means by which knowledge about a *domain* is stored in an expert system. Most expert systems in use today use either *rules* or *frames* for such representation, both schemes are possible and in more limited use.
LISP	A programming language popular in the United States, particularly in academic circles, for solving problems of artificial intelligence. The name is an acronym for LISt Processing, which is the language's primary strength.
loop	A series of computer program instructions that are carried out repeatedly as long as some predefined condition remains true or until such a condition becomes true.
premise	Generally, the IF portion of a production rule is referred to as the rule's premise. Some writers use the term to refer only to one of the conditions contained in a multiple-condition premise.

procedural	Computer programming and a description of programming languages that emphasizes describing to the computer how to solve a particular problem. Contrasted with *declarative* programming, procedural programming is the most commonly used method today and is exemplified by such computer programming languages as Pascal, BASIC, and C.
procedural control	The section of a VP-Expert program containing the ACTIONS block where commands not related to the knowledge but to how the knowledge is processed are collected.
Prolog	A programming language popular in Western Europe and Japan for solving problems of artificial intelligence, Prolog has gained some measure of popularity in the United States in recent years. It is a *declarative* language and is often viewed as a competitive alternative to *LISP* for solving artificial intelligence problems, though most researchers view *LISP* as capable of dealing with a broader range of such problems and limit Prolog to those involving logic. Prolog stands for PROgramming in LOGic.
rule	The means of *knowledge representation* used in expert system shells. Knowledge about a topic is stored in a series of rules that take the form IF-THEN-ELSE. (IF a condition is true, THEN some conclusion can be drawn, ELSE some other conclusion can be drawn.) VP-Expert uses rules as its primary means of knowledge representation.
shell	An expert system without a knowledge base. A tool for constructing expert systems.
slot	In a frame-based *knowledge representation* scheme, each *frame* has one or more slots. Each slot is designed to hold information about a certain characteristic of the object represented by the frame.

syntax	Rules that govern the statement of instructions in a computer programming language or an expert system. Each command has a syntax that must be followed for it to be understood by the program carrying out the instructions.
validation	The process of proving that the conclusions reached by an expert system are appropriate and that they coincide to the maximum possible degree with the conclusions a human expert would reach based on identical information.
variable	A symbol in a computer program whose value can change during a single run of the program or between runs. Contrast with a constant, whose value never changes without programming effort.

Index